Parenting Your Teen by the Spirit

Yes, your teen can reach the potential God intended

Sally Hohnberger

Pacific Press® Publishing Association
Nampa, Idaho
Oshawa, Ontario, Canada
www.pacificpress.com

Designed by Eucaris L. Galicia
Cover design resources from iStockphoto.com

Copyright © 2007 by
Pacific Press® Publishing Association
Printed in the United States of America
All rights reserved

Interior photos supplied by author.

Additional copies of this book are available by calling toll free
1-800-765-6955 or by visiting http://www.adventistbookcenter.com.

Library of Congress Cataloging-in-Publication Data:
Hohnberger, Sally, 1948-
Parenting your teen by the Spirit : Yes, your teen can reach the potential God
intended, ages 13–19 / Sally Hohnberger.
p. cm.
ISBN 13: 978-0-8163-2162-9
ISBN 10: 0-8163-2162-0
1. Parenting—Religious aspects—Christianity. 2. Parenting—Religious aspects—Seventh-
day Adventists. 3. Parent and teenager—Religious aspects—Seventh-day Adventists.
I. Title.
BV4529.H627 2007
248.8'45—dc222006050430

07 08 09 10 11 · 5 4 3 2 1

Dedication

This book is dedicated to the reader . . .

Who desires her youth to be cast in a different mold from what the world offers.
Who sees with a discerning eye what he does not want.
Who senses in her heart that the difference begins with "me."
Who will make raising their child into an adult his/her priority of life.
Who will look upon this work as the all-important work for his time.
Who is willing to do whatever it takes.
Who is willing to enter upon the path of being what she wants her youth to be.
Who desires to be an instrument in the hands of Jesus to redeem the mind, heart, and soul of his young adult to serve God and right.
Who is willing to take up this work with determination and courage under God.

This book is dedicated to you, the true in heart, to help you to say to your young adult from the bottom of your heart, "I am here for you!" Together, let's commit to let God lead us in that redemption process and not turn back from this all important work at this all-important time.

Acknowledgements

With deep gratitude, I want to thank my personal friend, Jeanette Houghtelling, for all her arduous, painstaking, faithful labors of love that have gone into editing and organizing each one of these chapters with me. Jeanette, you have been like my right arm.

I thank God for His inspiration, insights, and experiences upon which we drew. For without the Holy Spirit's guidance, our human reasoning would be foolishness.

May God take it from here to help each reader to see His hand working in their life to help them raise their youth to follow after Christ and not be susceptible to the pull of fleshliness and earthliness.

Contents

Preface

The turbulent teens—a time more dreaded by many parents than the terrible twos! This critical bridge between childhood and maturity was intended by God to be the most rewarding years of parenting. And yet Satan has sabotaged it. He has been all too successful in railroading our youth into a myriad of self-defeating detours.

He has accomplished this by hiding vital truths through misconceptions galore of how to raise children into mature adults. He has fed us a faulty program, and we have eaten it. The predominant child-rearing practices today are truly detrimental and do not produce wholesome, well-balanced characters.

So let us pull back the devil's curtain of deception and deceit to expose God's gems of wisdom for parenting teens. Let us dust off those jewels and hold them up to the light to see them for what they really are. Let us examine how to use them and reflect upon how they have worked in the lives of real parents and real teenagers of today!

Is there such a thing as a safe passage for our teenagers through the snares and pitfalls that surround them on every side? Yes, there is a way! And that way is Jesus Christ.

In writing *Parenting Your Teen by the Spirit,* I share my very real burden for our teens and young adults. As their parents, we have the privilege of making this transition easier if we are willing to take hold of certain important keys. First, understanding how their minds are developing right now, and second, grasping how to connect them to Christ in a very practical way. To put these keys into your hands is the purpose of this book.

Jesus Christ is our Teacher in this process. As you read this book, He will be by your side personally to show you how these principles can be implemented within your own unique and individual family. It doesn't matter what you have failed to do in the past or what the situation is right now for your young person.

God has a plan that will work for you if you are willing to follow Him. He is able to help each parent to prepare his or her young adults to meet their God with cleansed hearts, minds, and habits through faith in Jesus, their Savior and Friend!

Matthew, age 20, and Andrew, age 18, playing the guitar.
God wants to make our teens' lives to be like heavenly music.

Andrew, age 16, washing dishes.
Andrew and Matthew worked
together to install these cabinets.

Chapter 1

Unmet Needs

But they that wait upon the Lord shall renew their strength;
they shall mount up with wings as eagles.
—Isaiah 40:31

"Look who is coming up the street," I remarked to my husband, Jim.

Coming toward us I saw fifteen-year-old Chains Charlie sauntering aimlessly down the sidewalk with his sidekick, Misfit Murphy, fourteen. Following them in a lively conversation was Tough Tommy, age thirteen, and Abused Abby, probably fourteen. Lying Larry, Mad Music Mandy, and Despairing Dora tagged along, not wanting to miss a thing. What a sight!

As I watched where this group was headed, my fears, as well as my sympathies, were aroused. Not far from where we stood was Brooding Becki, an unhappy, vulnerable thirteen-year-old, talking with Cool Jace, whom I happened to know was trying to be a Christian, *without* success. Shy Sarah joined this twosome just as the first group arrived, and they all began to talk.

I saw Abused Abby, an outgoing, bubbly girl, reach out to Brooding Becki in an exchange of sympathy. Soon Abby's arm was around Becki, drawing her in with concern. Chains Charlie, his pants cascading with chains, was the obvious leader of this strange group. He approached Cool Jace with an air of authority that made introductions awkward. However, Misfit Murphy, who seemed to know Cool Jace, intervened, and soon all three boys were engaged in lively talk. Despairing Dora was drawn to Shy Sarah, who seemed taken aback by this motley group. Before long all of them were walking together down the street.

Do you see what is happening here? Which child is yours? Do you know some of the other young people in this group? Do you want your young people to adopt the ineffective problem-solving techniques, poor lifestyles, destructive habits, and vices of these youth?

Unmet needs in the hearts and minds of these potentially good kids make them vulnerable to what they see as love, acceptance, and caring by the rougher teenagers. Often *something* seems better than *nothing*! After all, *someone* is sympathizing, is caring, is listening, and is there for them, filling that void. But why isn't that sympathizing, listening ear a safe parent? Why are these young people so vulnerable to the kind of help that has a hook buried within it? Real needs are being met—but at what cost?

This scenario is happening not only in Los Angeles, New York, Seattle, Miami, and Houston but in every small city and many small towns today. Worse yet, these scenes are far too common in our churches as well.

What are we going to do about it? Are we going to stand idly by, our hands too full of other pursuits, while the current of worldliness sweeps away our youth? Is it

God's plan for Chains Charlie and Abused Abby to teach and lead our youth? No, no, no! A thousand times NO! That is the plan of our enemy, Satan, who wants to drown our youth beneath the waters of a self-directed life. And we need not let it happen! There is a better way. God has provided a lifeboat. Twenty-three years ago, Jim and I chose to get into that lifeboat and to help our sons get into it also. You can do the same, if you will. *Jesus is the lifeboat—our only place of safety.* Under God's guidance we can rescue whom we can—at least our own children, surely!

We need to give ourselves to our youth! Give our time, our hearts, our lives, and our interests to work for their best good and to help them know Jesus. We need to show them a better way, to be there for them. We need to learn how to be lovingly firm, to direct them without harshness or anger, to love and care for them, and to bring them out of wrong thoughts, feelings, and responses as God leads.

In order to do that, God needs to be the center—the very focus—of the parents' lives in a positive, attractive, and practical way so that the youth can see a demonstration of something better than what the world offers. Of course, this will require courage, fortitude, energy, a willingness to change priorities, and an openness to learn new problem-solving techniques!

But friends, the rewards far outweigh the seeming sacrifices. I can tell you from personal experience that you cannot put a price on being your young person's confidant. As you provide that sympathetic, listening ear and influence your teenagers to make wise choices—rather than abandoning them to flounder on their own with dubious companions—you can have the joy of seeing them successfully meeting the challenges of life under God's direction.

From eaglets to eagles

We all want our youth to fly above the pull of their flesh, don't we? We want them to have self-control and upright manners. How are these things inculcated? How is this accomplished?

The Christian life has often been compared with the flight of the majestic eagle. "But they that wait upon the LORD shall renew their strength; they shall mount up with wings as eagles."* The two wings of the eagle, when strengthened by frequent use, offer him a dependable vehicle with which to consistently defy gravity. The two wings of the Christian—trust and obedience or surrender and cooperation—with Christ's help, provide a means of consistently rising above the pull of his flesh.

Beyond these parallels it is obvious not only that the eagles are *masters* of successful flight themselves but that they know *how to teach* their youngsters to fly. Let's see what we can learn from observing them.

The parent eagle hovers over that little eaglet very closely, feeding it, protecting it from predators, and providing a good environment to grow in, as well as demonstrating eagle behavior that is worthy of imitation. Interestingly enough, the example of the parent eagle—*not* the eaglet's peers—is the greatest influence in transforming that eaglet into a majestic adult eagle. Isn't that God's plan for us, too? Eaglets learn

---

*Isaiah 40:31.

how best to fly, hunt, eat, respond in a crisis, and live happy, productive lives by imitating their parents' example.

Are our lives, habits, and character worthy of imitation? Do we demonstrate healthy, productive choices? Sadly, children following the example of a slothful, lazy parent will obey the perverted nature and have a miserable nonproductive life—avoiding responsibility, coming to want, and getting angry, all of which lead to destruction.

The transformation of my youth's character, behavior, attitude, and life must begin with me. I must let God change my character first. My youth must see me consistently spreading strong, well-developed wings of dependency on God and flying by His power. How can I expect my youth to fly well if I set an example of floundering on the ground much of the time? I must rise above the pull of *my* flesh for my youth to see and imitate how God empowers me.

The parent eagle's driving purpose in life is to raise the eaglet to carry on the majestic *heritage* it was created for—and, in turn, to pass this heritage on to the next generation. This eagle is not interested in keeping its offspring in the nest indefinitely. Neither will it allow the eaglet to leave prematurely. It provides both protection and challenge at the appropriate times with the purpose of seeing the little eaglet one day fly successfully—properly independent of its parents and properly dependent upon God.

As the eaglet grows, the role of the parent will change. At the beginning of the eaglet's life, the parent provides physical care and training in the basic habits of life. But before long the young eaglet is flapping its wings, stretching its muscles, and showing interest in the world beyond by peeking over the edge of its lofty home. Soon it scrambles up to get a better look and perches uncertainly at the edge of the nest, testing its wings against the wind while enjoying the scenery. At times, the wind buffets it back into the nest, but the eaglet clumsily climbs up again until it gains strength and balance to stand against the winds of its summit home.

Just like those eaglets, our children get on the edge of our home nest, don't they? They begin by saying things such as, "May I drive, Dad?" "I want to learn how to change the oil in the car!" "Mother, does my dress look right?" "What do you think of my new hairstyle?" "What do I say when . . . ?" "I'm thinking about having four kids when I get married, and . . ." "I can't cook the whole meal, Mother! That's scary." "Let's all go skiing in the dark." "We just want to hang out with the kids. What's wrong with that?" "What's wrong with this music?" "But this is the style today; everybody's doing it." "Wear these clothes? That's old-fashioned." "Yeah, that's the hairstyle I want. I think it looks cool."

The eaglet has closely watched how its father stands as he scans the horizon. It now imitates the same stance. Whom do our youth imitate? As they teeter on the edge of the nest, preparing to make life's decisions, whose flying patterns are they watching—those of their peers or their parents? We must allow God to show us how to help them as they learn to fly in this life. It isn't animal instinct we want them to follow. We don't want to leave them to themselves! Our flight training has eternal ramifications! Are we pointing them in the right direction—toward biblical standards irrespective of fads and fashions? Do they know how to connect to the empowering Jesus so that the air currents of worldliness do not take them downward?

Learning to fly

Mother and Father eagle look at each other with understanding. The eaglets are no longer babies. Parenting now requires meeting a *new* need: learning *to fly*. The eaglet is ready, so Flying 101 begins. Father gives his eaglet a gentle push, and the youngster finds himself airborne. Frantically flapping his wings, he plummets downward. Father eagle is prepared for this. He swoops down to catch his little treasure on his back and carry him safely back up to the nest—letting his offspring feel flight for the first time. Back in the nest, the young eaglet huddles briefly, recovering from the fearful sensation of this new experience. But soon the intrigue of the big world draws it again.

This time, Mother is soaring by and calls to her youthful eaglet to jump. When he hesitates too long, she returns to the nest and gives him a little shove—then intercepts him as his father had done. Now, like a puppy retrieving a ball for fun, these parents give the youthful eaglet *opportunity to exercise his wings* while providing a safety net. The maturing eaglet develops courage and gleeful trust in this way.

Are we there for our maturing eaglets in a similar fashion? Are we showing them that their parents and Jesus are their safety net? Are we encouraging them to practice flying—making right choices the right way? When they need us, are we swooping down to pick them up in a healthy and safe manner—before they are dashed on the rocks below? Do they see our help as loving? Are they learning to try again and again, choosing right over wrong until it becomes who they are?

On the other hand, are they hovering in the nest—fearing to choose, fearing to fall, or fearing to displease you because you'll yell and criticize their trying? If we demean their choices or give them a guilt trip for not doing what we would do, if we don't reason with them and tell them why we do what we do, are we helping them learn how to make good choices? If we are demeaning and denunciatory in our approach, we're pushing them away from us and toward their peers!

If we are inattentive and neglect the important training of these years, Satan will take up the slack. Do you really want that? If we don't decide to direct our youth to God, we are deciding to let Satan lead them! There is no middle ground. But if we will be attentive under God, He will give us His own courage and confidence to direct our youth to Him. We can replace our demeaning, fretful, faultfinding ways with wise restraint, loving direction, and sympathetic encouragement.

The eagle's driving purpose of life must become our own! Dedicated and focused like the eagle, we need to be teaching our teens how to become adults—how to make wise choices that will result in successful living. We open the textbook of *true flight* to our teens' minds when we help them decide to spend time with God, to learn to hear His voice in Scripture, in their conscience, in providence, and their daily walk. Will they participate or will they decline? Decisions for good or evil truly determine their destiny.

Pushing our young people off the edge of the nest is challenging them to apply God's principles in their daily life. When you call them to participate in washing the dishes cheerfully, scrubbing the tub faithfully, or preparing the meal willingly, you are giving them the opportunity to spread their wings in trust and obedience. Insisting that they do their schoolwork thoroughly or keep their room neat and orderly tests their flight skills. These challenges call them to a decision to obey or not to obey. They can choose to fly with God when Mother calls them to soar above the pull of their flesh—or they can sink beneath the gravity of self and be grumpy, unfaithful, disorderly, or rebellious. We are to be their safety net showing them how to fly, catching them when they fall, and returning them to the nest for another try until they get it right.

Flying requires defying the law of gravity while cooperating with the laws of flight. Being a Christian requires defying the law of sin and self while cooperating with the laws of heaven. When we ask our teen to do something that crosses self, they have the opportunity to choose flight or disaster. We must be there to pick them up and bring them back to try again. It's all right to fail. Trying and failing and trying again is called learning. Trying and failing and giving up is called quitting. We can love our youth by helping them to keep trying until they succeed.

We have an enemy, Satan, who tries to deceive these inexperienced eaglets. He, too, calls for flight—but flight of a very different nature—more like a death spiral. He confuses license with liberty and leads our youth into *abject bondage*. He inspires them with his own negative or rebellious thoughts, feelings, and emotions. He cries out to the eaglet, "Jump! Jump and fly free from restraint! Be unwilling to help! Go have fun with your friends! Do forbidden things! It doesn't matter! Your parents and God don't know what they are talking about. They are just trying to keep you from all the fun!" Many youth believe him and jump, thinking they are truly flying. But eventually, they find he was only leading them on until their crash course was set. Then he laughs as they flounder.

True flight comes when the eaglet makes the decision to filter all his thoughts, feelings, emotions, habits, and inclinations through Christ and His Word. The *art of flying* is choosing to listen to God's voice and to connect with Him for power as he jumps to obey. It is clinging to Jesus' back and flying in Him—not attempting to fly in the strength of self.

Pressing upward

Have you ever heard the eagle scream? When trapped in a narrow valley by dark storm clouds, the eagle swoops back and forth, sending its strident cry for freedom echoing from rock to rock. It can't see the sunshine, but it knows by faith that it is there. Soon with a shrill scream, the eagle darts upward into the darkest part of the cloud and wings its way upward to the clear sky above.

Our youth must learn first by faith (not by sight) and then by experience that he doesn't have to stay under the cloud of bad habits, bad attitudes, vice, or rebellion. It is a powerless Christianity that says we must live under the cloud. Our teens, like the eagle, can cry out to God, "I don't have to stay under this cloud of earthly negative thinking or feeling! Sunlight and life is just on the other side! I'm going to press through the darkness into the sunshine of life—Jesus!"

He sees nothing, senses nothing, can hope for nothing. But faith and experience tell him that there is sunshine and life (in Jesus) on the other side, and he longs for it. He pierces *through* the dark fog, the storm clouds of trials, difficulties, and selfish inclination. By faith he screams and flies through the clouds of uncertainty and finds *true freedom and life.*

Do you see it? Are you experiencing it yourself?

As the youth cries out to God, yields to Him and/or to his God-led parents, he applies all his effort. Jesus reveals His sunshine within, and His character shines without. The eaglet then becomes a diligent worker, a cheerful helper, a faithful team member in home duties. He learns to keep a neat and clean room and develops good study habits in school. With each choice to cooperate with divine power, his habits of right doing strengthen. Divine power attends his human effort and produces a life hid with Christ in God—real flight.

What better legacy could we give to our offspring?

As our young eaglets taste repeated success, they learn to like the challenge of flight. It's a newfound freedom to actually live above the flesh. They want to repeat this learning process because "in Christ" it works, whereas "in self" it doesn't. They are more inclined to cooperate with their parents in the important exchange of implementing good ways of thinking, feeling, or responding—and discontinuing the bad and harmful ways. They will find power to be all God created them to be. The sad become happy, the dishonest honest, the disobedient obedient, and the argumentative agreeable because God enables them to fly.

Experience with successful flight prepares them to navigate the challenges of worldly associates—both within and without the church. They will not desire wrong companionship. They will see it as shallow, empty, and not fulfilling, for their real needs are met—in their parents and in their personal, powerful God.

So the choice is ours, parents! Let's ask ourselves some pointed questions.

Is our flight training God-directed or self-directed? Is it Spirit-led or human-driven? Are we wisely seeing the need for positive direction to influence our youth in a good pathway of life, or are we letting them direct their own steps? Are we washing our hands of all responsibility? Are we too busy or preoccupied in other pursuits? Are we letting our teens dash themselves against the rocks below because it seems too troublesome to challenge their character weaknesses, self-experimentation, and unwise judgment? If this is you, realize you need not continue in this way!

God is willing to give us on-the-job training in flight instructions *if . . .* we will abandon our excuses and distractions and come to Him in the spirit of a learner. Much is at stake! Our youthful eaglets are wavering on the edges of their nests—preparing to launch into life sooner or later. Will we determine to do whatever it takes to loft them into the current of heaven? Or will we take the "easy" approach and watch them enter the death spiral of a self-directed life? Will we dedicate ourselves to meeting their needs as God planned, or will we let Satan fill the gap?

If we want to give our dear youth a better chance, we have some pretty important flight training to do. In the following chapters we will look more closely at different aspects of how to parent our teens by the Spirit. Come with me as we explore more closely how to meet more of those unmet needs we have neglected and save our youth!

THE LONE EMBRACE
A SPECIAL WORD OF ENCOURAGEMENT FOR SINGLE PARENTS

"I see unmet needs all over the place," you say. "How can I, one person, add anything more to my life, schedule, or duty list?"

God answers this question so simply, yet profoundly. "But seek ye first the kingdom of God, and his righteousness; and all these things shall be added unto you."[*]

Your attitude in this trial determines your altitude. Your seeking Christ first will give you the eagle-eye perspective, the big picture. Big things, insurmountable obstacles, become "small" through His eyes. Looking to Jesus' strength and not to your weakness is an important perspective to lift your attitude higher, and thus raise your goals and hopes as well.

God will put on you only that which you can do in and with Him. Fear not what is before you, for God will give you wisdom and enable you to do all that He asks you to do. Learn to walk and talk with Him as Enoch did. Read the Scriptures with God as your Interpreter. Ask Him to help you see the practical application of what you read. He is your faithful Teacher.[†]

This is your flight training—which you need so you can teach your youth. We can only teach what we ourselves know. When you have Jesus as your Husband, Counselor, Guide, and Friend, you have all you need to meet those unmet needs in your teen. They don't have to be left to the motley crew. And God will give you wisdom and a plan for how to draw them to your heart and His. He will multiply your efforts and empower your choices. You will see! So do your best under God and fear not. Begin by starting with your first step—make a plan with Christ to change in His strength.

---

[*]Matthew 6:33.
[†]John 6:45.

Chapter 2

Meeting Needs

Then answered Jesus and said unto them, Verily, verily, I say unto you,
The Son can do nothing of himself, but what he seeth the Father do:
for what things soever he doeth, these also doeth the Son likewise.
—John 5:19

*H*ow do we meet the unmet needs of Chains Charlie, Misfit Murphy, Tough Tommy, Abused Abby, Lying Larry, Mad Music Mandy, and the like?

Christ had true success in reaching people. He spent time with men and women as one desiring *their* good rather than His own. He sympathized with their circumstances and ministered to their needs, and in this way He won their confidence. Only then did He invite them to follow Him.

"Hey guys, how are you doing today?" Jim said to the group of youth.

"Pretty good. Why?" Chains Charlie responded.

"Oh, we feel sorry for you guys. You have all this energy. You want to do something fun and exciting, but it's hard to find something you really enjoy."

"So why are you interested in us?" Chains Charlie inquired suspiciously.

"I like young people. I believe most of them are just bored. They're not very interested in being Christians because they see so much hypocrisy in their homes and churches. They wonder why they should bother with it, since it seems obvious it isn't working. But the truth is that few of you have ever seen a real Christian and how attractive being one can be. Me?—I'm interested in caring for youth, getting them interested in something that will make their lives better. I'm thinking you would be a great house builder, Charlie. What do you think?"

"Well I helped my dad build a garage roof once—it was cool. But I don't have the opportunity to do anything like that. Most people don't want me around. So why are you interested in me?" he asked again skeptically.

"We just are," Jim replied. "Nothing in it for us."

The whole gang looked closely at this unusual fellow and his wife. One turned up his lip; a second furrowed his brow; a third rolled his eyes in disbelief. The girls just looked dubious.

"Hey, we live up the North Fork right near the river. Have you ever gone tubing down the rapids? It's great fun. How about coming up tomorrow? We can run the river and talk some more! If you want to, that is."

"Getting there costs money you know. I have a car, but I don't know if I can afford it," Chains Charlie looked cynical.

"It will take you about an hour and a half to get there from here. Costs about twenty dollars in gas, round trip. Here, I'll pay for your first trip." And Jim handed him twenty dollars.

Gaining the hearts of our youth requires an initial investment—of our time, our attention, our respect, and our interest. Most youth want someone to genuinely love and care for them. They want to belong, to fit in, and to be appreciated. It's a start. Then you build from there.

The kids all huddled together in a conference and then announced, "Yeah. We think that would be great fun. See you tomorrow!" And they shook our hands good-bye.

A worthwhile investment

The next day found us all on the river's edge, ready with our inner tubes. Jim gave safety instructions and asked. "Does everyone swim well?"

Shy Sarah and Tough Tommy didn't feel real confident, although they knew how to swim, so I offered. "I will go down the river beside you, Sarah, and make sure you're safe. You'll have fun; I'll let you know what you need to do. You'll do great, I'm sure."

Jim said, "Well, then, I'll go down with Tommy and show him all I know. I want the four of us to go first and the rest of you can follow. Have fun, but respect the river. It does have a very strong current."

Jim set off first with Tough Tommy following closely. As Jim floated backward, calling out a few more instructions to the rest of us, he didn't realize he was on a collision course with a protruding boulder. He got hung up on the rock, and the rest of us quickly floated past him, giggling at the surprised expression on his face.

"Hey, you guys, wait for me! You can't go ahead of your leader," he shouted good-naturedly. Everyone laughed.

Jim caught up with Tough Tommy just before we entered the rapids. "After this set of rapids, pull yourself to the right to approach the next set," he instructed.

The rapids were fun. Cold water splashed Shy Sarah in the face, and she shrieked fearfully. I pulled near her to make sure she was all right. Then I hit high-low rapids myself on purpose and got a big splash that covered me entirely. I shrieked for joy and turned to her. "It's really cold, isn't it? I just love this fun in the river." With each splash I squealed excitedly. Soon Shy Sarah was doing the same.

The first rapids finished, and pulling to the right, we entered the second set of rapids for more fun and splashes. The boys were having a great time. Jim was talking and playing with them, and they quickly warmed up to him because he was so much fun. He really seemed to care about each of them.

Next came a calm, deep area in the river we call "Beast Alley." Jim explained, "In this stretch of the river it's free game to dump one another safely. If anyone wants to opt out of this part, just put your hands up in a timeout fashion, and you will be left alone. This is supposed to be fun for each of us—so let's respect one another."

The free-for-all began, and in great fun most everyone was dumped at least once. Shy Sarah opted out, and Despairing Dora came close to see that she was OK. Chains Charlie dumped Tough Tommy, who came up coughing. Jim came over to make sure he was all right and instructed him how to remount the inner tube. Tough

Tommy opted out of his second dumping from Misfit Murphy, but Misfit Murphy was all for dumping him anyway.

Jim came alongside and said, "No, he asked to be left out, so let's respect him. That's fair. Why don't you dump someone else?"

Misfit Murphy began to respond angrily, but then thought better of it. Instead he turned his fun upon dumping Jim. Jim made a good game of it all and soon was out of his tube begging mercy. Soon we were approaching another set of rapids, and Jim called everyone to mount their inner tubes.

"Be sure to pick up your backside here as rocks are common on the surface. After rounding the curve stay in the middle for the wildest ride of your life."

"Hey that was great fun. Let's do it again!" Misfit Murphy said when we had gone through these rapids. And everyone agreed, even Shy Sarah.

So we did it again, and again. Tired, we all returned to our house, enthusiastically sharing what each liked best about our adventure. I made a little meal of fruit and bread; two of the girls came into the kitchen to help. We sat down in little groups and lively conversations began. Jim and I talked individually with several in the group, showing genuine interest in them. We wanted to get to know each one. Soon it was time for them to leave. We shook hands with some and hugged others.

"Hey, when can we do this again?" Abused Abby asked.

"Well, we'd love to get to know you better. Tomorrow I need to shovel this gravel on my driveway and do a few home projects first, but I can be done and go to the river about five-thirty in the afternoon, if that works for you?" Jim offered.

All would come who could, they decided. "See you tomorrow," they chimed together.

"Bye. Thanks for coming. Sure had a good time with each of you." I said, waving.

Involving them

The next day all the kids arrived early. They wanted to help us shovel the gravel out of the trailer and rake it smooth on the driveway. Jim talked and made working together lots of fun with interesting talk.

Mad Music Mandy came into the house, offering to help me with whatever I was doing. Oh, she was so sweet! We finished the cooking I was doing, folded the clothes, and swept the kitchen floor while we talked.

"So what do you want to do when you grow up, Mandy?" I asked.

"I don't really know; haven't thought about it much."

"Are you interested in the medical field, secretarial work, housekeeping, or do you want to be a mother?"

"Well, I do have some interest in the medical field. I thought about being an X-ray technician," she responded.

"What interests you in that?"

"My uncle is an X-ray tech, and he makes good money."

"Are you good at mechanics or taking things apart? How are your math skills?"

"I'm a dumbo with anything mechanical. I took a broken clock apart once and tried to put it back together. My father got real mad at me that I couldn't do it. My math is OK, but I'm not a whiz at it like my brother. Why?"

"I'm looking at what occupation would fit you—rather than what would make you the most money. It's nice to like your work. There will always be hassles in a job, but if you like it, that makes all the difference. Have you ever considered being a nurse?"

"As a matter of fact, I have. My family tells me I'd never be able to pass the classes because I'm too dumb." And her shoulders drooped.

"Well, I see in you a heart of helpfulness—from what you've done here to help me today. If you have a nurse's heart, I know you can do it if you apply yourself. It doesn't matter if it's hard, when you like it."

"You think I can? No one else thinks I can do anything good. I've sort of given up on the idea of being a nurse." She looked at me with a glimmer of hope in her eyes.

"You could try nursing—even now at fourteen—if you want to," I suggested.

"I could? How?"

"If you study and train to be a certified nursing assistant, you can work at a nursing home or a hospital as an aide and see if you really have an aptitude and liking for being a nurse. You'll get a feel, too, for the studies involved and whether you can keep up. If you have difficulty understanding something, I'll be glad to help where I can. I am an RN, and my family didn't think I would ever finish college either. They discouraged me from even trying. But I did it, and so can you, if you apply yourself. I just love nursing. Think it over."

"Thanks! I will. I'll think about that." She smiled.

We talked about different occupations that she could consider, but in the end, her highest interest was still nursing. "You'd really help me if I didn't understand something?" she questioned.

"Sure, I would. You're important to me. I would love helping you."

Under her breath I heard her say, "I wish my mom would care about me like this."

I prayed to God, "Should I pursue that or leave it alone?"

"Let's cover this area another time. She has a lot to think about already," God directed my thoughts.

"Lord, should I bring up her walk with You?" I inquired.

"No, not yet," He impressed upon my reason.

"You're a sweet young lady, Mandy. I really like working with you. I think it's time to get ready for the river. Let's see if the rest are done with all that gravel outside. I'm looking forward to the river tubing, how about you?"

"Yeah, what's not to like?" Mad Music Mandy was beaming because someone thought she had value and that she could become a nurse, and someone was there to help her when needed.

Stepping onto the back porch, we saw Chains Charlie leaning on his shovel in the empty trailer while Tough Tommy and Lying Larry were each leaning on their gravel rakes behind the trailer. They were involved in a very lively conversation with Jim about occupations and options for each of them.

"No one has ever tried to help me figure out what I want to be. I'm excited about getting into some construction work to see if it fits me," exclaimed Chains Charlie.

Tough Tommy was thinking about trying harder in school. He would like to run a sporting goods shop someday, and he knew he would need to improve his math to make that happen. Lying Larry wasn't sure what he wanted to be, but he sure was enjoying all this excitement.

Off to the river we all went. Riding the waves and dunking each other was even more of a blast this evening than it had been the last! Knowing each other a little better just added to the fun. Later, as we relaxed at home with a little snack, a bundle of questions arose from the boys regarding other occupations for their lives. They wanted to know more about apprenticeships and its benefits. Now they were interested in any advice Jim gave. When it came time to leave, no one wanted to go. They hung around . . . and hung around . . . delaying leaving. When they finally said Goodbye, we gave each a tender hug—no more handshakes. It was evident in their eyes that love and trust were growing. Jim and I felt this was such a sweet reward for caring and helping.

"When can we go down the river again with you all?" Lying Larry asked.

"We will be traveling for a week, but the following week we can go on Wednesday. Would that work for you?" Jim replied.

"We'll plan on it," they chorused.

Showing interest in them

On the appointed day they again came early to help with anything that needed to be done. They loved working with us; they felt appreciated. Getting instructions from us was a joy rather than a burden. The boys wanted to help Jim change the oil in the car, and they argued about who would get the privilege of being under the car with him.

"Let me show you a good way to resolve problems, boys, so everything's fair. *Real men* watch out for the little guy, right?"

"How is that fair, when I want to do it, too?" Chains Charlie asked.

"Well, a real man will give the younger fellow a chance. You were the younger fellow once, weren't you? Did you get a chance? Or did you always get put aside?"

"I always got put aside until I got bigger and stronger," he replied.

"A real man looks out for the younger ones because he is a true leader. He wants to be fair. So he plans opportunities for everyone to get a chance. That way no one gets hurt. It all works out in the end."

"That's a new thought. It seems right somehow. OK, I'll trust you. Let's try it."

So the youngest boy got under the car with Jim and helped change the oil.

Jim decided to have them all help wash the car. They got into a fun water fight, chased each other all over the yard, got soaked, and had lots of excitement, and the car got really clean.

There was still some time left over, so Jim took Chains Charlie to help him check out one of his brakes that was making noise.

"That looks complicated," commented Chains Charlie. "I never saw the inside of a brake drum before. But it looks like there is some gravel in there."

"That's the culprit, young man. Sure glad I have you here. You're one intelligent fellow. You can help me anytime," Jim encouraged.

Then we all went for some more river fun. The girls got cold, as the sun was hidden behind a cloud that night. So I started up the wood stove to warm them up. They were as warm and friendly as my own children. "Lord, how can I move them toward You?"

"Look for ways to meet their needs. I'm with you."

"Mandy, what are your thoughts about nursing these days?" I asked.

"Well, there is a class starting next week. I want to take it, but my mom is against it. She says it's foolishness and that I won't like it. Dad offered to pay for the class, but Mom's really down on it and got into a big argument with him. It was really bad. Guess I can't go after all. I'm real disappointed. The only thing nice that's happened to me is meeting you and your husband."

"Are you an active Christian? Do you know how to let God help you in this?"

"We go to church every now and then. The people there are just as mixed up as anyone I know. I don't see anything worth wanting there. The parents say one thing to their kids and do another. So I guess I'm not a Christian. I haven't seen God help anyone I know. Why would He help me?"

Getting deeper

"There *is* a lot of hypocrisy in the churches today," I agreed. "You're right. Most professed Christians don't know Jesus personally. And they fail miserably trying to be a Christian in the power of their own will. This is a pitiful state. But Jesus is *real* even if they are not. He still wants to help you and me out of all our troubles. He longs to talk with you through your conscience—not only about what is right and wrong, but also about the best way for you to follow in your occupation. He can change your mother's heart to help you go to the nursing class, if that is best for you. He can put the right words in your mind—the right approach—to speak to her about it. Or He may encourage you to be silent, as you learn to listen for His voice to your mind and heart. God doesn't speak in an audible voice; it's more like one of the thoughts that comes into our mind. When you give God permission to lead you, He will. Then, your part is to cooperate and follow."

"How will I know if it is Jesus speaking to me?" she asked.

"If the thought suggests that you do something you know is wrong or bad, you can know it's not God but your flesh or Satan speaking to your mind. So every thought is *not* from God.

"But if the thought is truth and has Christ's spirit with it, you can trust it is God speaking. We need to judge the thought according to the Bible—so we need to know our Bible, don't we? We must decide to follow it, and do it, too—that's experimentation. We must come to learn the voice of God through experimentation.

"So you can see the importance of spending time with God in the morning and committing yourself to be under His leadership rather than Satan's. Ask Him to show you what His will is for you. You can trust Him—he has your best interest at heart. For example, if He asks you to speak to your mother, do what He says and do it kindly like Jesus would, were He you. He will direct you. Try Him and see," I instructed.

"I will," she said simply.

We were all sitting around the warm stove enjoying the pleasant conversation when we noticed Abused Abby had a troubled expression on her face. Jim asked her, "What are you thinking about, Abby?"

"How I wish I lived here rather than at my home. How I wish my parents loved me like you do. I wish I could talk nice like this to my parents and tell them all my troubles and thoughts."

Then we saw her poor problem-solving techniques kick in for self-protection.

"But that is all right. I don't need anyone else. I am what I am, and that is all I am. I'll just enjoy being ugly old me. At least my friends here like me. They don't care that I'm damaged goods. They accept me. I don't need my parents. I'm just a bother and a pain to them anyway."

"We love you," we assured her. "So tell us how you are bad and a bother to your parents. How do you see it?" We encouraged her to talk more.

She was touched, and a little tear fell from her cheek. Gaining her composure she said, "Well my parents are always pointing out all my faults to me. We get into lots of arguments. I've tried for years to please them, but I've given up—I can't. They love me conditionally upon my performance. If I don't think or respond the way they think I should, it's another lecture, more downers, and more I need to work on to change. At times they play this saint stuff and show me what the Bible says happens to people like me. They're always yelling. To survive I have to tune them out, go to my room, and fill my head with loud music—or I get depressed. Then they get on me for my music. I don't care what they think anymore.

"At night I slip out my bedroom window to go and be with my friends and have a bright spot in my life. My friends care for me. They think I'm fun." And she straightened up.

"How often do you slip away from home? What do your parents do to you when they catch you?" Jim asked.

"I probably crawl out the window three nights a week, at least. I can't survive without my friends." And she glanced around the room at each one. "My parents catch me fairly often. My mom has given up on me, but Dad really gives me a verbal whipping, and sometimes he hits me. But I don't care what they do to me. One day soon I plan to be gone forever and get out of their hair."

"My heart aches for you, Abby," I said. "Were you abused as a child? You called yourself damaged goods—what do you mean by that?"

"When I was six years old my parents had my uncle baby-sit us kids, and he sexually abused me. He wasn't interested in my brother or my sister—just me. I was afraid to tell my mother and didn't. He would put my brother and sister to bed, and then he'd hold me on his lap and tell me he loved me. For a long time I thought it was all my fault. Now that I'm older I understand differently, but it doesn't change anything!"

"So did you ever tell your parents about this?" I asked.

"Well, I'd fuss and be nasty when we were going to be baby-sat, and one day my mother spanked me real bad, and I got angry and told her what he was doing to me."

"What did your parents do?"

"Nothing. That really burned me. Both my parents would talk so nice with both my aunt and uncle. It wasn't fair, I thought! It made me feel worthless. But it doesn't matter what my uncle did to me. It was just another rejection to add to all the rest."

"Truly that was unfair, Abby. Justice should have been done for you. If I were the parent, I would have done something. You need to know that you were the innocent one. The offender should have been called to make things right. God is that kind of Parent to you, even now! Do you know that?"

"No, I don't know. What do you mean?" she asked.

"Well, Jesus will bring justice in the end. All the unfairness we deal with here on this earth will be evened out when Christ comes. Jesus loves you with an everlasting love. He will come to bring justice then, especially if it doesn't come during our lifetime. You can be sure that God is calling for your uncle's heart to make it right. But he has the free-will choice God gave him to refuse heaven's entreaties to righteousness. Satan is prince of this world, and that is why we see so much evil and unfairness here."

Abby looked startled. "Really?" she asked.

"Yes, Abby. Christ is coming to redeem His people who decide they don't want to be under Satan's control anymore. Satan tempts us to do wrong and then taunts us with our failures. He leads us to think that God is the One who is making us miserable, when the truth is God is the One who is waiting to make us free and successful. God has given us a free-will choice to say no to Satan's wrong ways and lying thoughts, and to say yes to God and right. God will give us His power to do this. If we try to do the right without God, we fail. Every such effort in self must fail. Most of the Christianity you see today is done in self and not in God. That's why we have plastic, pretentious, and professed Christians—not the genuine article."

"I never knew that before." Abby was really thinking about what I was saying. After a quiet pause, she asked, "You mean God can be real and personal? Is there more to God than what I see at church?"

"Oh yes, Abby! Jesus is real and personal. He wants to come into your mind and reason with you about what is right and what is wrong for you. He will not force Himself upon you like Satan does. He gives you a free-will choice to choose to follow His suggestions or not. He wants to win you by His acts of love toward you that you do not deserve. He wants to lead you in this life to forgive your uncle, your mom, and your dad for all this as He leads you in His power, not yours alone. In Jesus you can do this and be freed in your mind and heart.

"As you accept God's forgiveness, you will find freedom from these things whether or not the people who have hurt you ask for forgiveness. You can be free. Free to be the Abby God intended you to be. Didn't Jesus befriend Mary Magdalene? Didn't He help her out of all her wrong ways, and heal her hurts? Only through forgiving will you find the happiness you desire and are searching for. You see, the love and happiness you desire is all found in Jesus. If you don't get it from others, that's all right because Jesus gives you all you need.

"You can be happy and at peace because you can please Jesus. He will become your heavenly Father and give you all the talk time, love, and parenting you need. He longs to spend time with you and heal you of your hurt. You can be at peace even amidst the storms in your home with yelling and rejection because Jesus is always with you. He will never leave you nor forsake you. You can be unruffled and free to be Christlike even amidst these storms—in Jesus. He will protect you in all situations of life and will make a way of escape for you. He will punish all the evildoers in due time."

"Are you sure?" asked Abby. "How can I really know that God will punish the evildoer?"

"We can know for sure, Abby, because God has promised it in His Word. God cannot lie! He says, 'Dearly beloved, avenge not yourselves, [don't] give place unto wrath: for it is written, Vengeance is mine; I will repay, saith the Lord.'*

"If you choose to come to Jesus, find Him as your Savior, and through Him forgive those who wronged you, He will heal you of those hurts. You can be freed from your history, not wounded afresh throughout your life. He can rid you of the cancer of bitterness working misery and death in you."

Abused Abby was in tune with what I was saying; her heart was longing for Jesus. "With all my heart, I want all you said. Please help me! What am I suppose to do?"

"Let's pray, Abby," I said tenderly. I knelt to pray right there, and Abby joined me. Jim went to his knees, and some of the rest of the young people knelt as well, while the others bowed their heads reverently, and we all prayed together in heart. First we prayed a surrender prayer, then a personal commitment to learn to follow God, and then a prayer giving Him access to work in Abby's family and home to make it better. She wanted Jesus to come into her heart, and He did right there for sure.

It was a solemn evening. Jim closed our time together with a beautiful, yet simple, prayer specific to each youth's home life, heart, and needs, giving God permission to work in them individually and to lead and direct them in their lives. It was heartwarming to hear from many of the lips there a personal affirmation that this was their hearts' desire as well. We exchanged warm hugs and sweet goodbyes.

---

*Romans 12:19.

Pursuing the example of Jesus does work! Our youth have real needs—they are not imaginary! When we follow God in ministering to those needs, their hearts open up to us—and to God!

After they left I said to Jim, "All of these hearts are being touched by God right now. I wonder what God's next step will be?" And Jim and I committed to pray for each of these precious youth as they seek to find the pathway to freedom in Christ.

THE LONE EMBRACE
A SPECIAL WORD OF ENCOURAGEMENT FOR SINGLE PARENTS

You want this experience for your youth, don't you? Do you feel inept to accomplish it alone? You don't have to do it alone—you can't! God is there for you, and He will see to it that all this is possible even for you, even under your forbidding circumstances.

In the heart of every youth is the desire to belong in his or her family—to be loved, appreciated, and cared for. Most youth are very merciful toward the failures of their parents if they see a change in a positive direction. They can be like a rubber band and forgive—won't you change with Christ and give them the hope they need so desperately? Your youth wants to talk with you like Abused Abby opened up with us, but many feel it is not safe for them now. Let God break down your walls and allow your youth entrance into your heart.

Our young people read the unspoken language that tells them they are a bother, are in the way, and are unloved. We must correct this wrong language with Christ leading, empowering, and dwelling in us.

We can become the parents our youth need—a parent who spends time with them, talks with them, listens to their woes, and gives practical solutions that work—respectfully, as this chapter demonstrates. We must learn how to give young people interesting, wholesome things to do. We must draw close to them, play with and enjoy them—not leave them to find these things in a group of peers who will accept them. Tell them how valuable they are to you by your words, your use of time, and your actions. Find their interests and help them reach their goals rather than yours. Directing them in their choice of an occupation is imperative. This will positively channel their time and energy. They need purpose. Let their schoolwork now have meaning so that they will apply themselves to it for their future goal. Inspire them that they can achieve their goals in Jesus and that you are there to help them wherever you can.

The youth described in this chapter turned around far more than this brief account indicates. Read on to see more of what changed them—and how the same approach can change your youth as well. It is so simple to meet our young people's basic needs. It just takes the right heart under Christ's leadership. And Christ is there for *you* today, this very moment.

God bless you!

Chapter 3
Abused Abby

Wash you, make you clean; put away the evil of your doings from before mine eyes;
cease to do evil; Learn to do well; . . . Come now, and let us reason together.
—Isaiah 1:16–18

The phone rang, and it was Abused Abby calling. She was a different person after last night. She was excited and just had to share with us. The night before, all the way home in the car, she had talked with God as though no one else were there, and through that conversation she became aware of how upset she was with her parents for doing nothing about her uncle's abusive behavior. She found herself talking at length with God about it all.

She committed herself to God's keeping and asked Him to open up and improve her communication with her mother—if that were possible—and to show her how to forgive both her parents and her uncle. She longed to know if Jesus was really there for her, as we had said He was.

The very next morning God provided an opportunity for her to talk with her mother. Abby shared everything on her heart. Her mother didn't see things as Abby did, but Abby felt she really listened—the first *real* conversation she could remember having with her mother. Now she had hope that maybe God could change her home. Maybe God *was* real.

We rejoiced with Abby and arranged to meet her in town over lunch the next day to talk further. She had many more questions; now she was on fire to do whatever she could to cooperate with God. He had showed His care for her so quickly. She realized He was truly there for her.

"So, Abby, you are almost fifteen years old now. What do you want to do as an occupation when you grow up?" Jim asked.

"I don't know," she said with downcast eyes.

We explored all sorts of occupations, looking for an answering spark of interest. Nothing seemed to attract her, so Jim pressed a little further.

"You're a very bright girl—more like seventeen or eighteen years old than fourteen. You're vivacious and a thinker. Abby, it is hard for me to believe you don't have something in that mind of yours of what you'd like to do. Come on! What's in your heart?"

She hesitated, and replied tentatively, "Well, I've told my dad that I want to be a mortician. I want to run a funeral home and make the people look real good after they die."

We had offered many ideas, but this was one we hadn't thought of! "That sounds good, Abby," Jim replied. "It's certainly different! You're a very unique individual, and God can use people in this profession too. What if I talk with your dad about getting you into an apprenticeship position in a funeral home so you can see if you have the stomach for such an occupation?"

Now it was Abby's turn to be shocked. "You mean you would do that? Do you really think my dad would help me? He's never been willing to help me before. You mean you'd really do that for me?"

"Sure I would. You've found Jesus now, and He will help you change and become anything you choose to be. You really want to do this, don't you?"

"I sure do! This is the most exciting thing that could ever happen to me. I can't believe this is happening." Her face flushed with the unexpected possibility.

"Well, Abby, there are some things you need to change in order to get this opportunity of a lifetime. You need to change the way you dress. You can't go into a funeral home to work dressing like you do. It's too provocative. I don't know what kind of men work in a funeral home, but we need to protect you from unwanted attention. You need to dress modestly, with no low-cut, tight-fitting tops, no mini-skirts, no tight pants or sloppy pants like you are accustomed to wearing right now. You must develop a professional appearance. Are you willing to do that?" Jim encouraged.

"I've never thought about that. I like the way Sally dresses; I could do something like that."

"Abby, you have Jesus now," I interjected, "and you can overcome all these things that seem so difficult right now—because Jesus is a *big God*. He will help you work through the changes one step at a time. Don't fear change. Jesus will begin with your thoughts and ideas, challenging some, suggesting new ways to look at dress. It may irritate or agitate you. But He will leave you free to accept or reject His ideas. Remember, though, He can help you only as far as you are willing to let Him lead you. You need to seek His will and learn to do His will. In following God you will find the happiness and joy of life you desire. God can change your likes and dislikes when you ask Him and let Him. You can become all you desire to be."

"Really, Sally? Is that true? God will work with me like that—even with my dress?" Hope mingled with disbelief in her voice.

"Oh yes, Abby. God cares about every little detail of your life! Whenever you want to know God's will, He will show you what you need to know, and He will allow you to exercise your *free-will choice*, which is of greater value than any forced submission.

"The devil will speak to your thoughts as well. He often pushes the emotional buttons of 'I don't like this or that.' 'Why do I have to change this?' Feelings of resentment will cloud the issue. Satan will not leave you with a free will; he will try to force and coerce you, often using your feelings, emotions, and passions as a very loud voice. If you don't follow his suggestions, then he will use more of the spirit of force and compulsion. This is Satan's voice. You'll need to experiment distinguishing between these two voices."

"I've started to see that difference already in my relationship with my mother," Abby reflected.

I continued. "You've tasted that following Jesus has good results with your mother; it will be the same with your dress. All you have to do is decide to dress for Jesus. Not for this or that group. Don't change for a church or a person, not even for me, but change for Jesus. Dressing for Jesus will make lasting changes because Jesus has the power that can change your thoughts, your feelings, your habits, and your ideas right down to the core of your heart—when you give Him permission to do so. You are free to be what you choose to be. This leads to stability. But if you dress to meet someone else's ideas, you will likely give it up down the line, be unstable, and wrongly think this is Jesus forcing you to do something you don't want to do. So sort this out with God."

"Well, I'm willing to try and see. If this is the cost for working with a mortician, I can do it!" Abused Abby said enthusiastically.

Ups and downs

Jim called and talked with Abby's dad, and when he grasped the potential positive influence in his daughter's life, he was willing to get involved. Abused Abby went home and had a lovely communication time with her dad. She told him why she slipped out of the house at night, of her need for acceptance and someone to listen to her, and her longing for this "someone" to be her parents. She asked why he didn't seem to listen or care. They had a good talk! Her mom still didn't seem to understand or care, but her dad had a listening ear and some compassion for her. This was good. This caring from her dad became a big motivation for her to consider being different.

Abby changed her dress in preparation for her great opportunity. She threw herself into studying everything she could find about being a mortician—even with no pay. Now she had no free time for getting into trouble. Even her schoolwork improved, for it had a purpose now. She was a very bright girl. Her interest level was high, and she felt she was in heaven—life was grand! Her parents talked more with her, and her home life was improving. She was hopeful and feeling more love than she had ever known from her parents.

One day she called me in frustration. "My mom is trying to be different after our talk, but it's like it just isn't in her to understand me. I have so much to be thankful for! I see Mom and Dad so differently these days. But *my* response to my mother is like a tornado, and that concerns me. It's like I react so nasty to her, without even intending to. I feel badly about it afterwards. I'm spending time with God each morning—well most mornings anyway—but this isn't changing. What's wrong with me?"

I replied, "One very important question to ask ourselves as followers after Christ is, Why do I react the way I do? To understand one's self is a great knowledge. Often we react violently because of our history inside us. Let me explain. You have grown up feeling unloved and unwanted because of your mother's nonverbal as well as verbal communication. Satan has told you a lie—that your mother doesn't love you—so often that you have believed it. These wrong thoughts have led you to set up a habit of responding in a self-protective manner. You've probably withdrawn emotionally from your mom over the years because you resent her lack of love toward you."

"You're right," Abby interrupted. "I'd go play outside the house just to be away from my mother. I'd go to my room or try to be with friends—anything to just be away from her. She was always on me, and I couldn't do anything right unless I did it her way, like a robot. I *was* protecting myself from being hurt anymore by her."

"Yes, that is our *history habits*. All those old *unresolved issues* push the tornado of emotions you described to me without your conscious decision. You are responding in an automatic mode of self-protection when your mother says or does something similar to the way she has acted in the past. You are reacting to all of that history of hurtful interactions in the only way you've known until now. You are obeying your feelings in this way.

"But God came to set us free from the wrong way of responding. He wants to help us think His thoughts, feel His feelings, and use His power to effect this change. He needs you to consciously give Him permission to take away this *history response*. In order to do that, He needs some time to talk with you about it—and you with Him. He wants you to understand why you respond that way. So He will lead you to reason this through often, using questions to direct your reason. Follow Him. If you get negative and emotional, it's likely Satan interjecting his thoughts to discourage you. When the mind wanders in this process, just bring it back to God. Say that you want to be under God rather than Satan. Does this make sense to you?"

"It sure seems logical. God is much like a parent, isn't He?" Abby asked.

"Yes, He is, Abby. God will also want to teach you how to forgive your mother. I'm sure if you knew your mother's history, you'd find it to be a difficult one and that she has baggage from the past. So God wants to teach you how to pity her because you realize that she responds to you the way she does and hurts you because this is a self-protection mode she uses to avoid being hurt herself. It's her *history habits* working. God will reason with your mind in this way, so you can have compassion and pity on your mother. Then He will teach you how to forgive her from your inner heart, by His grace working in your thoughts. To change your feelings, God needs your thoughts first. Cooperating with right thoughts from Jesus can create right feelings. Jesus came to redeem our characters, which consist of our thoughts and feelings together. God knows that *of ourselves* we cannot change them. He knows we need Him to re-create us. He awaits our will and consent for Him to perform this work. When God has our thoughts and feelings, He can redirect our responses. Our thoughts and feelings create and drive our response for good or evil. Do you see that?"

"I do! This makes so much sense. So I need talk time with God for Him to help me sort all these things out. He understands my mother and me. I didn't realize how important that morning time with God really was. And my mother did have a hard life growing up," Abby commented.

"God wants to help change your home for the better, but first He has to get someone—parent or child—to come to know Him, to recognize His voice, and follow Him. God needs you to cooperate with Him so He can free you. When you find freedom from your history, you can tell your mother what Jesus can do for her. And it won't be just rhetoric. You can share this very practically with her, from your experience. You will understand the struggles in her thoughts, feelings, emotions, and habits. Now you can encourage her by showing her what to do with her wrong thoughts and feelings and how to turn away from despair and turn to God. You can share with her how to be changed in Jesus. Few today really understand how God works with us, freeing us from these old ways."

"I want that!" Abused Abby exclaimed.

"This process of forgiveness will free you, Abby. As you forgive others in your life, you will be set free in Jesus to become Happy Abby. You need not have any scars from the wrongs done to you in the past, and your history need not hurt, wound, or hinder you anymore. You will be washed clean as only Jesus can do! God understands your situation of abuse. If you will admit your bitterness, He will forgive and cleanse you.* And thus the truth shall set you free, and you will be free indeed. God's new thoughts will replace your old hurtful ones. In this way you can become upright and live a happy life forever in Jesus even if the circumstances in your home never change or your uncle never asks for forgiveness."

"Really? I want that!" Happy Abby responded. "How can that be?"

"Well, when you know Jesus personally like this, He will reveal your wrong thoughts and feelings and help you to replace them with God's positive ones. He will be your Shepherd to direct you with new thoughts and empower you *to do* your right choices."

I continued, "For instance, instead of thinking and believing your mother hates you and that you are in her way, you can believe she loves you the best she knows how. God will lead your reason to have pity for her history that has contributed to her poor responses to you. God will lead you to have compassion for her and to appreciate what you can of her now. You'll recognize you can't expect her to change until she meets Jesus and finds the power to change. In herself, she cannot change any more than you could. In praying for her, seeing her from God's perspective, you are set free to love her genuinely. God will put His feelings of contentedness and prayerful support for your mother in you. Now you can be thankful for the love she can show. Wouldn't that be great?"

"Oh, yes! I'm beginning to understand more! I see my dad had a tough life too, like Mom. He's provided more for me than he had growing up as a child. That is his love to me, isn't it?"

"Yes it is! You're getting it now," I encouraged her. "Jesus came to free you from these lying, twisted, perverted thoughts that kindle your *old* pain. Christ's new thoughts will dispel the tornado of thoughts first. Then as you cooperate in right thoughts, He will dispel your tornado responses too. He pronounces upon you His 'peace . . . be still!' "

"I see it now!" Abby said.

Hope springs up

After Abused Abby understood the battle between Christ and Satan for her thoughts and feelings, she began to trust that God could complete in His own timing what He had begun in her and with her family. Hope replaced the former residents of despair, hurt, and hopelessness. She had an understanding of a personal Savior that was big enough for whatever might come into her life.

---

*1 John 1:9.

"As you come out of these lying, negative views of your life and find that God is cleansing you from wrong ways, Heaven's peace will flood your soul. Then God may use you to share this understanding with your mother, so that she, too, can find the same peace and freedom from her history and bad problem-solving techniques that you did. This is exciting!"

Freedom gleamed from Abused Abby's countenance even now without one single change in her parents' or her circumstances. She had understanding, purpose, and direction for her life. Preparing for her possible career gave her a sense of value. She also had hope that her family situation could change and that she need not have to respond like a tornado anymore. She was thankful for God's personal presence with her, directing her. She would trust Jesus.

At home, Abby and her dad pored through the yellow pages looking for funeral homes in their area. They drove by each one and noted which were closest to home. Then they began interviewing the various offices. Abby dressed modestly yet attractively. The staff at one funeral home appealed more to Abby than the others. She and her dad discussed it for a few days, and she prayed to God to lead her choices. Then she offered her services free-of-charge to the most attractive choice.

Again Abused Abby was so excited that she gave us a call to share all her excitement and joy. Jim encouraged her, saying, "Make yourself so valuable that they can't get along without Happy Abby. After two weeks' trial, sit down with them and negotiate your salary. Apprenticing this way is more like a free college education. How do you feel now?"

"Oh, I'm so excited! I can't say thank you enough to you for helping me get here! My dad and I are talking like never before. School subjects seem important to me now. I need to increase my math skills. My dad said he'd teach me some shortcuts to being quick with my calculations. The funeral home staff told me that anatomy and physiology are good to know too. I want to learn it all. They gave me some books that will be helpful to read, and so I'll work my way through them in my spare time. This summer I plan to buy those anatomy books to learn all the bones and muscles so I know what people are talking about when I work with them."

Parents, do you see how having a sense of purpose and direction brings focus and fun to those school lessons? Why? Now the young person has a purpose. Learning becomes a step toward a personal goal. Time is filled with good, essential things rather than idleness, evil thoughts, poor or bad activities, and unhealthy relationships.

Learning and growing

After a few weeks of apprenticeship, Abby was even more enthusiastic. She was learning lots of things. She would clean up, sweep, and gather equipment. She did a lot of watching and combing of hair before showings. Some things seemed a bit gruesome, but the end results were the goal.

"How are you doing, Abby?"

"Hey, it's going pretty good. They let me assist a little today. They want me to finish reading the books they gave me. I'm considering it my career education. It's a lot of work and takes all my free time in the evenings. They like me, and I like them. They hired me! Can you believe it?

"You know, things are going better at home too. There is a lot of housekeeping at the funeral home—like preparing for guests all the time. I'm learning to have a better eye for order and attractiveness. So I have changed my room from blasé into extraordinary. Mom really likes it that I'm taking such an interest in my room. She asked me to help her make our living room more orderly and attractive. Hey, I think that could be fun."

"How are you doing with your responses to your mom?" I asked.

"I've been really keeping my time with God in the morning—praying, reading, and talking to Him, as well as listening for Him to talk with me. I've had some good experiences too. Like when I felt like being curt with Mom, God got my attention and brought this thought: *'Abby, don't you want to respond differently this time?'* It helped me recall my alternate plan, which is to cry out to Him for help to know what and how to respond.

"He simply suggested, *'Be respectful to your mom.'*

"I did it. And it made all the difference. I didn't tick her off as usual. And God has put pity in my heart for her. I asked her about her growing-up years, one day. They were awful. She's giving me better than she had. She does love me! She just doesn't know how to show it like she should. I'm still learning how to give God my wrong thoughts and feelings, but I'm growing. When I get it down better, I'll share it with Mom—if she wants to listen."

"Abby, this is on-the-job training. It's like your apprenticeship job. You look to these people to help you learn the ropes, and by watching, reading, learning, and experimenting, you are learning. So, too, with God. You are apprenticing under Him, learning to recognize His voice day by day, and filtering through Him what you should do and how you should do it.

"You are learning useful labor and more efficient work habits. With Jesus, you are learning to deal with your wrong habits, thoughts, and emotions, which is *true* character development. You are carrying greater responsibilities in your home as well as learning to do so in the workplace. This is great. You are growing into a fine young lady! Do you like being this busy?"

Happy Abby smiled and said, "Oh, I love it. I feel useful. I feel needed and valuable."

And so Happy Abby continued to grow. She met hardships and setbacks. When her parents couldn't help her, Jim and I were there for her. She grew to see that God was there for her in all situations. She saw how the way she dressed could help her in dealing with men. She wanted to be pure now! She learned to persevere with God for a solution to the questions of how to make her home life happier, how to respond when anger or unfairness arose at home or work, and how to persevere in her studies. God even helped her to understand resentment when it arose and how to resolve it in her heart so that she was repeatedly freed from its plague.

She had looked upon God as stern and unjust instead of loving, caring, and helpful. She had always viewed herself as worthless, but now she learned that, in Christ, she has infinite value. She began to realize that she is capable and intelligent, and that she doesn't need to see herself as inadequate or stupid. She is becoming a hard, faithful worker at the tender age of fifteen. God is becoming real to her. She is getting down on herself far less often than formerly. She is becoming increasingly happy.

Busy hands are happy hands. Giving her purpose and direction eliminates the idleness that is the devil's workshop. As we come into a healthy, heart relationship with our youth, instructing them in the way to go, in an attractive manner, we make God real, personal, attractive, and helpful as He truly is.

"Can the Ethiopian change his skin, or the leopard his spots? then may ye also do good, that are accustomed to do evil."* Christ says, "Abide in me, and I in you. As the branch cannot bear fruit of itself, except it abide in the vine; no more can ye, except ye abide in me. I am the vine, ye are the branches: He that abideth in me, and I in him, the same bringeth forth much fruit: for without me ye can do nothing."†

Wind under their wings

The dreams and goals of our youth are the winds that beckon them to fly. Those aspirations can be the motivation for them to reach out to Christ in a personal way. As we lovingly enter into their hearts, we can encourage their good interests that will improve their lives and occupy their time in a wholesome manner. Use their needs to turn them to Christ, to discover His voice, His interest, in their lives, and His empowering grace that can make their dreams come true. An eaglet fully occupied in learning to fly is doing what God designed it to do. Flying is discovering that Jesus is my personal Friend, Savior, and Creator who is interested in every detail of my life.

These young adults at age fourteen, fifteen, and upward are learning the "art of flying." These early lessons, under our watchful care and Spirit-directed encouragement, are essential prerequisites to proper independence. The older they get, the more prepared they should be to experiment with their own flight program because they know Jesus personally and depend on Him to direct them. To give free flight to a youth who doesn't know God personally is a very dangerous thing to do. His attempts to fly will be impelled by his history and his own impulses. The success or failure of our youths' flight is heavily dependent upon the parent properly directing their steps in a life occupation and teaching them how to come under Christ themselves.

Discuss with your youth what his/her future career will be. Look at his talents. Look at her skills. What are his desires? What are her dreams? Inspire the aspirations upward. Tell your youth their value. Show them that they can do anything in Jesus. Be realistic with them in a positive way. Then give them the opportunities to experience what it would be like to be a nurse, a mortician, a mechanic, a doctor, or whatever. Every child does best when he has a goal or purpose in life. Discuss with your young person real, current issues he will face. Encourage him that he can face them

---

*Jeremiah 13:23.
†John 15:4, 5.

successfully and that you will help him to be the best he can be, that God will change what needs changing inside of him and providentially lead him in the best possible way. Point out what Jesus is doing for him!

Your goals and directives will change according to what you are raising. Are you raising a rocket scientist? You know that studies come natural to him, so be sure you balance his program with physical exercise and social involvement. God wants balance! Are you raising a surgeon? Let him fix all your cuts and bruises. Allow him to pull your slivers, to develop a tender bedside manner. Are you raising an engineer? Give him opportunity to build a workbench, to construct a cabin with someone, or to do some concrete work at your home or a job site somewhere else. If an occupation he pursues isn't really for him, how much better to discover this in his teens than later? Redirect his course into another area if the chosen field doesn't work out.

If you can't direct his or her steps in an apprenticeship, find someone you can trust who can. Fill your youth's time with all the good and best things of life. The good will crowd out—or at least curtail—Satan's inroads in his life. Teach him practically of a real Jesus who can help him, who is there for him, and who will walk and talk with him. Don't consider your inconvenience in this, for the ramifications are eternal. We must be there for our youth!

Above all else, we want to give our offspring the ability to fly above the pull of the flesh! Only by acquaintance and association with Christ can they find real success!

THE LONE EMBRACE
A SPECIAL WORD OF ENCOURAGEMENT FOR SINGLE PARENTS

When you are the solo parent, things happen in life you wish never happened. Abused Abby was wrongly treated in those young formative years. Don't deny that it occurred. Don't blame the child. Seek God for wisdom and strength to deal with it—first for yourself and then with your child. Give your child the emotional support he or she needs. Let her know you love her. If it requires that you come out of your "history habits"—then so be it! It's worth the necessary change to break the cycle of family dysfunctions!

God can erase the spots of sin, circumstances, bad judgment, and mistakes if we face them *in Christ.* To deny them or not deal with them leaves far-reaching and big scars that hinder hopes of a happy life in your child. To not deal with the abusing individual in your child's/youth's life is to send a loud message that you do not love him or her. This has very destructive and far-reaching ramifications. But remember God can erase these spots. Go to Him for the emotional healing that needs to be done. It is possible.

"Draw nigh unto God, and He will draw nigh unto you."*

---

*James 4:8.

Chapter 4
History Plays a Part

Behold, I was shaped in iniquity; and in sin did my mother conceive me.
—Psalm 51:5

Silly Sal from Siam! Silly Sal from Siam! Silly Sal from Siam!" taunted Dean, one of my brothers. I tried ignoring him, but he didn't stop. I finally snapped at him to be quiet. He could see he was getting under my skin, and his fervor only increased. So I slugged him. He slugged me back. I was a young teen, and this had been going on for years. He always won, and my resentment was growing. I always had to take his teasing with no recourse.

I was Walter and Vicki's fifth child and first daughter. While my parents were excited to finally have a girl, I soon became just another task on Vicki's To Do list and another mouth for Walter to figure out how to feed. They had little time to spend with me. While all my physical needs were dutifully attended to, I grew up sensing often that I was in the way. My mother was an at-home mom during my younger years, but seamstress activities consumed her time, attention, and energy. I learned early that I was expected to stay out of her way and entertain myself. I played with blocks, colored, and practiced acrobatics, finding companionship with the family parakeet or my brother Byron.

Brother Byron was a bully, but for some reason Mother seemed to pet and protect him. She consistently sided with Byron even though I would tell her truthfully about our spats. I was unfairly labeled a tattletale and liar. Children learn to accept their lot; they have neither the reason nor experience to do otherwise.

My three other older brothers were also busy raising themselves. To them, I was just a bother. Tyson, the oldest, was in the army reserve; when he came home on leave he'd pull my hair and tease me mercilessly—in fun of course. Dean and Sam, who were six and nine years older than me, were absorbed with school, friends, and youth activities. When they were home, I seemed no more important to them than a table or a lamp.

Although Vicki seldom went to church, Walter was concerned about his children's spiritual welfare and faithfully took them to a conservative Lutheran church. I fell in love with the choir's music. In church listening to the choir, I *felt* understood. Often the songs expressed the sorrow in my heart, and I longed for the healing and freedom the songs expressed. I was a very shy girl, hiding behind my mother's skirt on the rare occasions she attended church. More often, I would slink into a pew, hoping to not be noticed. My shyness only increased as I entered my teen years. In religion classes, fear of rejection and/or conflict hindered me from saying what I thought. Emotional anxiety was a way of life.

Ten-year-old Byron wanted to be with his friends and was irritated to have to watch over his little sister even though I didn't slow them down. As a seven-year-old,

I climbed with them to the second-story roof of the school building, played kick the can, and rode bikes as well as any boy. But one day Byron particularly didn't want to look after me. He talked me into playing cowboys and Indians—and I was the cowboy. The chase was on. Soon the "Indians" had captured me and securely tied me to a tree in the neighbor's backyard. Then the boys ran away. After a very long time, I realized I had been abandoned as well as rejected. No one was home, so tears didn't help. Finally I began to scream until help came.

Training the turtle response

Rarely could I talk to my parents about my trials. Oh, I would chatter about inconsequential things, but it was obvious my mother wasn't listening. Neither parent had the time or inclination to talk about problem-solving or feelings, or to suggest good responses.

Mother was the only disciplinarian in the home. When I did wrong, Mother reproved me with cold silence—a silence that left me to imagine what my offense had been. I often believed it to be much greater than it really was because no amount of asking, pleading, or apologizing relieved the tension. Desperate for Mother's approval, I would try to do some household chore, but Mother usually responded with criticism or would redo the task herself in a rash and angry spirit. The result was a deep-seated insecurity and uncertainty that led to self-destructive thinking. I learned very early to pull into my shell of self-protection—just like a turtle. I truly believed that I was no good.

Demeaning Dean regularly teased me, telling me that I was dumb, stupid, fat, and ugly. His negative remarks, spoken "in fun," only reinforced the lies I already believed about myself. Demeaning Dean would curse at me, but when I cursed back at him, he slapped me in the face so hard he knocked me to the ground. So for survival, I learned to maintain an outward self-control, but inwardly, resentment and revenge remained red hot. The only outlet I knew was to hide in my bedroom oasis and mull over this unfairness—to cry, to rehearse the occurrence again and again, to plan how I would get even one day—until the emotions exhausted me. I concluded something must be seriously wrong with me, for no matter what I did or didn't do I could never please my mother or brothers. I would throw myself on my bed and let hopelessness and despair whip me into an abject, mindless depression.

My father was diagnosed with cancer when I was very young. Needing extensive testing and surgery, he was often away from home for six months to a year, leaving my mother as sole parent. She had to work full time to support us five children. The nightmare at home alone with my brothers escalated, but I learned that Mother didn't want to hear about it. I would greet her at the front door with distraught tears, sharing my heartaches over my brothers' hitting me, teasing, being unfair or unkind. But since she didn't have enough energy to deal with my issues, these scenarios remained unresolved. To me the unspoken message was loud and clear—even though it wasn't true. "Sally isn't worth listening to. Sally isn't worth protecting. Sally isn't loveable. Sally is just a little tattletale." And worse yet, "Sally is a liar." That only added to my rejection issues. I finally learned not to even tell her what happened so that I could avoid the pain of being called a tattletale or liar. I tried to solve the problem by avoiding all conflicts. I played with the neighbor children, baby-sat, and petted my bunny or dog. When all other alternatives failed, I hid out in my bedroom so I wouldn't cause problems in the home. After all, *I* was the problem; I had been told that over and over—so it must be true.

My poor mother loved me but didn't know how to show it in these situations. And how could she correct her older boys when she was gone from home? Sometimes I would call her at work, desperate for tools to resolve these issues. But again and again, I found that she had none to give me. She didn't know what to do or how to direct me. Again the unspoken message was, *"I'm not loved."* She rarely believed me or defended me. My brothers were never restrained or punished. Where was justice in it all? There seemed to be none. My insecurities mounted with my feelings of unworthiness. I responded poorly when provoked, since all I knew was to obey my feelings.

Demeaning Dean would sneer as he roughly tousled my hair, "You are so ugly! Why don't you put a bag over your head so I don't have to look at you?" As his fun increased he'd say, "Silly Sal from Siam, you are just so dumb, stupid, fat, and ugly." Week after week, year after year, he continued to repeat this in singsong fashion. Often his teasing would end with a comment like, "As fat and ugly as you are, no one will ever be interested in marrying you!" And he laughed gleefully.

I believed these often-told lies; I had no way to know they weren't true. I'd look into the mirror and believe the reflection I saw was what a dumb, stupid, fat, ugly girl looked like. I was someone whom others would not love no matter how hard I tried to please them. I accepted my brother's picture as reality. Children and youth do this to a great extent.

This is my history. These were my thoughts, feelings, and habits, which formulated my character and my responses. I've learned that many children and youth, unfortunately, share a similar experience.

It's too bad there wasn't someone with the understanding to help me see what Satan was doing to cripple and hurt me mentally, emotionally, and spiritually. How I wish there had been someone to teach me that this was Satan's voice, that these thoughts were lies that I didn't have to believe! What a difference it would have made if someone had shown me what God thinks about me and that I could believe Him instead of my feelings. But that was not my lot.

I unconsciously set up barriers between God and myself because I saw no justice. I responded to God as if He were stern and unjust. Didn't He leave me in this terrible state of affairs? Because I didn't know God as He truly is, I *protected myself* just like a turtle does. I would pull into my shell, make myself scarce, not talk or share what I thought—for anything I said was dumb, stupid, or wrong. So I spent a lot of time alone, locked in my bedroom, until Mother would come home. When I needed to be out of my room, I'd avoid my brothers or pretend to be tough so that they couldn't hurt me. Inwardly, I harbored distrust and revenge, but seeing no chance for fairness, my hopelessness grew.

At times it seemed that life was getting better. My brothers would treat me decently for a time. I'd come out of my shell, be bubbly, laugh, and enjoy them. I'd forgive them and begin to trust again—only to find them reverting to the demeaning pattern of dominating and harassing me. Then I'd clam up out of self-protection, afraid to express myself. I'd begin thinking despairing thoughts. Once more I would become a victim, a beaten puppy retreating with its tail between its legs.

Roller coaster relationship

Since there was no parental supervision after school, Byron and I were often home alone with lots of time on our hands. He was both my best friend and my worst enemy. When he was good and kind, I would do anything for him. I had sweet, tender feelings for him because he was there for me when there was no one else. It seemed he loved and cared for me.

One day my brother had a disagreement with his friend next door. To settle the disagreement they ended up pitting this friend's brother and me in a fight. Out of loyalty to my brother I entered into that fight to show my love for Byron. I wrestled the neighbor's brother and won the battle for my brother. I'd do anything for him. Often, just to please him, I would play in the boys' games of basketball, baseball, football, hide-and-seek, and tag so they would have enough people for teams.

Those were the good days. But many days were not like that. Byron could be a terrible bully. He liked to wrestle, which was common play for us. We would arm wrestle, leg wrestle, and push each other around. This was fun to a point. Then Bully Byron got the bright idea to try out his bullwhip on me. He wanted to practice with me as the target. Having no idea what was involved, I played the part he told me to. After feeling the sting of the whip several times I objected, but he paid no attention. The chase began. I raced for my bedroom, but he caught me before I could lock the door. He wrestled me down; I struggled to get away. I fled outside, but he pursued me. I ran back inside the house again but wasn't able to lock the door in time. He kept chasing me until exhaustion forced him to stop. I was hurting from all the wrestling, bullwhipping, and resentful thoughts and feelings.

Now it was time to get the meal ready for Mother when she came home. The responsibility that day was Bully Byron's, but he asked me to do it for him. I refused. An argument ensued and was settled with the bullwhip. I begrudgingly peeled and cooked the potatoes, then resisted again. Angry feelings heightened and exploded into another bout of physical wrestling. This settled nothing; it only stirred up our passions to the point that I resorted to biting and scratching. He let go of me long enough that I was able to get loose and run to my bedroom. This time I managed to lock the door. I was physically safe unless he broke down the door. Should he succeed in that, I planned to escape out the window. I put a chair in place and opened the window—just in case.

Bully Byron pounded on the door and threatened me not to tell Mother what had happened. He cursed me and called me names. In my bedroom oasis fear, hurt, hate, and revenge filled my mind and heart to overflowing. It is in the crisis that our character is revealed. My character was being formed in the wrong direction. I needed God, but I didn't know Him personally.

Too bad there wasn't a parent present who knew God personally, who could have brought fair discipline into the home. Had our character defects and poor problem-solving techniques been dealt with then, how different all our lives would have been!*

Under God, parenting can stop the negative effect upon the thoughts, feelings, and responses of anyone in this kind of situation. God can help us develop right characters even in tough times. God has a solution for whatever our home life may be. He wants to redeem us from those wrong character traits by teaching us good responses. We must learn to trust Him and follow Him rather than our old problem-solving techniques such as withdrawal, silence, or attack.

History stays with us

Why do I share this peek here into my young years? Those years molded an image into my mind of who and what I am. The nonverbal as well as the verbal input synthesized my character. What is character? It's the thoughts and feelings about life, about oneself, about one's value, and about God—regardless whether those thoughts and feelings are real or supposed. Character forms the basis for how one reacts and responds to life's difficulties. There was no one to help me during my growing-up years—not Mother, Father, brother, or friend. God wasn't real to my family—so how could they share Him with me? God was seen as Someone who lives up in heaven with more important things to do than to help us down here.

My responses to life's trials were not good, but they were all I knew. Did God see me as stupid or ugly? No! Was it His will that I was in such an unfair situation or that I saw myself in such a demeaning, ugly light? No! Left to ourselves, Satan easily leads us down a very detrimental road of wrong thinking that wounds and discourages us. I did what I did because I didn't know what else to do. For me, back then, God wasn't a resource for solving my problems. I didn't know how to talk with Him. I cried out to Him, but I thought I was talking to myself. No one taught me that God was there for me. When He tried to direct me, I didn't know His voice and rarely followed His directions. Instead I'd escape emotionally—be untouchable and tough.

As I grew up, got married, and had my own children, I perpetuated the same thoughts, feelings, emotions, and protective responses I had learned in my childhood and youth. My history was active in my present. The giants I *did not slay* with Christ still possessed the land and harassed me over and over years later. My husband was not like my brothers, yet I responded as though he were. The thoughts and feelings I followed as a child were what I followed as a grown-up as well—even when they didn't honestly apply. Just a similar situation would throw me automatically into the old responses I had learned in childhood.

I'd withdraw and pull into my turtle shell when I didn't *feel* safe. Often I had a strong desire to run away like I used to do to my bedroom. In a potential conflict I'd automatically respond with silence, *fearful* to share my thoughts, paranoid that I'd be told I was dumb and stupid, wanting to avoid it. Feelings of being dominated would enter, and I would lash out. It seemed I had no choice in the matter. I often felt inadequate, dumb, and stupid. I would give up on myself and bemoan my hopeless

---

*Proverbs 22:6.

condition just as I did as a youth. I wrongly accepted that I was the cause for every disagreement or sad experience. This would lead me deep into the hopeless pit of despair again and again. My feelings and emotions were childlike and compelling. I felt I had no choice but to accept these ugly thoughts about myself. This was emotionally and spiritually hurtful and destructive, but I knew no other way as yet.

My inadequacies and fear of failure kept me from participating up front at church. I'd gladly do any behind-the-scenes work, but nothing up front. I wasn't hiding in my bedroom, but this was a form of hiding. I couldn't face my fears. I wrongly thought that whatever I'd say would be dumb or stupid. My lying thoughts and feelings still ruled over me. When asked to lead out at church I'd become very uncomfortable—even anxious. I didn't understand why I responded this way; it was an unconscious thing. I had decided I could never speak from the pulpit, for it was too fearful an experience. I was certain that I'd be put down again. Seeing myself as dumb, stupid, fat, and ugly hindered me in countless areas of life. The giant Despair was a familiar companion who followed me as my brother had in years past, echoing over and over the put-downs, whipping me into responding in the old way, and I submitted to him. Not until I came to know and communicate with God in later years did I connect this response to my childhood.

This is my history, like a legion of giants holding me in bondage through a deeply ingrained belief of lies. I wasn't free to be the Sally God made me to be. And this is true not just of me; it is true of most parents today. Our habits are a byproduct of our repeated self-protective responses learned in the circumstances of our life's trials. We are responding to life with the same childhood problem-solving techniques we learned apart from God. Our history often plays an unconscious part in the present. That's why we react in the negative, destructive way we do, and that's why we seem to have no power to change.

Rule of the giants

The negative giants that possess the land of our characters are familiar companions that need to be abandoned. They are our history of lying thoughts, wrong habits, appetites, selfishness, wrong problem-solving techniques learned in childhood or youth, self-protective mechanisms, dishonesty, unwillingness to look to our past and evaluate it, anxieties, fears, insecurity—and the list goes on. These giants wound, hurt, and attack us, making life miserable. Warning! Any giant, given residency or mercy, will grow and strengthen to wound and hurt, and in time destroy you.

Parents, look at and evaluate your youth today. Have you contributed to their wrong thoughts, feelings, and responses? Do you realize it is in your power to stop passing on to them the old family dysfunctions that have been handed down to you? God is there and longs to help you out of your history. And as you cooperate with Him, He will give you the wisdom to help your youth connect with Him for real change.* Take Christ's hand and you can choose to pass on the legacy of a life hidden with Christ in God.

---

*James 1:5.

God is working in your life as He is working in mine. He is always there with you, trying to direct you in a better way of thinking and responding. When we come to know God as He truly is, we can then look back and see His presence throughout our life, attempting to redeem us from wrong ways of fear or selfishness. We will see how our uncooperative spirit has left us in bondage to self. We'll also see how God has freed us from negative emotions or saved us from disaster as we have cooperated with Him and how our lives have been better as a result of that moment of choice. We'll wish in hindsight that we had followed God consistently! But we can make that change and gain its blessings for our family and ourselves now!

Take courage! God has promised us that we can live and inhabit Canaan, the Land of Promise. We can possess all of this goodly land that flows with milk and honey. It's ours, and God has commissioned us to go in and possess it in His strength, conquering the giants through Him. He has promised to be our General and to teach us how to wield the sword of the Spirit so that we can slay all giants in the land of our character. All wrong, lying thoughts can be denied occupancy and eliminated in Christ. God is not pleased when we lie down passively like a victim. Put on Christ's armor; let Him be your Commander, and go forward to slay the negative influences in your life and that of your family.

Let freedom ring!

THE LONE EMBRACE
A SPECIAL WORD OF ENCOURAGEMENT FOR SINGLE PARENTS

Our history must be looked at, examined, and understood to see how it molded us into what we are. God doesn't want us to remain in our dysfunction, our prisons of fear; He doesn't want us to remain in bondage under lying thoughts, appetites, or passions. Instead He wants to lead us out of this poor desert land into the Land of Canaan to be free to serve Him and righteousness and empowered to slay the giants in the land. He desires to set us free!

When we learn this process of union and communion with Christ, of surrender and cooperation under His leadership to slay these giants in the land of our character, we can teach this freedom to our children and youth—and more also.

With prayer and God's leading maybe, just maybe, our alienated spouse may desire and grasp this life-changing hope in Christ. What could happen then? Do you think if two adults heard God's voice and followed Him fully, that the two of you could fall in love the right way—God's way—and restore your broken family? Wouldn't that be something? If both parties let God deal with them at that level, what a change it would make! Christ within, through the Holy Spirit, is our only hope of glory. This is the most essential truth that we have to learn and enter into.

Or if it's not possible to resolve your family situation, He will still be there for you to fill your void and help you raise your youth in a way that will avoid leaving scars from all of this. God comforts the sorrowing heart.

Wouldn't it be wonderful to pass on to your youth a legacy of walking with God and coming out from under the domination of Satan and self? Could anything be more rewarding than for them to know the difference between the voice of God and the voice of Satan? Would any sacrifice be too great in order to see your young person knowing God as his most valuable Friend and Confidant? Realize that by neglecting to train them in God you are strengthening Satan's hold on them. You can choose today which legacy you will pass to your precious ones. God is there to direct your steps. Isn't knowledge of Him and His power what you want to pass on rather than the dysfunction, the damage, or the weaknesses you have? Of course it is.

Mother shares Andrew's exhilarating sky-diving experience.

Sharing Andrew's dream of biking up the "Going to the Sun Road."

Chapter 5

Let Freedom Ring

Come out of her, my people, that ye be not partakers of her sins.
—Revelation 18:4

Jim and I were snuggling together on the floor of our living room in front of a crackling fire as we reminisced. Jim pondered aloud, "How did God pluck us from the fires of the world? Considering our youth, it's amazing to me how God got through to us!"

"Jim, it's twenty years past my troublesome teen years. I'm thirty-seven years old, and it is only now that I can see how God led me away from so many wrong paths of life amidst those formative years. I didn't really know Him then, yet He was there guiding and directing my life. I am *beginning* to see the pattern in redemption. And what a difference it makes!

"I've been freed from the prison of fear of the bears. He released me from the dungeon of inadequacy and unworthy feelings. He led me out of the maze of fear of failure and my 'turtle response.' He got me into the pulpit to speak and to discover I didn't die, and that God is a Redeemer. I did have worthy things to say in Jesus. Little by little, the shackles of the lying thoughts that I was dumb, stupid, fat, and ugly melted away so that they had less and less control over me—until one day they were gone! More than that, I am learning to speak my mind with you even when I disagree!"

"You sure can, Sally. Are you sure that's a good change?" Jim teased, mischief gleaming in his eyes.

I suddenly tickled him in the ribs, and he rolled over feigning severe injury. I pounced on him and tickled him some more. He started tickling me back, and we wrestled playfully, giggling and laughing. Settling down again, Jim looked at me with his searching eyes. "Seriously, Sally, you are becoming a different woman, and I love seeing you find freedom. What has made the difference?"

"Knowing God personally has made all the difference, Jim. I didn't understand before how God was so personal and so involved with every one of us. He's right in the middle of our lives, and He is willing to direct us through it all. When I cooperate with Him, one choice at a time, He redeems me from the shackles of Satan. It's very simple.

"In my daily time with God, I settled into the truth that God loves me—even me. For me, that was one giant step of faith that brought me a degree of freedom. Intellectually I saw that I wasn't alone like I thought. The Bible could be believed over my feelings. I made the decision that I could trust God. He had my best interest at heart. Experience taught me tangibly that God did love me. He was there just like the Bible says, even if I couldn't physically hear, see, or feel Him.

"My biggest blessing came when I dared to experiment with thinking God's thoughts instead of my own in times of trial and temptation. It meant cooperating with God in trying new ways. I found that allowed Him to work a real transformation inside of me. Wrong thinking lessened its hold on me, and a new life was becoming tangible and desirable. Hope arose. It was God's power doing something inside of me that freed me from long term, wrong habits of thinking, feeling, and responding. The commonplace oppression, sadness, and hopelessness subsided. Choice by choice, God detached me from my former scars.

"As I've experienced God redeeming me from the inside out, He has led me to clearly see that He was there for me all along, prompting me to reach out to Him. I just didn't realize who He was and how much He could be trusted. So often I turned away from God, thinking His suggestions were ridiculous or foolish. How different my life would have been if I had listened more!"

Could it have been different?

Christ had always been *with* me—right? Yes. He says, "I will never leave thee, nor forsake thee."* "Lo I am *with* you alway, even unto the end of the world."† This is the first level of knowing God, and He takes this first step toward each of us. "Christ *with* you" is God's unconditional love toward every individual.

When I was an *infant,* God was there through the Holy Spirit speaking to my mind (thoughts) and heart (feelings)—telling me that when I was fearful I should trust my mother's comforting. At times, I surrendered to that still, small Voice and yielded up the wrong feelings and was truly calmed. But most of the time I didn't heed His voice and cried selfish or fearful cries. It seemed easy to yield my will to the rule of selfishness and fear—for it was a loud voice, but it was not a pleasant experience.

Notice that God was always *with* me—when I obeyed and stopped crying, and when I didn't. But He could change my heart (feelings) only when I responded with my will to obey the right. As an infant, I couldn't reason. Neither did I have a mother who understood how to teach and discipline me to heed God's voice over the voice of my flesh. The flesh was the loudest, most compelling voice, and this is the one I responded to most often. God stayed with me, trying to teach me a better way. But He could effect no change without my cooperation. I was left in "self."

God was also *with* me when I was a *child.* My mother would ask me to mop the floor. I didn't want to! I was selfish and uncooperative. It was easy to justify my course. "I will not mop the floor. It's Byron's turn—not mine. This isn't fair! I won't do his work." My strong ill feelings drove me to obey them. And I refused to help.

Now, God was still there *with* me, wasn't He? He continued to speak through His Holy Spirit to my conscience—my higher powers of reason. But God has given us a free-will choice. We can follow Him or follow sin, self, and Satan. I failed to

---

*Hebrews 13:5.

†Matthew 28:20, italics added.

decide for God, and not to decide is to make a decision. There is no neutral ground. When we do not consciously decide for God, we are choosing to have Satan and selfishness rule over us. How very sad!

God spoke to my heart. *"Sally, you love your mother. Why don't you show your love by helping her? Mop that little floor cheerfully. She needs you."*

But I refused this thought and reaffirmed my decision. "It's Bully Byron's job, and I'm not going to help. No!" And off to my bedroom I went.

Christ was *with* me, but I remained apart from God by refusing His ideas. Often I had thoughts that seemed in stark contrast to my own thoughts, ideas, and wishes. In a certain childish way I may have even realized this was God's voice calling to my heart to surrender my desires. The voice of my feelings was louder and compelling. So I refused His suggestions. God, who will never force anyone, had to leave me to my own will and way for the time being.

But God is love, and He didn't give up on me. He knew I had no one to give me practical instruction about Him. He understood my many misconceptions. He didn't want to leave me in my sin. He wanted to deliver me from it. So He gave me more chances to learn. An almost identical situation arose, and Mother again asked me to mop the floor.

Again, God spoke to me. *"You love your mother. Why don't you help her? What she is asking is only a 'little thing,' but it will bring her much happiness if you help her now. She is so tired. Can't you see it in her eyes?"*

"Well, yes, I see. I do love my mother. I do want to help her; she works too hard." Tenderness was awakened, and my heart responded to it.

"Choose to help her, then. You can choose to do right."

"But . . . it's not fair! It's Byron's job! I'm always doing Byron's jobs!" That loud voice of the flesh, that history, aimed to ruin these godly thoughts.

"And were you happy when you refused to help Mother last time, following your own will and way? Tell Me, was that fair to your mother?"

"Well, no. It wasn't fair to her." And in my bedroom I wasn't happy, either. I felt so guilty that I had let Mother down. But I argued with myself and decided I was not going to help Byron—that was the issue. And those old, unresolved issues with Byron, those unfair dealings of the past, were as though they were current. These emotions continued driving me.

God prompted me further. *"Love your mother, Sally, by helping her. That will make her happy. She needs your help."*

"All right! For Mother I'll do it!" I resolutely went to mop the floor without any discussion.

While I was mopping the floor, God called for my heart in a deeper way. *"Why are you so glum while you mop? Why don't you put on a smile and enjoy helping Mother? Do a good job. Think about what you love about your mother."*

"I can do this. I'm not mopping for Byron; I'm mopping for Mother," I decided and put on an outward smile. As I cooperated with these God-led thoughts—thinking about what I loved about Mother—I became cheerful inwardly about mopping. And this change was delightful!

You see, God works from the inside out to cleanse away our selfishness. It's our outward cooperation, putting our will on His side that allows Him to work within. He creates a new heart—something only He can do.*

As the Creator, God is well able to create a new heart in us, but He will never do so without our consent and cooperation. God will never force us against our will. Our part makes His part possible. We cannot change our ways apart from Him, but *in Him* we can. Even our thoughts and feelings can be upright.

Is "Christ with me" enough?

"Christ with me" can only woo me, tell me what is right to do, present to me what I can be, call for my decision—and then leave me to decide whether I will follow Him or my flesh. There is never any force or coercion. To walk the walk, it's not enough just to know what is right. Many of us know what is right, but we don't do it. To be changed requires more than "Christ with me." It requires "Christ *in* me."

"Christ in me" is that deeper relationship. When we give God permission to come in, He re-creates us into His image. We cooperate by thinking His thoughts, choosing to feel His feelings, and deciding to respond as Jesus would. We depend upon His creative power to make our choices real from the inside out. We let the Creator create us into His image—we cooperate. "God in me" is more powerful and can effect a change in my character, my thoughts, and even my feelings.

"Christ with me" is God's *unconditional* love for me. This is the first step of knowing God. I do not earn it or deserve it; it is God's love to me. When I respond with surrender and cooperation to God's call to my heart, I take the second step of knowing Him—my responding love. Then my free-will cooperation allows God to love me deeper, which is the third step of knowing Him. Divine power is unleashed, and He works within me to re-create me into His image. "Christ in me" is a *conditional* love dependent upon my cooperation.

"Because they have no changes, therefore [this gives evidence] they fear not [know not] God."† Knowing God is experiencing God changing me from within.

God transformed my heart inwardly so that it matched my outward smile—and mopping the floor became a real joy. I loved helping and pleasing my mother. "Christ with me" brought me to a decision, but it was "Christ in me" that gave me the power to change from my wrong thoughts and feelings.

Sad to say, I cooperated with Christ only on rare occasions—when I was frustrated enough to try a new way or when all other avenues failed. This is true of so many of us. We try God as the last resort, often because we do not understand the process. We do not understand that we don't have to obey our selfish feelings. No one has told or taught us this truth. This union and communion with God can set us free from our bondage. We can be living, happy, successful Christians from the inside out every day.

---

*Ezekiel 36:24–28.
†Psalm 55:19.

As a teen, God continued to call for my heart, trying to help me out of my troubles. Yet this same cycle of following my feelings and emotions instead of God and my conscience was common. God was always there with me like the Bible said. He offered better responses; He tried to tell me what was true. But I rarely followed.

Struggles and a Savior

Let me tell you the story of some of my teen struggles to illustrate how God was there for me so that you can see how God is there for you—whether you are a parent or a teen.

Sad Sally often got angry with one of her four older brothers. They were all bigger and stronger, and I had to bow down to what they said. Remember how Bully Byron chased me with his bullwhip until I was able to lock myself in my room? Let me tell you the rest of that story.

Even though I didn't know God, He was there for me and called to my heart. *"You don't want to hate your brother."*

"Yes I do!" I responded with heartfelt vengeance. "He just whipped me mercilessly! It's not fair! I do hate him, and I will get even with him one day!"

Of course, I didn't understand that this was God talking to me. It was not an audible voice; it seemed to be my own thoughts. But God was there and didn't give up on me for lack of knowledge or experience. I had no clue what God wanted to accomplish in me. But His love offered me a new and different option for responding to my current trial.

"Hate hurts the one who hates more than the one who is hated. I can teach you how to love your enemies."

I had been raised in our church with a basic Bible understanding and knew in my mind and heart that I should not hate my brother, but my present emotions were alive and active in the opposite direction. At this stage in my life, I knew how to respond only from my feelings and emotions. I knew nothing else.

So I questioned, "Why should I love someone who treats me like he just did?"

God didn't answer my question. My mind was silent momentarily. So I returned to thinking hateful, revengeful, hurtful thoughts until my head hurt so badly I had to stop.

"It does hurt to hate. You're right! I'm so tired of hateful feelings; it's so miserable. Why can't I have a happy home? Why doesn't anyone love me? Maybe if I exercise real hard I could get slim enough to not be so ugly. Maybe if I eat some candy, it would sweeten me up. If only I ate less at mealtime . . . but eating seems to be the only joy I have in life!" And I sank into despair with no hope of change.

"Why don't you rearrange your dresser drawers? You've been wanting to do that. Now would be a good time." God's thoughts came to me again.

God was trying to redirect my thoughts, to get me involved with something positive to replace all the negative thoughts and feelings that were ruling me and wounding me further right then. Everything good comes from God. He is always present with us to teach us better ways to think, feel, and react. He promises, "Lo, I am with you alway, even unto the end of the world."* God wants to re-create us into His image, to think His thoughts, feel His feelings, and respond in His power in a better way. God sees our free-will choice as most valuable and will not force or coerce us to do His will.

"OK," I responded. As I was rearranging my drawers, I recognized that putting my mind on this task was crowding out the negative, hurtful thoughts. But all too soon my mind returned to rehearsing what had just happened. "Why can't Bully Byron be kind to me? What's the matter with me?" I bemoaned, taking the blame as I typically did.

Just then God spoke again to my conscience. *"Why don't you think some good thoughts about Byron?"*

"That is ridiculous," I reasoned. And off I went, rehearsing not only the problems of that day but those of many other days just like it. I justified my feelings and protected those negative thoughts as though they were something to fight for.

"Sally, you are tired of those hateful thoughts; they wound and hurt you terribly."

"Yes, I am! What should I do?" I asked honestly from deep in my heart.

"Think of the good things about your brother. You say he's your best friend. How is he your best friend?"

It was difficult to shift gears in my thinking, but I persevered and found that God's grace empowered me to find some good thoughts even though I didn't know what grace was at the time. Then as I continued to reorder my drawers, more and more good thoughts presented themselves to my mind. As I cooperated with them, my emotional oppression lifted like a thundercloud and vanished. My spirit lightened. Good thoughts replaced the evil ones, and within five or ten minutes I actually had loving thoughts and feelings toward my brother. What a miraculous freedom amidst the storm! This is the mission of Christ for each of us—to redeem us from our wrong thoughts, feelings, and ways of self!

Just then, Bully Byron knocked at the door in an entirely new spirit and asked sweetly, "Sally, my friend and I want to go see a movie, but I don't have any money. Do you have some I could borrow—please?"

Amazingly, I walked over and unlocked the door without fear or hatred. I promptly emptied my piggy bank and lovingly gave him all he needed and more, well knowing I'd likely never get it back.

"You are a great sister!" Bully Byron said.

At age fourteen this was a miraculous turnaround, but I didn't understand then that it was God who had helped me. How did God change my feelings, emotions, thoughts, and responses so quickly? He used the *replacement principle*. He led me to follow His right thoughts, to choose His right feelings, and to respond to follow Jesus' leading. Above all else, we need to let God be in charge of us—to let Him take the steering wheel! With my cooperation, God was able to do His re-creative work inside me. He wants to do this for all of us. We are to have His character. It's Christ's mission to redeem us from serving self and to empower us to serve Him instead.

---

*Matthew 28:20.

Am I telling you that if you clean drawers when you have hate in your heart, you'll be freed? Am I teaching salvation by cleaning drawers? No! I'm saying that you can be saved from wrong ways of thinking and feeling by seeking and following God's will for you. Whatever He asks you to do—do it.* If He asks you to clean drawers, then clean those drawers. If He asks you to read the Scriptures, go for a walk, or write a letter, do it!

I had a number of experiences like this with my brothers. As I look back, I see these experiences of deliverance prepared me for bigger trials ahead.

From bad to worse

When Bob entered our home he brought violence, confusion, and untold heartache. My father was twenty-five years older than my mother and often away for long periods of time for extensive cancer surgeries. Initially, my mother found in Bob an oasis of badly needed friendship in the desert of her lonely life. Unfortunately, Bob was mentally ill and manipulated my mother by threatening to kill her children.

My mother often sent me to my grandmother's house on the spur of the moment to spare me from things that were happening. Not understanding why, I felt rejected and abandoned. I thought she did this because she didn't love me, that she didn't want me at home with her. When I'd return from my grandmother's, I would put out my "feelers," watching nonverbal communication, to see if home was safe or not. Should I watch TV with Mother or retire to my bedroom so as not to be a bother? The rejection I experienced was based more on my perception of events than on reality, but it *felt* real to me! I carried many wounds below the surface of my outward smile.

On one of those evenings when I was abruptly sent to Grandmother's house, Bob shot my mother with a rifle through the basement window. The bullet passed less than an inch from her heart, and she had to be hospitalized for a prolonged period. I endured much pain, heartache, and fear alone because I didn't know how to come to the Great Physician to sort out truth from error. God was *with me*, but without my surrender and cooperation with His leading, there was *no change* in my mental or emotional state. I just survived the violence.

After a year in jail with treatment, Bob was pronounced cured and released. He immediately began to try to convince my mother and me that he really was cured. Bob was a security driver and picked up the money every day at the bakery my mother managed. I frequently stopped at the bakery to avoid going home, and I resented Bob's presence and attention. Little did I know just how much of his presence I would have to endure!

Soon this paranoid, schizophrenic man began to manipulate my mother into marrying him. He threatened to shoot my father and us children if she didn't submit to his demands. After having been shot once by him, she took his threats seriously. She tried first to appease his unbalanced thinking, hoping he would give up the idea.

---

*John 2:5.

But finally, under great duress, she divorced my father and married Bob. My pain, heartache, and shame multiplied exponentially! Bob as my stepfather! The very idea was revolting! Perhaps you can imagine some of the trials and gut-wrenching heart-aches this brought. I'll share a few examples.

Mother came anxiously knocking on my bedroom door one evening. "Sally, you are always hiding here in your bedroom. You don't understand what problems you make for me when you do that. I want you to come out into the living room and be friendly. Come on now! I need you!"

I recalled hearing Bob and my mother tussling in the basement a few nights earlier. It hadn't sounded friendly, and I had worried about what he was doing to her. I had been too afraid to go to the register and see, so I had buried my head under my pillow. "What does he do to her? Surely he's hurting her." We never talked about it, so my imagination filled in the blanks.

"I don't want to go out there," I moaned to myself. "How I hate that man; how I resent all the hurtful things he does in our home. Now Mother wants me to be friendly to him. What should I do?"

God answered my questions. *"Sally, you love your mother. Why don't you do this for her? I'll be with you."*

"Well, I suppose I could. I do love my mother." My concern for her overcame my revulsion for Bob, and I ventured into the living room. At first I felt awkward, but soon Bob and I actually began to have some fun talking and playing.

Then Mother tapped me on the shoulder and even more anxiously whispered, "Sally, go to your bedroom. You don't understand what you're doing. You're mak-ing trouble for me! Go right now!"

I retreated to my bedroom, feeling like a failure. Once again, I had been unable to please my mother. I had no clue what I had done wrong. I began mulling over in my mind how much I hated that man! I suspected that he caused my dad to leave our home. The only time I could talk with Mother was when Bob was working. "Oh, I just hate that man, like no one else! Oh, I wish he'd have an accident at the railroad station."

"Sally, you must not hate Bob like that. You need to love him instead," God prompted.

"Love him? That is absolutely ridiculous. All he has ever caused is terrible havoc in our home. Remember, he shot my mother, and she almost died! And You want me to love him? Impossible! I don't even want to!"

"Sally, you need to pity him; he is a sick man."

"No, I won't do that. I hate him!" So God left me to hate. What a miserable life!

Much of my young life was like this. God was with me. He tried to help me out of my troubles and give me His peace in spite of my terrible circumstances, but I would not have it. I would not listen, nor would I surrender or cooperate with His thoughts. Thus I remained trapped in my troubles with no change. I miserably en-dured the torture, day in and day out. God did help me when I allowed Him to, but my stubborn lack of cooperation limited Him.

Another day Bob tried to help me with my schoolwork. I listened politely, but his ideas didn't make sense to me. He asked me what I thought, and I was afraid to tell him. My hesitancy provoked his rage, and he began stomping around the room—face red, neck veins swollen, yelling insults and threats. I fled to my bedroom once again and wallowed in the pit of discouragement. Desperate, I cried out to God.

"Lord, I want out of all this ugly stuff. I hate him; he's wicked! But I'm tired of hating, too. What can I do?" Not expecting an answer, I broke into tears on my bed.

Sally, you need to pity this man. To be a paranoid schizophrenic is not a pleasant life. I can help you pity him.

"Help me pity this man, then." I began to cooperate with the thoughts God suggested to my mind, and in a relatively short time the hateful emotions subsided. I began to feel peaceful and free inside—even with Bob's presence in the home. All the frustration and heaviness went away. God promises that "he [Christ] would grant unto us, that we being delivered out of the hand of our enemies [self, sin, Satan] might serve him without fear."*

This is exactly what happened to me as a teenager. "God with me" had offered deliverance. When I consented and cooperated, "God in me" wrought deliverance by divine power. Cooperation with God brought freedom from self's rule over me.

One evening Mother came to my bedroom and for the first time confided in me. Bob had threatened to kill himself and had locked her out of the bedroom. She was upset and wanted to help him in some way. My heart was drawn out in sympathy for my mother. What a terrible plight she was in! I felt she was giving me a chance to help her.

"We need to call the police," I said. "They know all about Bob. Surely they will help us!"

We were too intimidated by Bob to leave the house through the door, so we both crawled out my bedroom window and sneaked over to the neighbors. (What one does when one is afraid doesn't always make sense.) There Mother called the police and was transferred from department to department multiple times until at last she was promised, "We'll send two plainclothes policemen to your home right away."

In our living room, Mother explained to the two officers that Bob was locked in the bedroom threatening to hang himself. I very shyly tucked myself behind her, not wanting to talk, but wanting to be there to support her.

"I'm sorry, we can do nothing for you until he hurts either himself or one of you," they told us. They were sympathetic but restricted by Bob's civil rights. I was only sixteen years old at the time, and I became *enraged*! A flood of anger came in like a tidal wave. Hate and resentment overflowed my being like nothing I'd ever felt before. My thoughts were on a rampage—out of control.

"I hate that man with such a passion! He has made our home such a miserable place for many years now. I have had it. I'm going to do something about it! My brothers often threaten to do something to Bob. They never have, but I will. I will! We'd all be better off without him around, that's for sure." The arm of flesh had failed us, so I was going to take justice into my own hands.

---

*Luke 1:74, 75.

"God with me" called for my heart amidst rage and irrational thinking, saying tenderly, *"Sally, you don't want to hate this man. You need to pity this man."*

"Pity this man—phooey! He has hurt and maimed us daily. This is enough! It's about time he pays! He should die! I won't pity this awful man. I'll save my mother!"

"Sally, you need to pity this man."

"Pity this man? What is there to pity him for?" I responded sarcastically.

"How would you feel if you were a paranoid schizophrenic and hated yourself so much you wanted to kill yourself? You can love him as I love you."

The turning point

"Well . . . Well, that is a state to be pitied. I never thought of that." My heart was tender and responded to this different view of things. "Well . . . I'll choose to pity him. It would be awful if I wanted to kill myself. Poor man, we ought to pity him." As I cooperated with thinking these new thoughts, my tidal wave of emotions instantly dissipated into a calm, quiet pool. God can pronounce His "peace, be still" on any emotion if we let Him in. "Christ in me" was powerful enough to subdue the raging hurricane within me.

Then shy, quiet Sally spoke up in front of the two plainclothes policemen with a boldness never before seen. "Mother, we need to have pity on Bob because he hates himself so much he wants to kill himself. God told me not to hate him, but to pity him. And God put that pity and love inside me."

My mother listened and chose also to cooperate with pitying thoughts toward Bob. As she cried out silently to Jesus herself, love rapidly filled her heart. Her fear and anxiety were vanquished and replaced with peace. Oh, the peace, the wonderful peace, that God has for each one of us amidst our storms! While it passes understanding, it is nonetheless real. We can have the peace of God regardless of our situation. I have truly found 2 Corinthians 5:17 to be true: "Therefore if any man be in Christ, he is a new creature: old things are passed away; behold, all things are become new."

This was awesome! In a moment, my desires were transformed from murder to love. Only God can do such a work. My mother was changed as well. She was brought out of fear by letting Christ in to work in her heart! The only thing that hinders you and me from being changed is refusing to surrender and cooperate with Christ. When we hesitate, sin reigns. But if we yield to do God's revealed will, His power comes in to subdue the sin and to create us into His image. Then our thoughts and feelings reflect His. The choice is always ours—every moment. "Christ in me" changes all that is surrendered to Him.

The police left, seeing us at peace, although we remained in our fearful situation. The reality was that Bob could easily have come at us with knives or guns in his rage and unbalanced mind, but we were truly calm and at peace inside.

The world says that children are scarred for life when they go through a divorce or other major family trauma. Apart from God, this is true, but it doesn't have to be that way *in Him*. I want to testify to you that I went through two divorces in my home and that I have no scars today. My mother divorced my father. Then six years later the courts granted her a divorce from Bob due to his violence. From my youth until I was in my forties I did have scars. Scars are the poor problem-solving techniques, trained responses, misconceptions, and lying thoughts we obey that hinder God's re-creative, redemptive work in our lives. Only after finding a personal God did I find a way to deal with those scars.

Let freedom ring! I'm free; yes, I'm free in Jesus! Now I am truly grateful for the life my mother gave me. She loved and cared for me the best she could. She had her own baggage. There are many who have had to grow up with far less love than I had. My mother and I became real close, adoring and appreciating each other, and had open communication. It was my freedom that opened the floodgates to my mother's freedom, in Jesus, from her scars.

"Come out of her . . ."

God wants to get inside of us to restore us to His image again. But He cannot perform this miracle without our consent and cooperation. We, the parents, must understand the process of coming out of our childhood ways—our history—and gain freedom in order to help our young people do the same. Under Christ's guidance we can follow right responses. He truly is our best Friend!

Jesus came to save us from the old ways and show us His new ways that work. God is able to deliver you and me from whatever ails or binds us. Christ says to us all, "Come out of her, my people."* Come out of the history that binds us to Satan, sin, and self. Come into our liberty to follow Christ. Then our history can be made null and void, and we will be free to be upright. In Christ we need not obey the dictates, the bondage of our past any longer. We can grow up in Christ and become mature men and women. We don't have to stay in the old ways of thinking and responding any longer! We have God!

Many teens today are all tied up in knots with similar misconceptions, and God wants to set them free! They need someone who understands to help them. We help them identify their past issues honestly so that they can understand why they react as they do, but we don't grovel there. Identifying the origin of the lies simply allows us to break the shackles of old patterns of thinking, feeling, and relating. It sets them free to replace the lies with the truth as it is in Jesus.

What a blessing is ours! It's all because of "Christ in me" through my cooperation with His leading. I can talk of all these traumatic events today—not as a victim bemoaning my lot in life or even as a mere survivor—but as a victor who has discovered an inexhaustible source of love, support, and encouragement. I have plunged myself deep within the healing balm supplied by Christ, and I am free.

You, too, can have this freedom. When you give God your past with all its cultivated wrong thoughts, feelings, and patterns of relating—and decide that you will follow God regardless of the cost—He will direct your steps. Do you see clearly now the difference between "Christ *with* me" and "Christ *in* me"? Won't you take the next step in your walk with God and let Him come in to you and free you from all

---

*Revelation 18:4.

that is not right inside? You can be free to serve God without fear and without regard to your hereditary and cultivated tendencies to evil. It's just a choice away! You, too, can let freedom ring!

THE LONE EMBRACE
A WORD OF ENCOURAGEMENT FOR SINGLE PARENTS

Isn't it wonderful that God allows life to show us our weaknesses? Has He shown you some of yours? Then He can impart His grace to heal them if you consent and cooperate with Him. Cooperating with God's grace allowed me to forsake the history that made me what I was—fearful, timid, insecure, and certain I was dumb, stupid, fat, ugly, and useless. Heeding God's voice connected me with His strength and grace so that I could mop the floor cheerfully, forgive my brothers, and come out of resentment and hatred—even when offending parties made no efforts to apologize or make things right. And then God empowered me to yield bitterness, rage, revenge, and the desire to kill in exchange for His pity and love toward the unlovable and undependable. God did all the miraculous changes each time I consented and cooperated—even when I didn't really know much about Him. Then Christ brought Heaven's rest into my soul.

Your circumstances can't be much more foreboding than mine were. Even if they are, God is big enough for them! So trust that He can do the same for you that He did for me! Won't you open your heart's door and let Him in?

Physical labor makes a boy strong and manly. And work can be fun if the attitude is right. Andrew, age 18, shovels snow.

Chapter 6

Prerequisites

For which of you, intending to build a tower, sitteth not down first, and counteth the cost,
whether he have sufficient to finish it?
—Luke 14:28

If you plan to go to college, you must complete certain prerequisite courses. A college will not accept a student until he meets the entrance requirements. Hence, the academic dean tests applicants to discern their mastery, or lack thereof, of basic knowledge and skills. This is done, not to belittle the student, but to identify weak areas that need to be strengthened before advanced courses can be pursued successfully.

We cannot learn algebra and geometry successfully without first mastering the foundation skills of addition, subtraction, multiplication, and division. You cannot write fluent essays without first mastering the basic building blocks of language—the alphabet, grammar, and spelling.

This is true of our Christian walk as well. We cannot start at the top of Peter's ladder.* Many try to jump up to the top without learning to climb each step in sequence, but none are successful. We all must begin at the first step—faith.

Faith and knowledge of Jesus Christ as our personal Savior is step one. Step two is learning to connect to His virtue, which is His power to enable us to render true obedience. We need His virtue to heal our diseases of selfishness, rebellion, wrong attitudes, and bad feelings. We need His virtue to enable us to exercise true self-denial, self-control, and gain true knowledge. We need Christ in us before we can become a Christian. We need first things first, don't we?

Moving Marvin

One-year-old Moving Marvin is very active. He is so eager to be mobile that he just rolls to get where he wants to go. He doesn't want to take the time and trouble of learning to crawl. His wise mother calmly encourages him to crawl, but Moving Marvin resists. Mother prays for direction and continues calling for him to surrender. She prays with him, tells him what he needs to do, and places him on his knees beside her while she demonstrates crawling. Moving Marvin yields his impatient attitude and learns to crawl. It's fun! After a time of mastering this skill, he is happy because crawling is a much faster means of getting around than rolling! And so, too, with the more advanced phases of mobility. After becoming skillful in crawling, he learns to pull up to a standing position holding on to Daddy's fingers. In time, he learns to balance himself and then take his first steps. Soon he begins to run.

---

*2 Peter 1:5–8.

Now if Mother had skipped crawling and walking lessons and had tried to teach Moving Marvin to run before he learned to crawl, would he be successful? No way! There are prerequisites.

This is also true in raising our teens. We want them to be industrious, kind, helpful, respectful, and obedient. But we often don't find that to be reality. Instead, in most cases, they are indolent, selfish, uncooperative, and disobedient. The reason they are like that is that we have failed to train them to connect with God as a prerequisite. If they haven't been trained in their infancy and childhood to know God's voice, to recognize that they belong to Him, to surrender to right, to yield up wrong thoughts, feelings, and emotions, how can they learn now unless you take them back to learn these basic skills?

Selfish Sophie

Selfish Sophie had just turned thirteen and was accustomed to being in charge. She decided when she would go to bed and when she would get up. Yes, Mom told her to go to bed, but she didn't. Yes, Mom told her to get up for breakfast and school, but she didn't do it on time and missed the school bus. Mother lovingly drove her to school, but Selfish Sophie treated Mother as if it was all Mother's fault. Mother's frustration with her daughter had been mounting over the last few years.

"This kid just seems to have no gratitude for all I have done for her. She is so disrespectful. When I get up the nerve to ask Sophie to clean her own room, what happens? She turns the house upside down with her verbal tirades and attacks me for my 'unreasonable orders.' I've tried to reason with her and ended up arguing very loudly for over an hour before finally giving up. But then, I ask her to help me prepare a meal. Surely that's not too much to ask. I would think that a mother and daughter could enjoy working in the kitchen together, but she brings in such a grumpy attitude that I find it more pleasant to just do it myself. Maybe I do expect too much of her. Other young people are much the same, even at church. Maybe when she grows up she will realize how nice she had it here at home."

So Mother asked less and less of Selfish Sophie. She coddled, permitted, and nurtured self by allowing selfishness to be expressed.

As Selfish Sophie turned fourteen Mother's patience reached an end.

"All these years I've given into Sophie and look what it has gotten me—a heap of heartache. I walk on eggshells in my own home to avoid stirring her up. I've become her slave—cleaning and cooking, and she is never satisfied. Her disrespect has gotten to me more than anything else. I'm going to get firm with her."

And firm she got. She yelled, screamed, and hit in a vain, fleshly endeavor to bring Selfish Sophie under her control. Now, it is true that firmness is needed in raising teens—but never in such a spirit as this. This fleshly firmness only creates alienation.

After months of following this approach without gaining Selfish Sophie's cooperation, Mother enlisted Father on her side. Nevertheless, their combined efforts only reinforced a spirit of fleshly passion, which she artfully reflected back upon them.

In desperation, Mother consulted with friends and then adopted a new tactic—a sophisticated and disinterested program of removing privileges.

Mother began by going into Selfish Sophie's room while she was absent and discarding the music tapes she didn't feel were appropriate. Fifteen-year-old Selfish Sophie was livid when she discovered this invasion of her privacy. Mother remained cold and haughty. A verbal battle ensued that resulted in a tenfold increase of alienation, anguish, and paranoia while bringing about no positive change in Sophie. Instead, Selfish Sophie started becoming involved in unwholesome activities with an assortment of friends who further reinforced her selfish attitudes.

Mother did not give up. She rudely confiscated Selfish Sophie's provocative clothing. She expected Sophie to clean her room once a week, and when that wasn't done she angrily seized other special belongings until one day only Sophie's mattress remained in her bedroom. Mother kept vainly expecting this demeaning treatment to bring about willing obedience.

Do you see the errors of this supposed solution? Many parents have done something similar. Have you? This approach only engenders mutual distrust between parent and child. It fosters no interest in God or right living. It turns home into a war zone, and casualties are great on both sides.

Schoolwork declined. Sophie's feelings and emotions took her for a wild ride into the bondage of vice, sinful practices, bad associates, and appetite indulgence. She mistakenly called this freedom. When Selfish Sophie turned eighteen, she eagerly grabbed her supposed liberty and abandoned the battleground of her home.

Selfish Sophie is that little eaglet falling from the lofty nest, thinking she has freedom. In reality, the gravity of self is unerringly pulling her on a crash course with the rocks of sin below.

Her parents, with their disinterested removal of every possession from their daughter's life, also withheld from her real love, positive influence, and genuine teaching and training in the ways of Christ. Real consequences should have the effect of catching the falling eaglet and putting it back in the nest for another lesson. If the parent eagle is not there to catch this youth, if God is not acknowledged as present by this youth, who will save this youth from certain death on the rocks of selfishness?

There is an epidemic of youth falling in this very way. Why? The reason is that parents are trying to use Satan's tactics to win their child's hearts for God. This approach will never work. Instead, it only binds the teen more firmly as an emotional slave to Satan's kingdom.

So what do we need to do instead? There is another way.

Identify and retrieve dropped stitches

The first crucial step is to take the time to evaluate the methods and results of your child rearing. I can't overemphasize the importance of this step. It is absolutely vital to any real change. Evaluate the pattern of your youth's character and identify the dropped stitches. Do you know what I mean by "dropped stitches"?

I like to knit. The quality of the item I knit depends on each individual stitch being linked with the one next to it. There have been times I tried to knit too quickly, was inattentive, or otherwise distracted from my work, and I failed to connect one stitch with the next. The stitch was dropped. At some point—the sooner the better—I need to stop knitting and hold the item out where I can examine it and compare it with the pattern I am following. As I do so, the dropped stitches become apparent. As I see where the dropped stitches are, I can begin picking them up skillfully with my needle, twisting them in just the right direction and weaving them into their proper place.

Often, we leave "dropped stitches" in our parenting. The only way to identify them is to take the time to stand back and compare the fabric of our youth's ways with the Pattern—Jesus Christ.

There are some basic, necessary stitches that should be in place by age thirteen. A youth should be well versed in the Scriptures, know the voice of God as distinguished from the voice of his flesh, and have meaningful regular personal time with God. Linked to those stitches is his growing experience of God's power to change his bad thoughts, feelings, and behavior. Diligent work, a helpful disposition, a scheduled life, and willing obedience to God and parents should be habitual. Repeatedly choosing to trust God and to do His will in His strength forms a pattern of life that is both durable and beautiful. Isn't that what you want for your youth?*

If these basic stitches are in place, build on them by consistently affirming these principles. Nurture your youth in a proper independence from you and his peers as he turns his life more and more over to God's direction. When youth learn direct dependence on God in the home, they know how to turn to God automatically when beyond your supervision. Then Satan cannot easily trip them up.

However, if you identify dropped stitches, don't hesitate to change your present course of parenting. Accept the Lordship of Jesus Christ. Find the walk you desire your youth to have.† Then make a plan with God for instilling these missing traits. That's the second step—formulating a working plan that arouses within the youth a desire for something better and shows him how to make it his own.

Selfish Sophie, with all her baggage of selfishness, paid a short visit to my home. As we got acquainted, I showed genuine interest in her. I took her for a bike ride. She thought that was great, as her mother didn't like riding bikes. We played jump rope with my boys, and that, too, was fun. Later, when trust was established, she came for a longer visit and expected lots of fun and adventure.

In my personal time with God I wrote down a list of Sophie's obvious, detrimental character traits—selfishness, taking charge improperly, slothful work habits, ingratitude, and lack of perceiving the feelings and needs of others.

Then as I consulted with God, I listed the areas that were reasonable to address in a few short weeks. I wanted her to taste a new way of thinking, feeling, and responding under God. My list looked like this:

---

*For more detail, refer to my third book in this series, *Parenting Your Child by the Spirit.*
†You may find my first book, *Parenting by the Spirit,* helpful here.

1. God must be in charge of her life.

2. She must learn how to identify bad thoughts and feelings and how to replace them with good.

3. She needs to see that selfishness is like a cancer that kills fun and happiness and that it needs to be replaced with putting others first.

4. Gratitude must be cultivated.

5. Diligent work habits must replace slothful tendencies.

That evening, after worship, as we sat and talked, Selfish Sophie began to be sassy and disrespectful. "I don't go to bed until ten-thirty or eleven at night. I just can't go to sleep early. I want to sleep in this bedroom." She was being her take-charge self.

I sent a prayer heavenward for wisdom and a Christlike spirit. "Sophie, you may not sleep in my son's room—that is his room. We need to respect other people's things and not think they are ours."

"But that is where I want to sleep. He can sleep somewhere on the floor!" she asserted commandingly.

"Sophie, you need to stop talking and listen to me. We need to pray to Jesus and ask Him what He would have you to do. Remember that we read in our worship this evening how Jesus wants to be our God and that we are to be His people? Should we tell God what He should do for us or should we ask God what He would have us to do?"

Sophie began to whine and grumble.

Grizzlies

"Oh Sophie, that is a miserable way to be," I interjected. "Let's kneel down here and give these grizzlies to God. They are grizzlies aren't they? A grizzly bear's disposition is different from a black bear's disposition. A grizzly will just pick a fight without being provoked—she's just ornery! Have you ever seen these bears?"

"Yes! I did in a zoo!" Her eyes brightened. "A baby bear was acting real nasty. She would bite and growl and jump on her mother while she was trying to eat. And the mother got real rough and wrestled the little one down to teach her to behave."

"What do you think of that?"

"I wouldn't want that baby bear to come by me!"

"Well you don't want to be that grizzly bear either! Wanting my son's room is like being that baby grizzly. Jesus will help you get rid of those nasty feelings inside of you—the selfish ones that make you feel real yucky in here!" And I pointed to her heart. "You obey those feelings, but you don't like being ugly or unkind. I'd like to show you how to be happy in your heart by giving those wrong thoughts and feelings to God. Kneel down here with me, and let's pray to Jesus for help. We can change only with Him."

She nodded her head in agreement and knelt down beside me. I prayed, "Jesus take the naughty grizzlies out of Sophie's heart. She wants to give them to You right now. Teach her how to enjoy life by following what You would have her to do. May she let You be her God and take orders from You so she can find the happiness she wants and be one of Your people. May she sleep especially good tonight at our house."

"Sound good, Sophie?"

She hesitated. This was really different from what she was used to. "What time do you go to bed?"

"At our house we go to bed at eight-thirty—that's about fifteen minutes from now. Whoever stays here goes to bed at the same time with us. You will do fine, and maybe, like me, you will find out that going to bed early is a good thing."

"I don't know about that," she grimaced.

"I used to be a night owl, and God talked with me about changing. That didn't sound good to me at first, but once I cooperated and changed I found that it's much better to go to bed early and get up early. It's so special to have Jesus talk with you in the quiet morning. I'll teach you about that in the morning. Let's get ready for bed now. The bathroom is yours. Don't take too long, or you'll miss out on good-night hug time."

Selfish Sophie went to the bathroom, but she wasn't so sure about this visit now. She wasn't in charge, and that was a new, uncomfortable feeling for her. Still, she didn't want to miss hug time, so she got ready for bed unusually fast. It was a special evening, all snug and warm with a Christmas tree, little lights, and Christmas carols. The hugs were fun, and as I tucked her into her special bed in the living room, we discussed that a bit. She still wanted to be in the boys' bedroom rather than here. God impressed me to bring her to Him through prayer again, and she surrendered. God toned down the "I want" enough that she was content to sleep there.

Learning to recognize the voice of her Savior

In the morning, during our family's personal worship time, I shared my special spot at the table with Selfish Sophie. I had her read the story of the cleansing of the leper, and we talked about Jesus' power to heal him immediately. I helped her make the parallel that when self arises in our mind (thoughts) and heart (feelings and emotions), Jesus will immediately answer our prayers for deliverance from this leprosy. We experience that deliverance by obeying right thoughts and feelings rather than selfish ones. She grasped the concept. Then God had me challenge her to persevere in her personal worship time for the full hour when fifteen minutes seemed long enough to her.

"I want you to take some time to talk with God and get to know His voice to your conscience, your mind. Talk with Jesus about the story you read and ask Him to help you pick out four important thoughts to remember. Write down those four points on this special pretty paper and then draw a picture from that story of what you like best."

This felt awkwardly new to her. She didn't like all this new stuff. "Well, you have to give new things a try," I told her. "What if you had never decorated a Christmas tree or bought and wrapped love gifts before? Wouldn't it be fun, even though it was new?"

"Oh, yes it would. . . . OK, I'll try."

After a while she asked, "How do I know God is speaking to me? This seems kind of dumb to me."

"Jesus talks to us through our minds, as does Satan. We must learn to distinguish between Jesus' voice and Satan's voice." As we talked, Selfish Sophie understood and was interested.

"You know, Sophie," I continued, "Satan suggests 'grizzly' thoughts that make you feel agitated inside. He wants to make you unhappy. But you don't have to listen to him or obey him, do you?"

"No, I don't! I'm learning he's a nasty fellow. I didn't know about him before. Well, I've heard about Satan, but didn't understand it the way you are saying it. I would love to be a happy girl, but I'm not. Do you think Jesus could change me?"

"Yes, He can. But you need to let Him be God. He needs to be the One in charge—not you. That means you need to do His will rather than yours when your will goes against God's will. Satan will stir up your feelings against God. He'll imply that God is unreasonable and hard to follow. But that is not true. So you need to come to know God's voice to you. It is not an audible voice; it's a thought in your mind that matches what the Bible says and comes with the tender, sweet Spirit of Jesus. He never forces like Satan tries to do. When Satan speaks to you, he often speaks through strong negative emotions that feel compelling; he wants you to feel you have no choice but to obey them. Can you relate to that?"

Selfish Sophie pondered a moment and then looked at me with growing understanding.

"Here is a text you'll like," I encouraged her. "It's Jeremiah chapter thirty-two, verse twenty-seven. 'I am the LORD, the God of all flesh: is there any thing too hard for me?' It doesn't matter how loudly your flesh demands that you be selfish; Jesus can make you happy, free, sweet, and kind. He will free you from the bondage of thinking that you can be happy only when you have your own way. Nothing is too hard for Him unless you keep it from Him. He can make your selfishness smaller and smaller until it is all gone."

"That sounds good," Selfish Sophie responded.

She returned to her personal prayer time with God and liked what she found. God gave her ideas and thoughts. She wrote out her four points from the story and drew her picture. Her four points were (1) The lepers asked for help and healing. (2) God answered immediately with His healing power. (3) Only one leper returned to say thank You to God. (4) Life was happier when they were healed than when they were sick.

Sophie was tasting the joy of finding life's purpose and direction. She was beginning to understand why we do what we do.

Family worship proved to be a warm and practical discussion of how to cooperate with God to be changed from the inside out. As she cheerfully helped prepare breakfast, she continued discussing her talk time with God. It had been fun, she decided. She looked forward to tomorrow's time. Doing dishes, folding the laundry, tidying the house was fun as a team. She fit right in.

When selfishness was displayed as "I want" or "me first," we labeled her thoughts and feelings, identified God's will, and went to prayer for help. God repeatedly subdued her angry, irritated feelings as she chose to give them to Him and follow His leadership. When reason didn't work, consequences were lovingly administered until she decided to honestly follow God and right.

We played tag and learned to win and lose. She was beginning to see that obedience is fun and that God is there to change wrong feelings and emotions. She was happier in this new way of life. It was structured, disciplined, Christlike, and consistent.

Day after day we cultivated selflessness and compassion. Her feelings improved and became pleasant. Thankfulness to Jesus for His watch-care and help did wonderful things in her thought life.

At the end of two weeks, Sophie was an entirely different girl. We renamed her Selfless Sophie. In Jesus, she learned to be helpful and pleasant. She enjoyed reading her Bible and praying. The valuable plants of perseverance, diligence, and gratefulness were sprouting nicely. Replacing good for evil, right for wrong, cooperation for rebellion, thinking of others instead of thinking solely of herself, and talking with God instead of talking with self was her pathway to freedom. She just needed someone to show her how and to connect her to God, her power source.

Your teen needs someone to show him or her, too. Will you take up the work of teaching your young person the basic skills he or she needs for life on the wing? Will you give God your time and your ear for this purpose? If you do, He will guide you to understand yourself and your child and give you the keys to mastering the prerequisite of connection with God.

In the next chapter, let's look at how one teen chooses her destiny—and how your teen can, too.

THE LONE EMBRACE
A SPECIAL WORD OF ENCOURAGEMENT FOR SINGLE PARENTS

Introspection may not seem desirable, but it is the pathway to solutions. Stumbling blocks may obscure our pathway, but viewing them with God's eyes can turn them into steppingstones to your destination. God is a master at taking your adversity and turning it into His opportunity to touch you and heal you, to direct and guide you. His love is just that great. He is always there for you.

"And ye shall seek me, and find me, when ye shall search for me with all your heart."*

---

*Jeremiah 29:13.

Chapter 7

Choosing Your Destiny

What man is he that feareth the Lord? him shall he teach
in the way that he shall choose.
—Psalm 25:12

This chapter is unique. If you happen to be a teen rather than a parent, if you have been reading this book longing for your parents to pick up these principles—but they aren't—then this chapter is specifically for you. If your parents won't lead the way, God will fill the gap for you. Let me share how it worked in the life of one of my young friends who chose to follow God in spite of her parents' apathy.

Opportunistic Ona was always in charge. She used every opportunity that came along to slip away from the work her mother assigned her—whether that was making her bed, washing the dishes, or doing her schoolwork. Whenever her mother's attention was diverted and she wasn't standing over Ona, Ona would make a break for some fun. She truly was an opportunist—a real escape artist.

Opportunistic Ona took charge not only of herself, but also of her sister, Tag-along Tammy, who was two years younger. In her favor, Ona taught Tammy proper manners—how to eat and when to say "please" and "thank you."

In Tammy, Ona found a willing partner for her escapades, which led both of them into trouble. It wasn't too difficult to convince Tag-along Tammy that sneaking away to play was much more fun than tending to duty. As soon as Mother was preoccupied with one of her frequent, lengthy phone calls, the two would creep quietly out the front door or through the second-story window to enjoy some freedom and fun. At the tender age of five, Ona had learned that Mother would be oblivious to her absence for an hour or more and that the sharp reprimand that always followed was a small price to pay for the diversion.

Once, when she was only four years old, Opportunistic Ona was supposed to be taking a nap with Tag-along Tammy, aged two. But Ona wasn't sleepy. Her active mind toyed with various possibilities for fun and soon fabricated a wonderful idea. Climbing up on the bedroom dresser, she launched herself into the air and landed on a mattress below. She laughed quietly, but gleefully, while her little sister giggled and watched. Then up on the dresser Opportunistic Ona went again—and jumped.

"Come on, Tammy. Don't you want to jump, too?" Tammy hesitated, but her big sister coaxed until she found herself on top of the dresser. "Jump! Jump, Tammy! It's so much fun!" Ona urged.

Tammy paused uncertainly. It looked so scary from this position. But after a bit more urging Tag-along Tammy closed her eyes, held her breath, and leaped recklessly. The only problem was she missed the soft mattress and landed right on the hard floor. Her loud cries of pain soon brought Mother, who rushed her to the hospital. Tammy had broken her arm.

There were few situations in which Ona didn't find an opportunity for fun while evading work. In fact, for these two little urchins, this became their typical way of life—until Opportunistic Ona was about thirteen years old.

New thoughts stirring

It was then, at the beginning of her teen years, that Ona went with her parents and sister to a week-long camp meeting. It was such fun sleeping in a tent at night and going to meetings throughout the day. Between meetings, there was always time for playing with friends—both old and new. It was all so exciting!

"Girls, time for breakfast!" Mother called.

Both girls came tumbling out of the tent, sleepy-eyed but full of fun. Mother had prepared an abundance of delicious whole-grain muffins, cakes, and cereals for their camp meeting adventure, and the girls loved eating them. This was their reward for all the dishwashing they had done at home—that is, when Mother could keep them at it.

After breakfast, Opportunistic Ona ran into the tent to brush and floss her teeth. If she were very thorough with her teeth, Mother and Tag-along Tammy might have all the dishes done before she had to help. If not, she would buy more time by visiting with the girl next door. Then she'd innocently join the family for the next interesting activity.

Later that day, she heard about a lady speaker—Sally Hohnberger. Even though she had never met her before, Ona felt strangely drawn to her and wanted to hear what she had to say. The problem was that Sally's meeting was at the unearthly hour of 6:00 A.M. "I don't like to get up so early," Ona argued with herself. But she resolved to do this hard thing and not miss her opportunity. Her mother wanted to go, and she managed to convince Tag-along Tammy to go as well.

That early morning meeting opened Ona's mind to things she had never heard before. This lady had moved to the wilderness of Montana to find a personal God. Her adventurous story, "Yoking Up With Christ," illustrated insights about how to have a genuine walk with God.*

Sally and her husband had used a human yoke to pull great big trees out of the forest. Her husband would give her directions with words, looks, and a wave of his arm so they could work together effectively. Then Sally shared how Jesus invited her to "yoke up" with Him to do hard things—like move Giant Fear or Giant Despair out of the forest of her thoughts and feelings. How He worked with her reason to help her properly label good thoughts and lying thoughts. How He directed her not to obey the lying thoughts. How Jesus guided her with His eyes, His impressions, His hand, and His Word—much like her husband had. In yoking up with Christ, she showed how Christ had removed those lying thoughts and how God can move big stubborn things from our lives when we yoke up with Him.

---

*This message can be found in the CD series "Christ All and in All" available through Empowered Living Ministries.

Ona listened intently. New desires and hopes began to spring up in her heart. She began to realize that, although her parents had told her she was a Christian, she really knew nothing about working together with God. She determined to learn to yoke up with Christ. She wanted to walk and talk with Him in this way. The stories Sally told captivated her interest. She planned right then and there to be at the early morning meeting every day—and she would bring her sister!

As the days went by, Opportunistic Ona began to admire this lady more and more; she wished Sally were scheduled to speak more often than she was.

Ona's mother, being a very social lady, invited an old friend to lunch one day. "Could I bring Sally along to lunch as well?" he asked. "I'm sure you ladies would enjoy talking. Did you hear her talk on child rearing today?"

"Yes, I did. It was wonderful. Sure, bring her, too. We'll all look forward to that."

Opportunistic Ona didn't know of this change in plans and was surprised to see Sally walking into *her* tent site at lunch time and being warmly greeted by her own parents. Ona suddenly felt unusually shy. She withdrew to a safe distance but lingered close enough to listen in on the adult conversation. The things Sally shared about her family fascinated her.

Sally's family even had wild animals for pets, and she showed them her photo album to prove it! Opportunistic Ona ventured near and pored over Sally's pictures of pet deer, bears, and other creatures. Forgetting her shyness, she bubbled over with questions. Ona saw that heaven was near to earth, and she joyfully imagined what wild pets she could have at her home.

As Ona began exploring other photos of Sally's home and family, her mother asked questions about keeping her girls focused on tasks at home. "They are so easily distracted from their duties," she confided.

Ona wondered if Mrs. Hohnberger would look down on her when she heard this, but instead she smiled in Ona's direction as she began sharing with Mother. She discussed principles she had found worked with her boys—teaching them how to have a personal walk with God, training them to govern themselves, and cultivating the right in place of the wrong.

As Sally told of the results of this training in her sons, Ona was all ears! She could hardly believe that *boys* could take full charge of meal preparation for the entire family. Or that they were only thirteen and fifteen years old and had been doing that for years!

Sally went on to add that even while she was speaking at this camp meeting her boys were at home, taking full responsibility for running the household—doing the laundry and ironing, the cooking and cleaning—while keeping up with their home schooling. All without her supervision. They knew the voice of God to their own souls and had been taught and trained in this way.

Sally laughed that her husband had told her he was gaining weight with all the lovely extra treats the boys were including in their meal preparations. Then she said that when she returned home she would be having guests the very next day and that the boys were doing extra cooking in preparation for this event. "What a blessing these teen years can be!" she exclaimed.

Opportunistic Ona was supposedly studying while the mothers talked, but she was getting a higher education by listening. In her heart was a mixture of feelings she as yet did not understand.

On the one hand, she was indignant! "Just think of that—boys my age are more adept and capable in housework than I am. That isn't right! They do more cooking than I do. How can that be? I'm the girl. I'm supposed to be the housekeeper and cook in the home—not boys. I've never cooked an entire meal in my life. I don't know if I even could. And run the home? That's way beyond me."

On the other hand, Ona was scared. "I kind of like being a good escape artist! It gives me a certain feeling of freedom. Changing would mean a lot more work and a lot less fun!"

The Spirit and the flesh wrestled within her. God was calling her higher, while her natural inclinations struggled to maintain the mastery.

"Do I want to relinquish my escape artist degree? . . .Yes I do!" Ona decided. "I won't let a boy keep house better than me! I'm going to do it—at least I think I will."

The next morning began as usual. "Ona, I need your help with breakfast this morning," her mother called.

Automatically Ona began to respond, "I would help you, Mother, but I need to . . ."

"Remember your desire to change your ways?" God interposed.

"Well yes, but . . ." A feeling of strong resistance rose up within her; she could feel it all the way down to the pit of her stomach. It had seemed so important yesterday to make a change. But now . . . Then she remembered Matthew and Andrew—Mrs. Hohnberger's sons.

"If boys can do this, so can I! OK, Lord, I'll do it. Will You let me yoke up with You to teach me?"

"I'll be right there, Mother," Ona finished out loud. She put away her study things, put on her jacket, and left her tent with a new resolve.

"Matthew and Andrew learned to do this work cheerfully, and so can I. Right, Lord? Please take away the resistance I have. Give me Your mind and Your ways."

"Be assured, I am with You," God affirmed.

Ona's first try at this new change was a success. She not only helped prepare the meal, but also volunteered to wash dishes—and did it all with a willing attitude instead of her usual begrudging air. She wasn't smiling, nor did she enjoy it, but she was resolved to do it.

Opportunistic Ona didn't always help her mother with meals during their camp meeting stay, but a new resolve was settling into her mind. As she continued to go to all the meetings, she picked up more and more new ideas, which she determined to implement at home. Surely this was a better way of life and more in line with what Jesus wanted for her. Somehow, with God's help, she was going to change!

Hard battles

To Ona's pleasant surprise, her mother bought materials to take this message home with them. At home, Ona made use of these materials when her heart was so inclined. Yet, with each small choice she made, she was settling into the truth and learning to let God be in charge by responding when He called for her heart. Each time she surrendered in thought and cooperated with God in action, it was pleasant. And when she didn't, it wasn't pleasant. She was learning.

Opportunistic Ona faced a recurrent battle over sweeping the floor. So God chose this place to train her in a new way.

"Ona, you can sweep the floor for your mother. That would be very helpful."

"Mother hasn't asked me to do this."

"It needs to be done, don't you think?" God added.

"Well yes, it is very dirty, and I don't like things to be dirty or messy. But I was just going outside to play. It's not fair! I've already helped with the dishes this morning. Isn't that enough?"

"I'm calling you to do this. Won't you do it for Me? You read this morning that I want to be your God and want you to be My people. Don't you want to be one of Mine?"

"Well, yes, I do. But not at this price!" Her mind and heart were stirred regarding right and wrong. God appealed to her reason, intellect, and conscience—and this time, she decided for God!

"All right, I'll go sweep the floor for You, Lord." And away for the broom she went.

"Sweeping can be fun if you choose it to be fun. Do you want Me to help you discover this?"

"I don't know. 'Sweeping can be fun.' Isn't that a bit ridiculous?"

"Ona, any task I ask you to do can be fun—even sweeping! What about Sally's boys? Didn't you hear how pleasantly they learned to run the home?"

God was leading her to a deeper surrender found not only in yielding her will to do this unpleasant task, but also in allowing Him to clean out the ugly feelings of resentment locked in her heart. God wanted to give her a new freedom—found, not through *escaping* duty, but rather in *performing* it in His Spirit.

"That's right," Ona agreed. "So my thoughts are lying thoughts, and like Sally said, I don't need to obey them. OK, Lord, what would You have me to do?"*

"Think how surprised and happy your mother will be when she finds you've swept the floor without her even asking you to. Think of being in training to be the best mother and housekeeper on this earth—this is the beginning."

That was just what Ona needed. She cooperated, and soon pleasant thoughts produced pleasant feelings.

"I like feeling this way. Jesus must have done something inside me," she reflected contentedly.

Her satisfaction remained even when her mother was only mildly pleased with her surprise and didn't give Ona all the approval she was hoping for. Instead, Mother expected even more from Ona now. Nevertheless, Opportunistic Ona felt good anyway. She had pleased God even if she didn't entirely please her mother. This successful experience prepared the way for the next.

---

*See Acts 9:6.

Opportunistic Ona was thoroughly absorbed in reading when Mother called her to do the dishes. Ona's heart sank. It wasn't just a joke that her mother used every dish in the kitchen when she cooked, and this had been no exception.

"No way," Ona resolved darkly. "I'm not doing the dishes this time! Tag-along Tammy isn't working. Mom's on the phone. Why should I have to do the dishes? It isn't a bit fair. I'll slip out of the house and go read in the woods where Mother can't find me."

Then, God called for her heart. *"Is that honest, Ona? You don't want to be dishonest and carry that guilt. It's a little thing, My Little One. This is learning how to be a good mother and to give of yourself."*

The struggle in Ona's heart was fierce. The old feelings and inclinations were so strong. And yet, she had gained so much with Jesus and liked the new way. Did she want to quit now?

"Well . . . all right, I'll go," she decided.

"In everything give thanks," God urged.

"You want me to give thanks too! Ugh! Well, that's what Jesus did. It's the least I can do. It is a little thing."

As she cooperated with Jesus in her thoughts and washed the dishes, she found the true joy and freedom that come only in the path of duty.

Moving forward

Ona's next pivotal point came during her fourteenth summer. For a month, she worked in an office that produced a weekly Christian magazine. This experience opened her eyes to the importance of being responsible, faithful, and thorough in order to do a job well. When others lacked those qualities, it put more pressure on her. And her irritation at their deficiencies showed her how much she was still in charge—rather than Jesus—and led her to yield this area to Him to change also.

One of her duties in the office was to help proof a booklet titled *Way of Baptism,* by Matthew and Andrew Hohnberger.* (Here were *those* boys again!) This booklet was running as a continuing article in the weekly magazine, and as Ona worked on it almost daily, she was both inspired and disturbed. She liked the idea of taking responsibility for her own walk with God, but the practical understanding of "dying to self" touched some areas she wasn't sure she wanted to examine.

For example, she began to see that she had been baptized at age nine with the youth in her church just because it was tradition—not because she was ready or called of God. She began to realize that she had no practical understanding of what baptism really meant, and she was strongly convicted that she didn't understand the death of self, true surrender, nor how to cooperate with God. The more she read, the more disconcerted she became. It had been five years since her baptism, and she had only recently begun to let God be in charge of her life. She still didn't really understand how to die to self.

Even more painful were her guilt feelings about how she treated her sister. At the table, Tag-along Tammy chewed loudly with her mouth open, and when Ona re-

---

*Also available through Empowered Living Ministries.

proved her, Mother would not support her. Resentment grew. Embarrassed of Tammy, Ona would push her away, ignore her, or just send her away when friends came around. When they were at home alone, Ona would often be rude or refuse to play with her sister.

She resolved that with God's help she would change her attitude toward her sister as well as continue improving her work habits in the home. Over time, God made drastic changes in Ona; she and Tammy became inseparable best friends.

After her summer job, Ona felt a deepened resolve to go the distance with God. It bothered her that Mother wasn't as enthusiastic about this matter of overcoming as she was. She longed to have a mother who would help her step forward into these new and better ways. How could a teenager figure it out alone? Her anxious thoughts were soothed when God assured her that He would personally teach her when her mother wasn't inclined to do so.

Months later, a *big* test came that brought about deep changes in Opportunistic Ona. It was Friday—the family's cooking and cleaning day. While Mother worked in the kitchen, she expected her two girls to clean the 2,300-square-foot home.

Thirteen-year-old Tag-along Tammy was assigned to clean one bathroom. She mixed all the household chemicals she could find in the toilet to see if she could make an explosion—which would also clean the toilet, she reasoned. She enjoyed playing with the chemicals, and she made some awful smells, but no explosions occurred. The toilet remained dirty until Tammy was finally convinced she would have to scrub it herself. In the meantime, fifteen-year-old Ona scrubbed the other two bathrooms, vacuumed the entire house, mopped the wood floors and dusted the intricate woodwork—all with a cheerful, willing attitude. Then it happened.

Mother called, "Ona, come wash dishes so I can have some clean counter space to work. Come quickly."

"Can't Tammy help you, Mother? I've done so much work today already."

"OK. Tammy, come help me do some dishes."

No response was forthcoming from Tammy.

Ona's heart sank as she realized what had happened. Tammy had slipped out of the house, just like they both had done together countless times before. Later, she would just say, "I never heard you call, Mother!"

"Ona, you will have to come. I don't know where Tammy is. Come right now!"

Ona suddenly felt like a Cinderella—endless duties abounding with unfairness. Her lips were ready to give a sharp reply.

"Ona, don't give in. Not after all you have done right so far. I'm here with you. Don't give up now! Jump and fly, little eaglet. You can fly!"

"I don't feel like flying. It doesn't seem fun just now."

"What happens if you don't fly with Me?"

"I fly with Satan and self and crash on the rocks below." Memories of the previous Friday flashed through her mind. Ona and Tammy had slipped away while Mother was on the phone, and as a result they didn't have enough time to clean the house or to wash dishes. Facing the mess the next day was dreadful.

"It doesn't matter that it is unfair, does it? It doesn't matter that Tammy escaped alone this time without me. It doesn't matter that I don't feel like washing dishes. I can choose to take Your hand, and You will walk this path with me, enabling me to be content and happy doing what is right in You."* And she laid down her dust cloth and went to wash those *"endless dishes."*

Opportunistic Ona may not have gone to a ball like Cinderella, but she gained something far better than dancing with a prince! Jesus redeemed her heart from old, selfish ways and filled it with His own sweet character and presence. Washing the dishes with Jesus was more delightful than being arrayed in an elegant dress—and much more satisfying than riding in a pumpkin!

She was still an opportunistic girl, but now she looked for opportunities to follow God rather than self. Before, she took every opportunity to shun responsibility. Now she watched for the chance to be of service. God was teaching her true flight above the pull of her flesh. She was using her opportunities to change from serving evil to serving good.

Little by little, Opportunistic Ona was learning how personal Christ is. She found Him interested in every detail of her life and willing to be her personal Teacher.† Her experience demonstrates how *true* character development occurs—one choice, one step at a time, in Jesus. Through this daily exercise, Christ's character was becoming hers.

It's up to me

Ona's next step was to take charge of her own personal study time. She began spending thirty minutes a day in study and prayer; soon she increased that time to one hour. Her home life was less than cheery and ideal. Ona longed for it to be happy, like the Hohnbergers' home, and she was willing to put forth any effort to see that happen. So when her mother, who tended to be fanatical, suggested spending two and a half hours daily in personal study, Ona cheerfully accepted the challenge. She believed this would change her home and family. What she overlooked, however, is that it is not so much the *amount* of time spent in study that transforms the life, but rather the surrender and *application* made of what is learned under the direction of a personal Savior.

Much to Ona's dismay, the dynamics of her home did not change for the better. Her parents still carried baggage from their unfortunate upbringing. Although they provided a better home for their children than they had experienced, it remained far short of God's plan. Arguing and strife were common. Father was unwilling to face and change his fiery, dominant, demeaning personality. Mother was impulsive, and while more physically affectionate than her husband, she, too, was emotionally dominating and demeaning. Ona felt she could never please her mother—no matter how hard she tried. Ona strove for excellence but still could not get a "well done"—only suggestions for improvement.

---

*Psalm 25:12.
†John 6:45.

Ona's parents committed to many outward reforms, trying to make their family what it ought to be, but they never dealt with the heart—the only thing that would have notably changed the atmosphere of their home! No outward change can replace the necessity of facing old ingrained patterns of thinking, feeling, and relating in the inner heart. As long as these dysfunctions are not acknowledged, faced, and dealt with under Christ's leadership, they will continue to dominate the life.

Thus it was with Ona's family. The religion of the Pharisees ruled. They sought to gain God's approval and find peace through outward reforms.

Moving to a country setting and building a home together only increased their strife and heartache. They implemented extremes in diet and dress; their exacting study program dictated that they rise at 3:00 A.M. no matter when they got to bed. This caused countless difficulties emotionally, physically, and relationally. Poor health and insecurities abounded. While the parents grew more and more distant, the two sisters bonded even closer. Their only stability, outside of Christ, was their relationship with each other.

Opportunistic Ona was growing slowly in her experience of dying to self. Her life seemed so difficult—one endless exaction after another. All her hours of study only brought her more information that she wasn't sure how to apply, which resulted in deeper guilt. All the outward reforms she participated in with her family brought no inward peace and no lasting change in the unhappiness of her home. She even tried rebaptism.

"Where are You, God?" she cried out. "I want out of here. My home is a mess. My parents argue regularly. I do all they say and still feel so oppressed. Get me out of here—please!"

"Ona, I cannot release you from this position until you become content and learn to appreciate your blessings here."

"You don't want me to jump ship, do You? I could jump from the frying pan into the fire, and that would not be good for me either! Then You will have to transform my thoughts and feelings here at home, as You have in other areas of my life. I give You permission to work."

Over the next few years, Ona faced many trials. She began learning how to respectfully disagree with her parents when their expectations would lead her to compromise obeying God. She found peace in her heart in the midst of her unhappy home by surrendering to do God's will in each situation that presented itself. She began to be God-governed and even learned to appreciate the blessings she did have in her home.

Stepping out on her own

Then she was given an opportunity to attend a Christian school away from home. Although she was no longer looking for an escape, she discerned that this was the next step in God's plan for her. Her experience at school taught her some very valuable, though difficult, lessons of following God rather than men.

At age nineteen, Ona began working as a baby nurse. Living in other people's homes, she depended on God to be her Parent. Responsibility was now well ingrained, and so God began to touch on other emotional weak areas. He challenged her inadequacies and poor problem-solving techniques and replaced them with true thoughts and better ways. As she cooperated, the strong emotions that had tortured and debilitated her for so long, faded away. She faced her fears with Jesus, and He gave her confidence in His ability to bring emotional freedom choice by choice.

She had grown up believing that she had no value. God, with the help of dear friends, nurtured in her the truth that she was priceless. She began to blossom into a very competent, energetic, and skilled baby nurse.

God then challenged her indecisiveness. Her parents' dominating personalities had stifled her individuality, and she feared thinking differently from those around her. To avoid conflict, she would ask the people she was working for what they thought and agree with them whenever possible. God began to teach her better ways of relating. She learned that it is possible to disagree without losing friendship. As she compared her history with God's manual for successful relationships, she tried His ways and found greater freedom to soar like an eagle.

From the time she was nineteen to twenty-one, God challenged her habit of generalization—avoiding being specific with people for fear of conflict. This habit had grown out of her belief that something was wrong with her because of her sad home life and that to reveal this to anyone would make her vulnerable to further rejection. God provided special friends with whom she could safely work through these issues. She became an even better baby caregiver. She could now be specific in helping mothers get on a feeding schedule and discuss why. Now, she could present this information and not feel personally rejected if someone didn't accept her information.

In time, her work expanded into helping entire families with child-rearing issues. She became sought after for her expertise of reaching the heart of a child and connecting them with Jesus to find the power to overcome wrong ways of thinking and feeling. She taught these techniques not only to children but also to parents. This proved to be her God-given work.

Ona's parents had disciplined her when she was living at home with the militant Pharisaism they had embraced. Now, her mother regressed in many of the dietary and dress reforms that she had instituted in their home. But Opportunistic Ona reached a point in her personal walk with God that she could choose for herself how to handle each area of her life. She found joy in conforming to God's balanced view of the true Christian walk. Even though her parents abandoned their standards, she would continue following what she knew to be right. Not in a demeaning attitude toward her parents, but in an attitude of freedom—freedom to follow God and have proper independence while maintaining respect to her parents.

Opportunistic Ona chose her destiny, didn't she? Step by step, she followed God, and He chose her for His own. Choice by choice, she jumped out of the nest of her comfort zone and found flight in Christ. When her parents were not there for her, Jesus was. He became her constant Companion and familiar Friend. She filtered her thoughts and feelings through Him and cooperated when He challenged her misconceptions. With Him, she learned to soar.

Every youth today has a similar opportunity. You can choose a destiny of success regardless of your parents' choices. You can learn to fly with Jesus and overcome all your shortcomings. Jesus will personally adopt you into His family and take you into His nest to train you to fly above the pull of sin. If your parents accompany you in this, you are truly blessed. But if not, you can still seek God for yourself and choose your destiny.

THE LONE EMBRACE
A WORD OF ENCOURAGEMENT FOR SINGLE PARENTS

Father, Mother, you, too, can choose your destiny. You can choose to let God teach you how to overcome your history, your weaknesses, and your shortcomings. You, too, need to learn to fly above the pull of your flesh. You especially need this as a solo parent and especially if your spouse opposes your efforts to raise your child in Christ. When you are forced to shuttle your child between the conservative and liberal side of religion—or between religion and no religion—it is a very trying situation for both you and your child.

The best way you can help your children and youth is to give them their wings in Jesus. They need to know personally how to discern the voice of God from the voice of their flesh. They need to see you demonstrate the advantages of following Christ rather than the fleshly nature. The freedom is worth the battle. Teach your youth of a personal God who is with them even when you are not. Ask for His protecting hand over your child while he is subjected to opposing influences. Teach your youth how to follow God in practical ways like Opportunistic Ona learned. Then they, too, can have the proper independence to follow God even when they must do so alone. Help them find the *real* God who can empower their choices.*

Matthew, age 14, cheerfully washing the dishes.

*Deuteronomy 30:19.

Chapter 8

Lost in the Fog

For God is not the author of confusion, but of peace.
—1 Corinthians 14:33

*H*er wedding day dawned glorious and bright—just perfect for the momentous event that had been in the planning for nearly a year! Twenty-year-old Valueless Vicki tried to relax as she soaked in the morning sunshine, savoring deep breaths of fragrant summer air. She mentally went over the numerous festivities that were already in motion.

She had just returned from a catered brunch attended by all the wedding participants. The large college church was being filled with flowers, greenery, ribbons, and candles. The organist, pianist, harpist, brass quintet, string quartet, harpsichordist, and vocalist were well-rehearsed to perform the special musical arrangements orchestrated just for this special wedding. The area's best photographer had been hired to make permanent record of the day's events—both still photos and video—and was arriving and setting up for the day.

Other friends were busy preparing mountains of food for the reception. Vicki's mother had worked for months filling the freezer with special goodies just for this day. Over five hundred guests were expected—some traveling many miles to be present for this occasion.

Her tiered, southern-belle gown waited in its lacy perfection for that moment of a lifetime while her five bridesmaids were even now pressing the final touches into their flowing azure-blue gowns. She could imagine how attractive they would look next to the navy blue tuxedos of her groom and his five groomsmen. The flower girl and Bible boy were prepared to look and act their parts perfectly, while her two cousins, in their blue-and-white long dresses, were poised to light the many candles.

Lying there in the sunshine, Vicki knew she should be excited, but a familiar confusion filled her heart. Something was just not right.

Her troubled thoughts kept rehearsing that moonlit evening when her groom had proposed. Somehow, when he asked that magical question, "Will you marry me?" she had known she needed to say *no*. But she couldn't bring herself to say it—the word stuck in her throat. Her suitor interpreted her hesitation as breathless ecstasy, an inaudible *yes*. And so, their engagement had begun. She had played well the role she felt was expected of her while trying to quiet the qualms that rose up so often about their relationship. Surely once they were married, he would truly *begin* to love her.

Now, the turmoil filled her heart again—even more disturbingly than before. Tears welled up in her eyes as she recalled his demeaning treatment even that morning at the special wedding brunch. Something within her said, *Run! Run now before it is too late! Your parents will help you, if only you tell them!*

Just then, the patio door slid open, and Vicki's mother stepped out. Her smiling face clouded as she noticed her daughter's tears. "Vicki, what is wrong?"

Vicki couldn't seem to find the words to express her doubts.

Her mother continued. "Vicki, if you don't want to marry him, you don't have to. It doesn't matter that we've spent all this money. Your father and I will help you. Just say the word."

But then, the familiar picture loomed up before Vicki—the high expectations of this wedding. Her groom and his family, her relatives and friends, all the musicians, photographers, florists, caterers, all the money that had been spent, all the plans for her future of working as a nurse to support her new husband through medical school. How could she disappoint them all?

Feeling trapped in the fog of others' expectations, she stuffed down the turmoil, married the man to whom she had been too afraid to say no, and entered a marriage filled with emotional, verbal, and physical abuse. Seven and a half years later, after the loss of one child and the birth of another, her marriage ended in a nasty divorce.

Floundering on the rocks

Vicki was like a fledgling eagle, launched into the air without adequate flight lessons in knowing and following Jesus. She desperately tried to flap her wings alone but was unable to stop the downward spiral onto the rocks of defeat and divorce. Unmet needs and incomplete training brought her to this unenviable position. Is this you?

Once on the rocks, Vicki floundered to regain the air, feeling sure she was now a worthless individual. Driven by gnawing insecurity, she found herself once again helpless to resist the advances of a man who seemed to offer her the attention, love, and acceptance she so desperately craved. Once again, when marriage was proposed, the word *no* stuck in her throat, and her hesitation was assumed to mean *yes*. Lost in the fog of desiring a man to love her, she married this man less than three months after her divorce was final. She expected bliss to begin. Instead, she soon realized that she had only jumped from the frying pan into the fire. Although physical abuse was no longer present, emotional and mental abuse was the rule. Vicki was horrified. She felt trapped again by her unwise commitment. Her inner emotional pain was almost overwhelming, but she had no idea how to deal with it. She had no tools with which to set proper boundaries. She did not know a personal God to teach her and direct her in better ways. Instead, she used the best problem-solving tool she had—compliance and performance.

She accepted the irresponsibility of her second husband and did her best to pull both his and her load in the family as well as repairing the emotional damage inflicted by his tirades. She earned a good income as a home health nurse and kept up with the housecleaning, cooking, laundering, shopping, and bookkeeping. She cared for her son and was responsible for the visits of her new stepson. At church, she became very active as pianist and personal ministries leader. She led an active campaign distributing Christian literature, conducting cooking schools, and raising money for worthy Christian projects. She demonstrated deep concern for the waning piety in the church and actively agitated issues. Her conservative, striving habits gave her the appearance of being very religious.

But the inner pain only intensified. Feelings of rejection loomed over her in spite of all her striving and performing. Valueless Vicki had lived with insecurity all her life. That insecurity motivated her compliant patterns of relating, of taking responsibility for others, of not being able to say no when she needed to, and it drove her to become enmeshed in destructive relationships. She had not felt worthy of the stable men that had pursued her in college. Vicki had believed a lie, perpetrated on her from infancy, that she had no value, that she was not welcome in this world. She often felt guilty for occupying space on the earth and using resources to sustain her life. Where could she find relief? She must try harder, perform better, and comply more sweetly.

But the thoughts, feelings, and emotions that she tried so hard to avoid would not go away. Instead, they became more demanding. Her deep insecurity was triggered any time she was around another woman who seemed to her to be more attractive than she was. In her mind's eye, Valueless Vicki would deteriorate into a faceless blob with no intelligence—unable to look anyone in the eye or to speak in a normal voice. Then her survival mechanisms would kick in. She would withdraw into resentment, jealousy, envy, and bitterness. She would treat her husband with either icy coldness or hot anger. These episodes were followed by deep despair and hopelessness. She must try harder in self to measure up, to perform, to stuff down these explosions.

If she could somehow never see another attractive woman or even think of one or if she could keep her husband from ever noticing one, then she would be all right. But it's impossible to control outward circumstances so that our buttons are never pushed.

Why?

Why did this happen to Vicki? No one who knew her in her childhood and teen years would have predicted such struggles. She was talented and accomplished and had enjoyed many advantages.

Her parents had given her much more than they had received from their parents. They lived in a comfortable home in a country setting with miles of wooded hills and canyons to explore. They paid for a costly private Christian education—grade school through college. Years of expensive music lessons supported her striving for excellence as a pianist and vocalist. Mission experience in New Guinea and Africa offered a rich cross-cultural background while a high level of involvement with church programs and community events inculcated the principle of service to others. Lots of companions and wholesome activities ensured a superior social life. Interesting family vacations with friends built wonderful memories—exploring places such as Death Valley; the Grand Canyon; Yosemite; Baja, California; and the Sierra Nevada mountains. Year-round recreation included backpacking, camping, hiking, swimming, waterskiing, and snow skiing.

Valueless Vicki had never been one of those foolhardy or rebellious youth that people just "knew" were headed for trouble. She loved her parents and teachers and listened to their counsel. She was an industrious, dependable worker and was eager to please those she worked for. She was a straight-A student and had graduated from college with a degree in nursing. She loved her church and her Bible and had cultivated her talents to bless humanity.

What was missing from her training? Why was she so susceptible to relationships that well nigh derailed her for life? Why wasn't she prepared to make decisions for successful flight?

The key to understanding Valueless Vicki is found in 1 Samuel 16:7: "man looketh on the outward appearance, but the LORD looketh on the heart." No one in Vicki's life probed beneath the surface to find out what was motivating her good behavior. Her parents didn't know how to talk about feelings and the deeper thought processes associated with them. Vicki thought something was wrong with her because she had emotions.

How often do we overlook the quiet, cheerful, compliant teen? We think all is well because it appears so outwardly. But God looks at the heart and understands the lack of *a vital connection with Him* at the level of the thoughts and feelings. Unlike many parents, God is not satisfied with mere outwardly good behavior. Good behavior may be nothing more than a Pharisaical routine. He is concerned with motivation. We, as parents, need to pay attention to the same. We need to thoughtfully inquire, *Why does my youth behave the way he or she does?*

One needful thing

Jesus told Martha in His conversation with her so many years ago that "one thing is needful."* Nothing can replace that one needful thing. It provides the solid foundation upon which all the other good things are built. All the other good we can supply can never replace this one vital thing, and we cannot hide its lack.

That one needful thing is to sit at the feet of Jesus and learn of Him. This means far more than gaining intellectual knowledge. It means opening the entire heart to Jesus, allowing Him to search and reveal the hidden motives, to expose lying thoughts and replace them with truth, to cut through the tender emotions and nourish the real needs beneath. How does a person learn to do that?

Open communication between parents and teens is vital. If a young person doesn't find it safe to open his heart to his parents, it will be much harder for him to grasp how to do that with God. But when a parent understands the deeper heart work and can help the child identify what is troubling her and can lead her to Christ for real answers, for effective problem-solving techniques, for a changed heart—that youth can find freedom at the core of her being.

---

*Luke 10:42.

It wasn't until Valueless Vicki was in her thirties that she began to realize what that "one needful thing" was. The one essential ingredient that would have made all the difference in her life would have been knowing and belonging to a personal God that could direct her thoughts and feelings and could help her sort out life's misconceptions. Vicki thought she knew God. Her entire life was built around her religion, and she considered herself a superior Christian. It wasn't until she found herself tucked into a quiet country setting, out of the main thoroughfares of life, with few human resources around her that she began to realize that while she knew a lot *about* God, she didn't *know* God!

The quietness of the country thrilled her at first—but then sent her into a panic. The world was passing her by, and no one seemed to miss her. She was going to be swallowed up in oblivion! She wasn't needed! She could no longer numb her pain with activities. All the loud voices of expectation were silenced, and the tranquility was almost oppressive. Then she began to discern one still, small Voice gently calling to her heart. As she began to listen, she realized that Voice had been there all along. It had been drowned out by the more insistent voices crowding around her.

As she began to open her heart to Him, she discerned His Spirit in the breeze rustling the pine trees. She felt His warmth in the quiet sunshine. She observed His lessons in the little creatures that frequented her yard. More so, she began to grasp His care for her through the attention she saw Him lavish on the humble wayside flowers. She learned of a life hid with Christ in God from the little seeds she planted in her garden.

Her quiet time became a gold mine of real heart-searching, of investigation and testing of long-held assumptions, an unlearning of old ways as well as a learning of new ones. As she studied God's standard of character, she began to realize how far short of the mark she fell. It became evident that God desires truth in the inward parts and not just a correct outward routine. She realized her complete helplessness to break the shackles that bound her to her feelings, thoughts, and behaviors of worthlessness and insecurity. Shame and remorse intensified her desperate search for a solution.

About this time, she began to memorize Psalm 139. As she meditated on the thoughts she was committing to memory, it suddenly became very clear to her that it was completely safe to be transparent with God—to admit to Him and to herself just what she was and what she was not. She found that instead of continually striving to rise above her lost condition, she could sink down into the arms of a loving Savior. She found such a sense of relief just in knowing that she no longer faced her pit of worthlessness alone. God loved her and accepted her just as she was and assured her that He was there to help her. He said to her, "him that cometh to Me, I will in no wise cast out."* For the first time in her life, she began to feel a sense of belonging and security.

God became very real to her—not merely as a distant, important person, but as a close Friend, Savior, Lord, Father, and heavenly Husband. He desired to deal with

---

*John 6:37

her at the level of her wrong thoughts, feelings, and emotions. Her life and character began to change from within.

Her deep insecurity was still very real, and she began to see how inconsistent it was with Christian character and yet how utterly helpless she was to do anything about it. She could more easily change the color of her skin than to change her thoughts, feelings, and behavioral responses. Oh sure, she could stuff them down for a while or even vent them and then feel better momentarily, but she could not change them in any lasting way.

Untangling the tangles

Then God began untangling the hidden thought processes that had kept Vicki in this lifelong bondage; He revealed to her that in spite of professing to honor His law, she consistently violated both its first and last precepts. God wanted to deal with her at the level of her thoughts, because when the thoughts are corrected, they will, in time, cause the feelings to be correct and will correct the wrong outward behavior *in His power,* not in hers alone.

She began to see that the first commandment, "Thou shalt have no other gods before me,"* meant putting God in charge of her life. She had always thought that God was too busy with important things to be involved in her life. And so she had substituted the expectations of others for the guidance of God. She then tried to meet those expectations in her own strength, apart from God. She became a people pleaser. The more people she could please, the more satisfied she was with herself. And the more people she upset, the more stressed she became.

It was a major breakthrough in her life when it dawned on her that Jesus was not a people pleaser. In fact, the people around Him often misunderstood Him and were displeased with Him. Jesus worked to bless those around Him. But He lived to please only one Person: His Father. Blessing others does not always mean pleasing them.

Jesus said to Vicki, *"You have been carrying a very heavy burden—a galling yoke. This yoke is man-made, and you don't have to carry it anymore. From now on, you don't have to try to please anyone but Me. Give Me the burden of ordering your life—from the broadest overall direction down to the smallest detail. When someone makes a request of you, you don't have to agree right away. Wait until you have checked it out with Me and you know how I want you to respond."*

Vicki accepted Christ's offer, and although it wasn't easy, she learned, under Christ, when and how to say no gracefully. God began to agitate her mind concerning what things in life are essential versus those things that are merely urgent. She discovered that often the urgent crowds out the essential—the "one thing needful." She decided that if anything was going to be crowded out of her life, it would not be that "one needful thing"—her time at Jesus' feet and the experience of learning to walk and talk with Him all day! She began to find peace, purpose, and a sense of control in her life in His power.

---

*Exodus 20:3

Then God began to reveal to her that she was not living out the tenth commandment, "Thou shalt not covet."*

Covetousness is simply being discontented. Valueless Vicki longed to have value. And she believed that she would gain value if only she could grasp certain things. She was not content with the person God had made her to be. Her mind often ran in the *if only* track:

"*If only* I were taller, more slender, had darker, curlier hair, smoother skin that tans. . . ."

"*If only* I could be a concert pianist and play in a large symphony, I'd be important."

"*If only* I had a sparkling personality that everyone was drawn to. . . ."

"*If only* I knew how to dress more impressively. . . ."

"*If only* I had a brand-new car and lived in a beautiful house with a perfectly landscaped yard, I'd be respected."

"*If only* I could attain all these things, I would feel valuable and could be happy and content. I'd be looked up to."

Slowly, Vicki began to recognize that these inner desires were based on the devil's lies. She began to see that the remedy for her perceived lack of value was not based on anything she could be, do, or possess but was rooted, instead, in Calvary. When Christ died for her, He established her value for all eternity, and it is not negotiable.

Christ said to her, *"Let your conversation be without covetousness; and be content with such things as ye have: for he hath said, I will never leave thee, nor forsake thee. So that we may boldly say, The Lord is my helper, and I will not fear what man shall do unto me."*†

Vicki saw that Satan had been leading her on with a vaporous mirage while Christ offered her present rest and contentment through His own sweet presence. He is the Creator. He owns all things. There is nothing too hard for Him. He loves each of us just as we are and doesn't judge us for the things we have no ability to change. When Vicki placed herself in God's hands, a heavy burden rolled off her back. Jesus loved her for who she was! She could be content.

"Thou shalt not covet" means being content with who God made you to be and with the personal presence of Jesus.

Vicki saw how those two commandments—the first and the tenth—complemented each other: She saw that when God had the throne of her heart, uncontested (the first commandment), she had everything. She could be content (the tenth commandment). Trusting God freed her from serving the old ways.

In the beginning of this learning process, Vicki was still not free from her insecurity. Circumstances would arise that put her back in the abyss of worthlessness and fear, and it seemed she had no choice about it.

"Lord," she cried, "I thought I was supposed to have a choice, but it doesn't seem like I do. Satan pushes my buttons, and—boom!—I am in the pit, and I'm not sure how I got there. Can't You help me, God?"

---

*Exodus 20:17
†Hebrews 13:5, 6

Naked porcupine?

Then the day came when a situation came up that pushed her button of insecurity—hard! Vicki was expecting the usual quick slide into that hated pit. Instead, there was a pause this time, and in that moment, God spoke to her heart. "*Child, if you will consent and cooperate with Me, I can pull this ugly thistle of insecurity out of your heart—roots and all. And in its place, I will plant My own love. Will you let Me do it?*"

Vicki broke into a cold sweat. She knew what this would mean. She would have to give up all her old familiar defense mechanisms—her jealousy of other women, evil thinking, and resentment. She would not be able to speak sarcastically to her husband, accuse him, or try to control and manipulate him. She wouldn't even be able to withdraw. She would have to let all of that go and love him instead.

She felt like a porcupine being asked to surrender his quills. Can you imagine how vulnerable a porcupine would feel walking naked through the woods? It felt like she was being condemned to death, to cutting off her right arm, to gouging out her right eye.

Yet, Vicki chose to yield and cooperate because she had discovered that one needful thing—heart union with Jesus—and she didn't want to give that up. If Jesus would stay with her through this new experience, she could face anything.

"Yes, Lord, You can have my insecurity."

Amazingly, she didn't die! Instead, wonderful warm peace flooded her heart. A few moments later, however, the old thinking process hit her with full force again. In her mind's eye she could see her feet right on the edge of the dreaded pit, and she cried out to God to save her.

"*Go get those Scripture cards you've been memorizing and prop them up in the kitchen window and think on them while you wash the dishes.*"

Vicki did that, and the peace returned.

All through that day, Vicki faced that pit repeatedly. And each time, God gave her something tangible to do that would replace the wrong thoughts with right ones—quote Scripture, sing, listen to sermon tapes, help someone else, or clean the house. The funny thing was, Vicki had tried all these things before, and they had not saved her from her pit of insecurity and despair. The difference this time, she realized, was the "one needful thing"—the presence of Jesus. When she *put Him in charge* of the battle and depended on Him for direction, her obedience gave Him permission to cleanse her on the inside. Her hand in His hand made all the difference.

Vicki realized that the acid test of her victory would come when her husband came home from work. "Lord, what will I do? Everything in me tells me to withdraw, to be cold, to give him the silent treatment. That's how I protect myself from being hurt."

God impressed her heart, "*Go meet him at the door. Smile into his eyes, put your arms around him, hug him, and kiss him on the lips.*"

"Oh, Lord, are you sure that will be safe?" she responded timidly.

"*Trust Me. I am with you.*"

Vicki chose to trust God and did just as He said when her husband came home. The victory for that day was complete. No resentment tainted her heart, no ill feelings for her husband's demeaning words soured her joy, and no fear of what woman he might have talked to that day ruined her peace. She was free!

Vicki faced the pit many times after that, but she had found that "one needful thing"—a personal Savior—and she never went into that pit again.

Finally, one day, as she went for a walk to talk with her best Friend, He said to her, *"Vicki, you are not your own. You belong to Me. You are in My care and keeping, and I will never ever cast you aside. I have removed from your heart that giant thistle of the fear of abandonment. You will no longer be known as Valueless Vicki, but as Valuable Vicki. Satan will constantly attempt to plant the seeds of fear in your heart again by insinuating doubtful thoughts. But if you will stay close to Me, I will alert you when he is attempting to do that. And if you give those little seeds instantly to Me, they will never take root in your heart."*

Vicki knew it was true. God had reached deep down into the inner core of her being and healed that wound—that insecurity—and replaced it with a secure sense of belonging to Him.

Eight years later, Vicki is still free from that insecurity. It is merely a bad memory from the past. She can see other attractive women and not feel threatened at all.

This was only the beginning of God's work in Vicki's life—a work that could have been easily accomplished in her infancy, childhood, or even her teen years. Had Vicki been given that "one needful thing" in her youth, it would have saved her and others untold suffering and heartache. However, she is learning that, with God, it is never too late for a happy childhood!

God used this first major victory in Vicki's experience as a foundation from which to continue restoring her soul—teaching her proper boundaries, developing her own individuality, dealing with deeper issues related to value, bringing balance to her relationships with other people. Vicki is still learning; she's not done growing. But she is satisfied and happy because she has now found that "one needful thing" and no one can take it away from her. Christ within has transformed her into Valuable Vicki.

The fog of confusion

Yet a nagging question remains: Why did Vicki's parents not supply her that "one needful thing" while she was growing up? They were conscientious to provide every other good thing within their power. Why not that which she needed most?

Many have expressed the sentiment that this "one needful thing" cannot be passed on; that each individual must discover it for himself or herself. That statement is partly true. You cannot give to your youth what you yourself do not possess. However, this experience is available to all who will seek for it, and it can be passed on as you are learning it yourself. It is called on-the-job-training!

Vicki's parents had excellent knowledge of the Scriptures, and they passed that on to her. They had a passion for service and missions, and they passed that on to her. They enjoyed wholesome activities with like-minded friends, and they shared that with Vicki. But the experience of opening up at the inner heart level—of validating emotions, of identifying needs, of teaching boundaries, of taking Vicki to Christ for a changed heart—was lacking. How could that be?

Valueless Vicki was born at a time when her parents were extremely busy. Her mother was a senior nursing student, and her father was a senior medical student. Her mother would try to nurse her in one arm while she steered the car with the other as she raced to the babysitter's. What emotional message does an infant perceive when parents are too busy to give her their undivided attention, when the stress and demands of their life crowd out time to create a secure and happy home life? Doesn't it imply to the child that she is an unwelcome inconvenience?

One evening, Vicki's mother needed to attend a class and planned to take her to the babysitter as usual. Her father said, "Don't take her to a babysitter. She's my little girl. I'll take care of her."

He thought, "Babies sleep while medical students study. This will be no problem."

So her mother fed her, diapered her, and left her with her father.

When she came home after her class, she was greeted with a somewhat humorous sight.

Vicki's father, being very mechanically inclined, had rigged up a lawn mower motor to vibrate her crib back and forth to lull her to sleep. Vicki hadn't liked that arrangement at all and had expressed it so loudly that her father had securely taped her mouth shut! There Vicki was in her crib, face red, tears streaming down her cheeks, mouth taped shut, yet screaming as loudly as she could!

Where was her father? He was right there beside her. He would never allow any harm to come to her, but he needed to study. So he sat there beside her with his eyes glued to his book and his fingers in his ears!

What is the significance of this cute little story? Does it shed any light on why Valueless Vicki floundered so in her teen and early adult years?

Oh yes, it does. Vicki's thoughts and feelings in infancy were forming her character—which is the core of who she will be forever. This little experience implanted fear and rejection in her in a startling way. What is learned in the first seven years goes with our children for life, unless they find a personal Savior who can correct these misconceptions and empower them to change within. Is it any wonder that Satan works in parents' minds to belittle the importance of these early influences? In this way, he can gain a great advantage over the thoughts and feelings of the child, instilling fear and rejection into his or her thought processes.

You see, this little story is a vignette of Vicki's relationship with her father as she grew up. Her father always provided the physical necessities of life and was faithful to intervene in major crises, but he didn't understand Vicki's need for emotional connection. She needed her father to be a safe place to go, someone with whom she could share whatever was in her heart—not just those things that lay within the parameters he was comfortable with. She needed his acceptance and validation. She needed to know that her emotional well-being was a priority to him. However, he was too caught up in *his* work and hobbies to meet her real needs.

Vicki grew up expecting God to be like her father—providing the necessities and intervening from time to time in major crises, but not interested or involved in her daily temptations, her emotions, or her hopes and dreams. From her earthly father, she learned both to fear his occasional outbursts of anger and that conflict is *never* resolved; it is only buried. To dig it up again means you will hit a brick wall.

Vicki's mother, driven by her own issues of rejection, kept very busy with missionary projects, sewing projects, school projects, and home projects. In this way she crowded out, or at least dulled, the pain of her own unresolved issues. Tasks are good things in their proper sphere when done for the right motives and when they do not crowd out the more essential parenting work of dealing with your own heart and then with the heart of your child. However, when tasks are used to avoid the deeper work, they are a hindrance.

Vicki's mother also had a hot, hasty temper. When Vicki did not perform as her mother expected, she could lash out very quickly in irritation and anger. Vicki's mother reacted this way because that is how her own mother had treated her. This is one way in which the "sins of the fathers" are transmitted to following generations. Vicki's mother was unwittingly communicating to Vicki the same message she had perceived from her own mother: "I cannot accept you unless you perfectly meet my expectations. Since you don't measure up, you are rejected."

While feeling rejected she could quote the Scripture, "The eyes of the LORD are upon the righteous, and his ears are open unto their cry."* She did not believe that God's eyes were upon *her* or that His ears were open to *her* cry. She pictured God to be like her parents—preoccupied, distant, and performance-oriented. She didn't know she could truly express herself to Him. It was like her mouth was taped shut; to avoid rejection, she had to *perform and comply* with the expectations of those she needed to love her. This is nothing more than a thinly veiled form of salvation by works. And salvation by works inevitably produces insecurity because performance will always fall short somewhere, sometime. This need to perform in order to avoid rejection made it impossible for Valueless Vicki to learn to set appropriate boundaries. How can you say no to someone if doing so means you will displease him or her and thus lose your sense of value and be overwhelmed with feelings of rejection?

What could have broken through this fog of confusion? Only one thing—the *one needful thing!* If Vicki or her mother or her father or her siblings had gone to sit at Jesus' feet to learn of Him, the fog could have been dispelled. Sitting at Jesus' feet means more than reading our Bibles, praying, and attending church. It means more than acquiring facts and becoming skilled in the use of Scripture. It means to throw open the whole soul to God. It means to search our hearts, asking God to uncover the thoughts, feelings, and habits of relating that cause damage to others and ourselves, keeping us in bondage.

Vicki's father needed to inquire, "Why do I react the way that I do? Why do I bury myself in work, hobbies, or books? Why do I find it difficult to look into the eyes of my children and try to understand what is happening in their hearts? Why do

---

*Psalm 34:15

I stuff down my feelings of resentment only to have them explode from time to time? Is there a better way?"

Her mother needed to inquire, "Why do I react the way that I do? Why do I fear aloneness? Why am I bossy and domineering at times? Why do I lash out so strongly in irritation and anger? What motivates me to be so busy, busy, busy? Lord, what would You have me to do?"

Such an evaluation would have made them aware of their need of a Savior, for none of us can change the inner workings of our hearts. God would have revealed Himself to them, and as they connected with Him by faith, they would have found strength to experiment in the new ways He suggested to their minds.

It was not necessary for them to master all this at once; they needed just to begin the journey with a present, personal Savior, redeeming them from old ways and leading them into new ways, binding their hearts in a close and tender union, and enabling them to connect their children with the Creator.

If you are a teen, or the parent of a teen, ask yourself the question, "Do I possess the one needful thing?"

If you don't, what is keeping you from Jesus' feet? He bids you come to Him just as you are. He will not shame you, reproach you, or reject you. He will embrace you with open arms and cleanse your heart. He will help you sort through the misconceptions that hold you in bondage and make you a prey for Satan's snares. He will redeem you from any pit.

Give Him your time. Give Him your ear. Give Him access to the inner workings of your mind. With Him as your Savior, you need not become lost in any fog.

THE LONE EMBRACE
A WORD OF ENCOURAGEMENT FOR SINGLE PARENTS

Single parenting can increase our awareness of our need for God. We need a partner as we face the challenges of life in general and of our youth in particular. And God is there for you—regardless or your history or circumstances. Don't delay to come to Him!

If you do not possess that "one needful thing" yourself, make finding it your first priority. Let it crowd out the urgent things that seem to press unendingly upon you. God can help you sort out what is truly essential in your life from those things that are only distractions that Satan uses to keep you from the very best.

When you find a personal Savior for yourself, you will then be able to offer Him to your youth, giving them a real heart-changing foundation in Jesus Christ. If they accept that "one needful thing"—a genuine experience with a personal Savior—they will have a Guide that pilots them safely through their adult lives.

If you have the "one needful thing," the trials, difficulties, and insecurities won't matter in your life for you will have Jesus, the Problem Solver, on your side. Seek Him. Don't delay to start today!

Chapter 9

From Governor to Counselor

For the kingdom is the Lord's: and he is the governor among the nations.
—Psalm 22:28

We live in a quiet wilderness valley bordering panoramic Glacier National Park. There are no electric lines to our area, so we have our own "power company" in our garage. I flip a switch at my desk to turn on the generator when we need to charge our batteries or run a large appliance. Since I'm not very mechanically inclined, I call on my husband, Jim, when the system needs attention.

"Honey," I called on one occasion. "The power quit while I was running my blender, and the generator won't start again. Can you fix it?"

A few moments later, in the garage, Jim pointed out to me a flashing red warning light. He showed me how to reset the generator. The warning light went off, and the engine started to fire—but then shut down again.

"The generator has a governing motherboard," Jim explained, "to *protect the engine from misuse* and to keep it performing at its best. It lets me know when a spark plug needs to be replaced or when the oil is low. And when something isn't working right, it shuts down the generator to *protect it from damage.*

"The red light is there to *get your attention* that something needs to be evaluated and corrected. In this case, the generator was overtaxed. You were running the washer, dryer, vacuum, and blender at the same time. That's too much, so the governor shut down the generator until you figure out the problem."

I returned to the house and turned off the dryer until I finished using the blender. The generator did just fine, and I was empowered to get my work done. I had learned a new lesson.

"Isn't that just like parenting?" God began to kindle my thoughts.

"This generator is an object lesson, isn't it, Lord? My children and I need a power outside of ourselves to walk after Christ. Sometimes it seems like Your power gets shut off. I wish that reconnecting with You was as easy as resetting my generator."

"Sally, it is! When you yield to temptation, you disconnect from your source of power—for I withdraw when another god is on the throne of your heart. A red light comes on through your conscience, telling you that what you have done isn't right. All you have to do is come to Me and ask to reconnect. This is your reset button. I will receive you and instruct you, and as you yield to Me, you will have all the power you need to live a godly life.

*"Your child's misbehavior, too, is a warning light that he is following self and needs to reconnect with Me. I'll instruct you how to help him do this."**

---

*John 6:45.

I continued pondering. "When my boys tune me out, argue, act wounded, or behave offensively, I am seeing a warning light that should get my attention. It's telling me that self has gotten in the way and shut down heaven's power."

Andrew didn't want to wash the dishes. "It's not my turn. You always ask me. It's unfair!" he sulked.

The red light of misbehavior alerts me to check to be sure that I am connected to heaven so that God can direct me out of this difficulty in the right spirit. It is interesting that God is *my* Governor, and it's under His direction that I'm prepared to be a good governor over my youth. God will guide me to the correct reset button so that my son can have power restored to live uprightly.* Without God, I make a mess of it.

As I evaluated my son's thoughts and feelings expressed in his words and actions, I thought at first he was just being stubborn. God led me to probe a little deeper with questions, and I found the root issue was slothfulness, not stubbornness. God knew! Andrew had a fouled spark plug that was producing a slothful attitude. He needed an attitude adjustment, so I addressed his lying, slothful thoughts with the truth, led by God.†

Andrew chose to yield to reason this time and went to God in prayer to clean this spark plug of attitude. The reset was easy. The red light went off, and like a well-oiled machine, Andrew washed the dishes with a cheerful attitude, helped by the Holy Spirit.

Later, the red light of misbehavior came on again. This time it was Matthew's attitude. "I won't iron those clothes! You can't make me!" It appeared that the fuel mixture was at fault; too much playtime had allowed selfishness to take over.

I pushed the reset button as before, using prayer with mild reasoning. This time, however, it didn't work. It provoked only a torrent of disrespectful words. This engine was full of the wrong fuel. Acts 9:6 was my only recourse, "Lord, what wilt thou have me to do?" God knows how to reset and reconnect this engine.

God didn't seem to reply to my need with a distinctive impression. Was He too busy? No. The Bible says, "[He] will never leave thee, nor forsake thee." He's with me always.‡ So I did the next best thing *by faith*. "Lord, help me reason this one through."

Self is on the throne of his heart—this is the problem. Matthew doesn't want to choose to have Jesus be his Master and submit to Him. I need to go to firmer measures to motivate him in the right direction.§ I could send him on a grizzly run or to his room to talk with God, or there is weeding he could do in the garden to use up some of that selfish energy. I chose the later option, praying that God would nurture Matthew to choose the right.

After the consequence was given, I again reasoned with Matthew. His heart was open this time. He said he was convinced that the wrong way was not worth the

---

*Psalm 32:8.
†Romans 12:21.
‡Hebrews 13:5.
§Ecclesiastes 8:11.

effort. He yielded his selfish thoughts and feelings to God in prayer and regained his connection. Prayer pushed the reset button.

Then God prompted, *"Now you have to turn on the generator to see if we fixed the problem."*

"Matthew, would you please iron these clothes?" The oil of the Holy Spirit balanced the fuel mixture so completely that Matthew willingly ironed the clothes while cheerfully visiting with the rest of the family. His heart was completely free to be upright like Christ.

Whatever the warning light, our children and youth often need help to see that if they choose to obey self, cooperating with slothful thoughts, selfish feelings, or disrespectful attitudes, they make Satan lord in their heart. They need to be led to choose to come back to God. God can transform any wrong thought, attitude, or feeling that is yielded to Him.

Governing with a goal

Parents, we are much like the governing board in my generator, managing all aspects of our child's thoughts, feelings, habits, and responses to keep the heart generator running smoothly under God, not self. In this way the whole family can become what God wants it to be—a well-oiled machine empowered to be Christlike in thought, word, and deed.

"Behold also the ships . . . are driven of fierce winds, yet are they turned about with a very small helm, whithersoever the *governor* listeth."* Good parent-governors are personally governed by Christ and direct their youth into heavenly ways. A parent-governor apart from God leads the youth into disastrous self-directed ways.

Governor-parents manage all aspects of their children's physical, mental, and spiritual development. We want to train them in the way of the Lord rather than in the way of their flesh. We want them to exercise heavenly attitudes while doing their home duties, to be honest, helpful, and faithful team members, and have good problem-solving and study habits. This is preparing them to run their own home. The purpose of governing is to train the child for *self-government* under God. Notice that as the child increases in these abilities, our role shifts to that of counselor. Lets look at the role of the parent at the differing ages to see this cycle of change.

The governing role of the parent should be strongest in infancy. Parenting at this stage requires total care of all the child's physical, mental, and emotional needs— governing *every detail* of his or her life. It's time to get up; it's time to go to bed, time to eat, time not to eat, time to work, and time to play. Parents are to be mind and will for their infants. It is crucial at this age to build within them the foundations of character—trust and obedience.

As the infant becomes a toddler, the parent begins in gentle ways to instill work habits and Christlike attitudes. We teach them how to walk and talk, how to care for their toys, how to dress themselves, and how to eat properly. There are times to talk and times to be silent. We hover closely, nurturing every good habit while lovingly

---

*James 3:4, italics added.

restraining and eliminating every wrong habit. These are the key character-building years, so cultivate every right thought, feeling, and response.

We encourage them to persevere in doing right even in the midst of trials. When our children are despairing, uncooperative, or defiant, we parents must lead them to look up and see God as their Helper, to yield up wrong feelings, and do right. Just like the generator mixes fuel and air in the right proportions in order to run properly, so we parents must regulate firmness and softness in our discipline as needed for proper character development. Instill right thoughts under God.

In childhood, we deepen the teaching begun in infancy and toddlerhood. At this stage, our children are learning self-government, and our caretaking is reduced notably. It is not God's plan for the child to always need total care. They can, and should, learn to care for themselves and to lighten the home duties. They can assume responsibility for getting out of bed, caring for their personal needs, and having their own worship. They can help with all the practical home duties. We can cultivate in them good taste in music, reading, and dress and inculcate heavenly character traits such as honesty, timeliness, industry, and orderliness.

They can be taught to know right from wrong, to recognize God's voice to their conscience, and how to respond to that Voice as Samuel did. We train them in pleasant manners, helpful dispositions, and good work skills. This is the time to establish good study habits—both for school and personal Bible study. In childhood they need skillful training to become good helpers in the home.

In the early teen years, we must begin to foster a greater yielding to God. We need to focus strongly on their personal walk with God; it needs to become practical, tangible, and habitual if it isn't already. This relationship or the lack thereof will decide their destiny. If we are doing our work right, our teens should skillfully and efficiently manage their own personal worship and school studies—and find them both interesting and fulfilling. By this time, they should enter cheerfully into all the practical household duties, being prepared to take full responsibility for the laundry, meal preparation, and house cleaning without parental assistance.

If this is not the case with your youth, don't hesitate to pick up those important dropped stitches under God's governorship, working to help them gain both the skills to work efficiently and the heart desire to do so as well. Useful work is essential to keep idle hands from becoming the devil's workshop. All this training is preparing your youth to successfully run their own household or business one day.

During the teen years, we need to lessen the reins of total control and management *a little at a time* to nurture self-government and personal initiative, as well as to see how they do on their own under God. Help your teens develop good problem-solving techniques, and then give them the opportunity to fly with God, without you. You will still instruct and discipline as necessary, of course. Come back to being a governor when needed. But your teen needs to begin to perceive from you the message, "You have what it takes, under God, to be separate from me."

During these years, we are to begin to become a counselor and guide instead of an absolute governor. The childhood lessons listed above have been mastered. Now our training focuses on helping our youth to make right decisions led by God. We begin by allowing them choices within safe parameters to see how they analyze problems and arrive at conclusions. Then we can help them improve their thinking and reasoning skills. When they make poor choices, the governor will intervene to give input, to redirect, and to point them back to Christ. Our training aims at developing their minds more directly under God and stimulating them to exercise their own wills on the side of right to be God-governed, not man-managed.

Must the teens be terrible?

Satan has sold many of us a wrong perception of youthful independence and its fruits. I had to wrestle with it as my sons approached their teen years.

"Lord, Matthew is going to be thirteen in a few months, and I dread what might come. Our program of teaching and training, under You, has brought us thus far, and Matthew is learning to make good decisions. Thank You for being my Governor in this process. But doubts keep coming up in my mind about the teen years. Others keep warning me that these years are a nightmare—and that this is normal! They say teens must sow their 'wild oats' before they can find You. Is it true that all youth must go crazy? Is this truly normal behavior?"

"*What do you think, Sally?*" God wanted me to express my faith as His child!

"Well, Your Word says that you reap what you sow.* I've been sowing seeds of trust in You and obedience to Your voice, so I should reap the fruit of Christlikeness. All that seek You will find You and be empowered to do right. Although neither my boys nor I am perfect, we are seeking You, and we are finding that You can change our thoughts and feelings when we submit them and cooperate with You. We are discovering that we can follow Your will against our flesh. Our family has changed drastically over the past seven years because of learning this. If I train my boys to know Your voice and to heed You, I need not fear the teen years, falsehoods, or hormones."

"*You have said well! This is the truth. Remember that Satan insinuates doubt to unsettle you, to discourage you, to lead you to withdraw from your youth out of fear and superstition. And in this way he can have unhindered sway over your youth.*

"*Satan doesn't want parents to call upon Me for wisdom and help. He doesn't want parents to ask their youth what they are thinking so they can direct them to Me. Above all, Satan wants parents to avoid bringing up thoughts about Me or what is right and wrong for fear of losing their youth. He lies to parents that teens need freedom to 'find themselves' and that sin is 'normal oat sowing.' Thus he binds them up as his subjects in vice.*"

"Yes, Lord. It is absurd to consider it normal for our youth to have to taste sin and vice in order to choose You for themselves. This can't possibly be Your will. You didn't want Adam and Eve to know good and evil. Look at the bad effects of their experience. So, too, with our youth. It can't be good for them to be scarred by bondage to sin and vice before they come to You! How much better to introduce them to the best first so they don't want Satan's garbage. I think You want to save them from replaying Adam and Eve's experience."

---

*Galatians 6:7.

"Without *Me, it may be 'normal' for sin to have sway—but not* with *Me! Under My direction, anyone can live an upright and happy life whether they are thirteen, thirty, or ninety. Righteousness is heaven's norm for all ages. I leave all free to choose whom they will serve. It is not necessary to sow 'wild oats.' "*

I pondered such thoughts until Matthew's thirteenth birthday. I looked for a negative change but didn't see one. We continued the same structured program in our home with Christ as the Head. We restrained wrong habits and nurtured godly ones. As a result, Matthew turned to God with his trials and temptations and found answers, under God, that brought peace.

Over the following year, my confidence in God's principles escalated. Instead of becoming a monster, my teenage son continued developing into a dependable young man one could truly enjoy. He could work almost as efficiently as I could and was increasingly sensitive and obedient to the voice of God. Our home experienced joy immeasurable. When Andrew turned thirteen, I observed the same about him.

What's really normal?

I concluded that it is neither normal nor necessary for teenagers to "sow wild oats." Sowing good seed instills a distaste for the evil. Satan's agenda was clearly exposed to me now! He wanted me to stop training my boys to know a personal God so that he could send them on a long detour right at the beginning of their life's journey and bring much heartache into our home.

God's norm and Satan's norm are entirely different. Parents *must* take the time to evaluate whose norm they are operating under. You can always trust the Word of God, but Satan is a deceiver who mingles dangerous errors with at least some truth. So beware! God can help us discern Satan's snares if we are willing to give Him our time, our ear, and our reasoning faculties.

"That they may walk in my statutes, and keep mine ordinances, and do them: and they shall be my people, and I will be their God."* Because we accepted God's norm, our boys' teen years were some of our most rewarding years of parenting. Under Christ, their abilities strengthened and developed as God taught Jim and me where and how to give guidance and where and how to give freedom.

When Matthew and Andrew were thirteen and eleven respectively, they had been earning money doing odd jobs for the neighbors for several years. Now they wanted more steady work and talked with Jim about it one evening.

"You boys need to let all the neighbors know about your desire and availability. How can you do that?" Father probed. "Andrew, what do you think?"

"I suppose we could visit them all and tell them. We could walk to those nearby and drive to everyone else's house."

"Or we could design a letter and mail it," Matthew suggested.

"That would save you a lot of time," Father replied. "What do you think you need to put into this advertisement?"

---

*Ezekiel 11:20.

All gave input. The boys created a flyer that included their names, address, and hourly wage, a description of their experience and skill level as well as their willingness to learn new skills. Father looked it over with them and helped them fine tune it. Then the boys copied and distributed it. They soon had as much steady work as they wanted.

Jim was very wise. He recognized the beginning of some adultlike thinking in the boys and viewed this new venture as an opportunity to foster it. When challenges arose related to their jobs, he didn't just tell them what to do. He probed them with questions to help them think through the issues. He encouraged them to ask God for wisdom and to make decisions under God. God put it on our hearts to train them to be thinkers instead of mere reflectors of other men's thoughts. To foster this mature thinking, Jim allowed them freedom to do things differently than he would do—as long as no moral principle was violated.

When neighbors came to ask questions about the boys' work, Jim referred them to Matthew and Andrew. At times, the boys found this uncomfortable, but with practice, they developed good communication skills and learned how to work effectively with customers. This experience was a good flight lesson in proper independence.

Once in a while, the boys got out of sorts with each other over who would do a particular job. The red warning lights of jealousy, selfishness, or dominance would flash, indicating that they were disconnected from their power Source. Their character (thoughts, feelings, and responses) needed to be cleaned, adjusted, or oiled by the Holy Spirit. The governing side of parenting would then predominate as Jim and I tried to motivate them to deal with their misunderstanding in a Christlike spirit. Sometimes we needed only to reason with them. Other times, firmer measures were required. Our aim was to help them reconnect with God so that they could continue their advancement toward independence under Him. We would address their wrong concepts and faulty expectations as God led. We did not allow the conflict to remain unresolved. Harmony would be restored to our home, not by indulgence, but by a heart resolution.

One of the jobs the boys took on during this period was on our own property. Three Christian brothers were building our guest cabin. Matthew and Andrew learned carpentry as they helped with the project at ages fourteen and twelve. In the evening, we were interested in how their day went and what they were learning.

"They are really nice guys to work with," Matthew shared with us, "and I'm learning a lot from them. I really like it. But, Father, their music is really bad—rock and all. I sure don't like listening to that all day."

Jim prayed silently for God's help and wisdom before he spoke, so as not to demean his boys. "Did you say anything or ask him to turn it off?"

"Yes, I did ask him to turn it off, and he did. But how can I teach him about good music? Wouldn't that be better?"

"Well, tastes in music vary a lot today. What did God ask you to do?"

"I'm not sure; my thoughts are so confused on this. I guess I need to pray about it in the morning and see what God says to me. What would you do, Father?"

"Well, I'd likely explain what is wrong with the present music if he's open . . ."

Andrew interrupted. "Why don't we take some of our *Beside Still Waters* music for him to listen to instead? When we come home for lunch they can listen to their music, and while we're working, we could take turns listening to the music we want."

"That's a great idea, son. Check with God in the morning and do as He leads you."

That's what they did. Those builders respected our sons for their good work habits and moral principles and entered into a lively discussion regarding music. They shared their thoughts, listened to our sons' thoughts, and even agreed with them on some points. That evening the boys shared all about their conversations and experiences and then brought up another issue that disturbed them.

"Mother, they drink Coca-Cola, and Wayne said that if you put a nail in it, it will eventually eat up the nail. That's terrible. Is it true?" Andrew asked.

"Yes, son, I understand that to be true."

"They can't drink that stuff then. Why do they do that?"

Matthew interjected enthusiastically, "We need to bring some homemade lemonade to them tomorrow and give them a better alternative. We sure don't want them to get sick."

"Check what God would have you to do. I'll be glad to make up some lemonade for you to take, if that is what God asks of you." And this they did.

These men enjoyed and encouraged these interchanges—another success. The boys were growing in decision making and confidence in God's leading them independently of their parents.

After this, they began working with another crew and became known as being very straight boys. At times, they were put on the spot with tough questions, and God gave them some good answers. God was guiding them personally on the job site. Becoming comfortable speaking what you truly think awakens and exercises individuality, prayer, and tact. We had our usual family evening discussions with Jim and me taking the counselor approach and giving them room to think, solve problems, and determine God's will.

One day the builders yelled some words the boys had never heard before. They didn't know what those words meant but sensed they were not good. We discussed why people use those kinds of expletives and some better alternatives. One evening, Matthew was excited to share his story.

"Father! One of the carpenters, George, was hammering on the roof. All of a sudden, he stopped hammering. There was this long pause, and I wondered if he had smashed his thumb. Then he yelled some of those nasty words. I didn't say anything, but I did pray for him. While we were eating lunch, George asked me a question.

" 'Matthew, what are you permitted to say when you hit your thumb with the hammer?'

"I told him, 'I say, "Ouch!" '

"The conversation shifted to other things, and I didn't give it much more thought.

Then later that afternoon, George smashed his thumb again. There was a long silence. Then he yelled out real loud—'Oouucch!' And he told me later, he was surprisingly satisfied with that."

We all laughed, then praised God at how He can lead and direct our youth to speak His will and show grown-ups a better way of life. How we live and talk does influence people. And God can lead our youth to make a difference—if they personally know Him!

Tough experience–good lesson

The boys did construction work for about five years. They earned a solid reputation as skilled, dependable workers and were in high demand among the builders in our valley. After they helped one of the crews construct a beautiful home, Mr. Barry, the homeowner, offered them a great opportunity. He hired the boys, at that time fifteen and thirteen years old, to clear a huge area of woods surrounding his newly landscaped home with a promise to pay nicely when the job was done.

That evening, we discussed the opportunity as a family, and Jim advised them to collect payments every week or two instead of waiting till the end of the job.

"It's not good business to do it the other way," he cautioned.

The boys approached Mr. Barry on this, and after a long discussion, he consented. At the end of the first week, the boys turned in their hours, but Mr. Barry couldn't find his checkbook. The next week they turned in their hours again, but he never got around to writing them a check.

"Did you get paid this week like Mr. Barry promised?" Father asked after the third week.

"No, Father! Mr. Barry said he paid a big bill and he needed to go to town to make a transfer from another account. He promised to pay us next week."

"Son, I don't like this scenario. I sense dishonesty. You need to talk straight with him."

"But we have, Father. His wife is real nice and gave us some juice at lunchtime," Andrew protested. "I just hate to push him. I think he'll come through, don't you?"

"I think he wants to get a lot of free work out of you and has no intention to pay. You need to ask God what you should do. I wouldn't work anymore for him until you get paid."

The next morning the boys went to work with heavy hearts. They wanted to trust Mr. Barry—that's the Christian thing to do, isn't it? However, their prayer time with God seemed to suggest doubt about trusting this man. They felt confused. Would God want them to be skeptical of his intentions? They talked with Mr. Barry again, and he promised payment. So, they worked that day. The job was almost done, and still they had not received even one payment.

The next day when they went to work, Mrs. Barry said her husband had left for his diamond mines in Australia so that he could get some money to pay them. By lunchtime, the boys felt they were now sure of God's will, and said to Mrs. Barry, "We can't work any longer for you. When you pay us, we'll come back to finish the job."

"Mother, we felt so guilty doing this! We just don't think a Christian should doubt others. But we also felt God wanted us to stop working, that something wasn't right."

This gave us the opportunity to talk about true and false guilt, the voice of Satan and the voice of God, and the need to make a decision. We discussed such ideas as, God would rather we make a wrong decision than no decision at all. God can direct when we decide. A Christian is to trust those who prove themselves trustworthy, but there is also a time to distrust those who have shown themselves unworthy of trust. Some people have no problem telling lies. They even calculate to say the right words for the purpose of deception. We are told, "by their fruits ye shall know them."* We judge by what a person does—not only by what he says.† God does not want us to trust a serpent and snuggle it into our bosom; we'll be bitten. There is a right and wrong trust. God will lead us aright as we seek Him.

We soon learned that Mr. Barry had fled the country because there was a warrant out for his arrest. He was guilty of fraud against several local merchants and contractors. Jim encouraged the boys to apply to the courts for their part of the settlement. Mr. Barry was put into jail. While there, he wrote a check to the boys drawn on a Swiss bank to pay them four hundred dollars each. The bank said it was good, but by the time it processed, it wasn't. They got a bill from the bank for processing the nonpaying check! This was their pay for all their hard work.

In the following evenings, we discussed forgiveness as well as the lesson of "by their fruits ye shall know them." We talked about discerning the voice of God in difficult situations and how He does not always tell us just what we might expect. We evaluated the firm side of being Christlike as it relates to collecting our proper wages and withholding services when the employer is not keeping his end of the bargain.

After working it all through, the boys said it had been an uncomfortable, but worthwhile, lesson. They learned that judging the character of another could be done without hate or vengeance when God is in the equation. They chose to dwell on how they benefited rather than on what they lost, and to let God take care of the injustice.

Isn't it great that God allows us parents to work with Him in the practical lessons of building character in our teens through life's experiences? We have the privilege of teaching and training our youth to work through problems that arise and to replace misconceptions with a proper balance. What beautiful flight lessons my boys gained in their working experience. Their working environment was not perfect and pure, but they learned how to speak up, change what they could, and be content with what they couldn't change. They learned how to talk with people, follow their heart regarding what is right, and seek God for wisdom for what to do next. How I would have loved this type of training before I got married. Wouldn't you?

---

*Matthew 7:20.
†Proverbs 20:11.

Yes, parenting takes on a new, different perspective when your children reach their teen years. We want to nurture the emerging adult aspects of our youth. We want to give them freedom to fly alone from time to time, under God, and strengthen their flight feathers, while awakening in them a sense of God's reality in their lives. Being personally responsible makes them keenly aware of their need; they call out to God and make decisions—as our boys did in their business dealings.

When this freedom is misused for unrighteousness, the governing board should shut down the engine so that the bad habits do not cause damage. Then, the parent must reconnect this engine to God to restore the proper function.

Over and under managing

Have you ever seen a butterfly straining to come out of its cocoon? Have you ever felt so sorry for one that you helped him along? And what happened? His wings were crippled because he had been deprived of the essential strengthening exercise of breaking out of the cocoon on his own. He couldn't fly correctly and became an easy meal for a predator. Trying to protect the butterfly in its cocoon too long will result in its death. Stretching, growing, and changing are essential patterns of life.

So, too, with our youth—if we aid them too much, hover over them, making decisions for them like they are still infants and children, they will not develop their wings in Jesus and will be easily taken down. On the other hand, if we give them too much freedom too fast, without Christ, they will be easy prey for Satan's temptations and snares as well.

Youth is the time for them to exercise their newly developing wings under God's direction, while their parents are still overseeing their training—just as the eagles do. It is the time for them to perfect their characters through communing with God and seeking His will for their lives. It is the time for them to make decisions to serve God and right. When they fall, parents and/or God can lift them back up to try again before they crash on the rocks below. We don't want to help them too little or too much. We want to use life's situations and duties to begin to put them under God's care. If we don't, we will cripple them for this life and may ruin their chances for the next life.

John the Baptist said it well, "He [God] must increase, but I must decrease."* I think this well describes parenting teens. Our role as governor needs to be decreasing increment by increment as we attach them more and more firmly to God. We are still there as counselors. We are still teaching and training, but God must eventually become their ultimate Teacher.

In this way, we can raise a Luther who will stand under God rather than blindly submit to papal politics. We can influence a Peter who will obey God rather than man. We can prepare an Esther who will follow God rather than her feelings.

"Lord, help me to find in You the balance of governing and counseling my youth. Lord, show me how to manage them in their teens!"

---

*John 3:30.

THE LONE EMBRACE
A WORD OF ENCOURAGEMENT FOR SINGLE PARENTS

As a single parent, you may be inclined to be all governor—and not a counselor. You may feel the need to hover over your teen, overprotect him, and make decisions for him. After all you have been through, you fear they will make the same wrong decisions, and you want to prevent that. Consequently, you attempt to control their lives in order to save them—you think! Or you may be so overwhelmed by the responsibilities of single life that you have no time or energy to counsel or govern your youth. Either extreme—overmanaging or undermanaging your youth—is detrimental to his destiny.

The only question you need to ask and find an honest answer to is, "Lord, what wilt thou have me to do?"* If you allow your own emotions and human reasoning to lead you, without regard to God's direction, your youth may follow you—but he won't learn to follow God. And apart from God, he will have no safe guide for his life. Sooner or later, he will end up on the rocks of "self." Your actions may seem right in your own eyes,† but the ends thereof are the ways of death.‡ Take the only safe course: Follow God and let Him help you find the proper balance of governing and counseling.

The most important purpose of a parent-governor is to teach and train the youth to know God personally using Scripture and life experiences. Above all else, they need to be able to distinguish between the voice of Satan leading and directing them through their flesh, and the voice of God leading and directing them through their mind and heart. The teen years are the time when they are choosing what religion will be their religion, which god will be their god. Which god are they most attracted to and comfortable with? Familiarity with one or the other master often determines their destiny. So let the God of heaven be the God they know best. Teach

them that God is their supreme Head—not self or any other person. God will personally teach you the way to do all of this. He is your Head, your Husband, and your children's heavenly Father.

Andrew, age 21, designed and built this garage to house his vehicle. Construction builds men.

---

*Acts 9:6.
†Judges 21:25.
‡Proverbs 14:12.

Chapter 10
Horse Training

O Lord, I know that the way of man is not in himself:
it is not in man that walketh to direct his steps.
—Jeremiah 10:23

My father was a real horseman. His favorite horse was Courageous, a spirited black stallion. Courageous loved my father. Whenever he saw him coming, he ran eagerly to him and nuzzled him affectionately. He was overjoyed when my father had the saddle and bridle with him. The two of them were like one as they cantered easily through the forest, splashed across the creek, galloped along the meadow, and jumped over the hurdles. Courageous willingly carried my father wherever he wanted to go.

Courageous loved nothing more than serving my father. Why was this? Was he born naturally affable and obedient? No, he was not. You see, Courageous was *properly trained*, and that made all the difference!

Are you making the parallel, even now, to your children? Are you despairing because your filly and colt are of a different spirit? Would they be more aptly named Spunky Sam, Tom the Terror, Independent Ivan, Halting Harry, Stubborn Stella, Fearful Florence, No Brain Billy, or No Work Nelly? You would just love to have a stallion like Courageous—obedient, affectionate, and willing for service—but that isn't possible for your teen—or is it?

You are underestimating God! You, yourself, don't understand that the way of man is not in himself.* You don't know the program of redemption. Yes, it is possible! With Christ, all things are possible! I believe, unhappily, that one of the best-kept secrets in Christendom today is the practical experience of how to commune with God, how to cooperate with Christ and be changed from what we are to what God wants us to be.

In this chapter, I'd like us to look at horse training to gain insights into how God wants us to work with our children. We can prepare them to serve the kingdom of God joyously, affectionately, and enthusiastically—just like Courageous served my father.

My father used two simple steps to train Courageous. The first was earning the horse's trust. The second was applying a consistent *training program* of right behavior using a balance of firmness, fairness, and gentleness.

Where do we start?

Every child at birth is like an untrained colt or filly that needs this kind of program. Perhaps you didn't understand that when your children were born. Perhaps, instead, they have been allowed to follow impulse and inclination like a wild horse

---

*Jeremiah 10:23.

on the prairie. You have failed to give them sufficient practical instruction in God-directed ways. Consequently, they have developed a self-directed character. They find no joy in restraint or direction and run from burdens. Now they are teens, and you are wondering if it is too late. Let me assure you, it is never too late to begin God's program.

The cowboy rounds up a wild horse and drives him into his corral. This untamed stallion stomps and bucks and chafes at his unexpected restraint. He is used to going where he wants to, when he wants to, and for how long he wants to. He is *not* accustomed to surrendering his will, and he does not want to change. Trust has yet to grow.

As Trainer Tom comes to the captured horse, the horse may pace desperately, toss his head fearfully, or rear up defiantly. Different personalities respond differently. Have you seen this in *your* youth? The trainer studies the horse's disposition, all the while asking God for wisdom to win the heart of this horse. He knows that gaining trust is the first step and that trust cannot be commanded—it must be earned. Accordingly, he asks God for insight into how to approach this horse in a way that will communicate trustworthiness. He sees not just what the horse is now, but what he can be when he is properly trained. He gives him a name that will fit his new character*—Come-Along Casey.

He enters the circular pen, his hand in Christ's, his ear tuned to heaven for direction. The trainer has been taught of God the necessity of demonstrating to Come-Along Casey in a tangible way that he loves him, cares for him, and will make life good for him. His movements are gentle and deliberate; he speaks to Casey in calm, self-assured tones. He does not carry a whip, nor does he yell harsh commands. He wants the horse to become comfortable with his presence. After a time, he patiently tries to approach, but if the horse isn't ready, he backs off and waits. When Casey finally trusts Tom enough to let the trainer approach him, Tom rewards Casey with some grain, an apple, or a carrot. Then Tom begins to touch the horse and to draw close to him—increasing his trust. In time, Casey yields to the pleasure of being combed. Each increasing level of closeness, experienced safely, builds Casey's confidence in the trainer.

Our youth must be approached similarly. We are not to come to them with the whip of a sharp tongue that kindles fear and fight. "A soft answer turneth away wrath: but grievous words stir up anger."† "And, ye fathers, provoke not your children to wrath: but bring them up in the nurture and admonition of the Lord."‡ We are not to be militant and aim to break our youth's will, but to bend and direct it in a good path. We are not to dominate, force, or compel the spirit of the youth, but to win their hearts. Isn't that how God is toward us? So we must begin with our youth. Trust is earned, not commanded, forced, or extracted with a guilt trip.

God impresses Trainer Tom that there is now sufficient trust to put on the bridle and let Come-Along Casey get used to it. He slips on the reins and begins to lead the

---

*Isaiah 62:2.

†Proverbs 15:1.

‡Ephesians 6:4.

horse around the circular pen. Round and round they go, the trainer leading, the horse yielding to follow. Repetition strengthens habit. Next, the blanket, then the saddle is gently placed and cinched down. As the horse becomes comfortable being led with the saddle in place, God impresses Trainer Tom to drop the reins. He calls the horse's name and walks around and around the pen. Come-Along Casey follows willingly without hands on the reins. At the end of each day's lessons, Tom rewards Come-Along Casey with his favorite grain, corn.

One day, Trainer Tom failed to give Come-Along Casey his grain. Casey whinnied questioningly and pawed the ground. Tom was puzzled until the Holy Spirit reminded him of what he had forgotten. "What shall I do now, Lord?" Trainer Tom inquired.

"Get the grain but do not give it to him just yet. Turn your back to him." The God of heaven knows the heart and how to help this horse take another step forward in trust, surrender, and love. We just need to follow God, and Tom did.

Come-Along Casey tossed his head and pawed the ground. Do you see the value of consistent training? Horses like dependable routine. Then Casey trotted up to Tom of his own accord and nuzzled under his arm. Trainer Tom again filtered what he should do through the all-knowing God. Tom turned toward the horse, hiding the grain behind his back this time. The horse nuzzled the trainer some more and a sweet bantering continued until Tom gave Come-Along Casey the grain. A closer bond was knit, and in this way the joy of companionship and love was nurtured day by day, week by week, and month by month.

"You have his heart, his affections, and sufficient trust to begin the real training today. I am at your side. Keep your ear tuned to Me, and I will direct your path to deepen what you have begun," God instructed.

Trainer Tom climbed into the circular pen, and Come-Along Casey warmly nuzzled him. Tom put the bridle on as usual and then introduced something new: a fifteen-foot long leader, designed to teach a horse to obey from a distance. The horse accepted it trustingly, so Tom proceeded prayerfully to train the horse to obey hand and word signals. He had to use a whip now to guide the horse to stay on the outer perimeter of the circular pen while he remained in the center. (The rod of correction is to be used to train, not to hurt or punish.) It took several days for the horse to understand clearly the trainer's will and to settle in comfortably to the new program. Tom's consistency and Christlike approach brought success. Casey learned obedience to his trainer while exercising greater independence.

In time, Come-Along Casey didn't need a pen to hold him or a bridle to lead him. These had been only a means to bind heart to heart, to communicate Tom's will, and to establish proper habits, until the horse wanted to be by the side of Tom the Trainer—pen or no pen. Casey's trust and loyalty grew under the consistency of training.

It doesn't always go smoothly

Riding lessons were interspersed along with the bridle training. Now, the riding lessons didn't go as smoothly at first as did the bridle and leader training. Tom tied

Casey's reins loosely to the fence and then began to gently climb into the saddle. He had one foot in the stirrup when Casey reared up, yanked the reins loose, and bolted. Tom was thrown to the ground, bruising his hip, and Casey almost trampled him. A flood of anger nearly overwhelmed him, and Tom was about to go after that "stupid horse" and give him the whipping of his life. But God called to his heart. *"Do not weary in well doing, Tom. You need to evaluate why Casey reacted the way he did. Was that normal for him?"*

Tom cooperated with God by recalling what was special about this horse and why he chose to go through the arduous process of training him with love and firmness rather than with force and harshness. He affirmed again his conviction that the training would work and that he'd have a better horse this way. How much more valuable is service rendered from love and free will rather than service forced by physical dominance. "I will not give up on this horse, myself, or on what God can do if only I can steer this steed's heart fully to me through God's leading," Tom promised.

"Why did he respond *so* painfully to me just now?" Tom questioned himself. "That is not like Come-Along Casey. *Painful* . . . that's it! Perhaps I missed a burr that was under his saddle. I'll check."

Back in the pen with the horse, Tom calmly approached Casey, talking to him reassuringly. He petted him on the nose and then began to stroke his neck. He gently moved his hands back towards the saddle and noticed that Casey started to tremble and look at him with fearful eyes. Carefully, he removed the saddle. Sure enough, there was a clump of burrs. And underneath the burrs was an ugly open sore. Evidently, the weight of the saddle on the burrs had been tolerable, but Tom's weight pressing the burrs into the open wound was just too much! No wonder Casey reared up!

Tom continued to speak tenderly to Casey while removing the burrs and treating the open wound with soothing salve. After a few days of treatment, the wound festered and required debridement. Although expressing the puss was painful to Casey, he sensed he needed it and submitted to the tender care. Tom had no idea how deep this wound had been until he patiently worked through the healing process. He was thankful he had listened to God and walked away rather than beating and yelling at Casey when he felt so provoked. He realized that he would have forfeited the trust he had worked so hard to gain. Attentive, kind, and faithful treatment brought healing.

So, too, we must work with our youth. Often our teens have issues with us because we are the burrs under their saddle, and they balk, kick, and bolt. Maybe we have abandoned them, rejected them, abused them, were harsh and belittling to them, were indulgent and not there for them—whatever. Whether they react because these issues are real or supposed doesn't matter. The burrs need to be discovered and removed, and a healing salve needs to be supplied until the wound is healed. Satan effectively speaks lies to their minds, and often they adopt them, and these lies are the cause of negative reactions and behaviors. God can direct you to discover them. He'll show you just what you need to do to change and restore these matters. Go to God.

The time came to try the saddle again. Come-Along Casey's fearful eyes reflected his memory of the former painful experience. Tom worked him through it with reassuring words, gentle touches, and an extra long combing. Casey trembled when the saddle was lifted to his back and cinched down. He turned cautious eyes on his trainer as Tom slowly stepped into the stirrup. When he realized it didn't hurt this time, he relaxed, and the training continued. Casey was a gem. Confident in Tom's love, he learned quickly—first walking, then cantering, then galloping. He was very sensitive to Tom's wishes and learned quickly what Tom meant through leg pressure, verbal commands, or use of the reins. Tom was delighted and let Casey know that. Come-Along Casey was becoming a most wonderful, faithful, and loyal horse. But there is a price to be paid in order for these qualities to grow, isn't there?*

In time, Tom galloped Casey through the pasture and out into the very hills where Casey had grown up. Casey could feel old impulses rising within—the call of the wild was very strong. Oh, to be free to run as before! But then he remembered the rider on his back. The bond between them now was strong. Love and loyalty won. Casey chose to serve Tom and be his faithful and true companion.

One day Trainer Tom took Come-Along Casey out as he fixed some fence posts. As he worked, his horse followed him, carrying all his tools and waiting patiently at each stop. No tied-up horse. He munched grass along the way, but his eye was aware where Tom was at all times like a child who admires his parent. After lunch, Casey lay down, and Tom leaned up against him for a pleasant nap. At home Casey would follow Tom around while he did his chores—just wanting to be with him. He loved to work, to run, to play, to always be with Tom his trainer. Why—because love had awakened love. Service from love far outweighs the value of blind submission.

This well depicts the relationship God, *our* Trainer, wants to have with us parents and teens. God wants to train us to become happy and free like Come-Along Casey.

Tom, in turn, enjoyed being with Casey and always kept his favorite treats on hand—corn and carrots. Casey especially loved carrots. Tom would look into Casey's eyes with a fondness that the horse just ate up. Other horses were curried by the *hired hands*, but not Casey. Tom did it himself, and so they lived happily ever after with mutual respect, love, and service one for the other. Was all this effort to establish the foundation of true training worth it? By far—yes!

Don't you want that kind of relationship with your youth? You can have it. The same two steps apply. Maybe you have a Cool Jace, an unsettled, defiant stallion. Or maybe your teen is fearful and distracted like Despairing Danny. Read their stories in the following chapters and see that whatever your teen's need, under God, you can win his trust and apply the training program that fits him. Your stallion, with God, can be all that Casey was—and more!

---

*Proverbs 18:24.

THE LONE EMBRACE
A SPECIAL WORD OF ENCOURAGEMENT FOR SINGLE PARENTS

Every youth that is not carefully and prayerfully disciplined will be *unhappy* in this probationary time and will form such unlovely traits of character that the Lord cannot unite him with His family in heaven. A spoiled child carries a great burden all through life. And it is so easy to spoil them, to be lenient regarding their weakness in a separated, divorced, or solo-parent situation. But ill training produces bad fruit. When trial comes—or disappointment or temptation—the poorly trained youth will follow his own undisciplined, misdirected will. Children and youth who are allowed to have their own way are not happy. So we must see that there is love in proper correction and debridement of bad habits. There is love in training for good habits and in being willing to put in the necessary time to do that.

A horse is limited in its understanding, but you can go further than an outward training of manners and submission. You can connect your youth personally to God by your influence and example. Don't you want them to know the Trainer, Jesus, personally for themselves? Don't you want God at your youth's side to instruct him? Of course you do. Then you need to individually make a choice to seek, hear, and follow the Trainer, Jesus, yourself. You want God to be always with your youth, even when you are not there; you want him to be accustomed to hearing, knowing, and following the Trainer's voice.

So take courage! Jesus is with you. He is the heavenly Trainer who is at your side to comfort you, direct you, and bring balance to your imbalance, wisdom for your confusion, and strength for your weakness. God will be your personal Trainer.

Matthew, age 19, blowing snow as part of household duties.

Chapter 11

Cool Jace

Grace and peace be multiplied unto you through the knowledge of God,
and of Jesus our Lord.
—2 Peter 1:2

Cool Jace, age fourteen, sat submissively on the couch next to his parents, but there was something disquieting in his expression. As Jim and I visited with the parents, we'd also reach out to Jace in a friendly, interested way. But Cool Jace responded with considerable reserve. He was polite and answered our questions, but his heart was not in it. Underneath his cool demeanor, he seemed restless—like that newly penned stallion, looking for an escape.

"Let's go for a walk to the river, and we can talk some more," Jim suggested.

Matthew and Andrew, seventeen and fifteen, walked ahead with Cool Jace and his brother. Jim and I walked together behind them with Jace's parents. They began to share their difficulties parenting Cool Jace. They were looking for some answers, and this was the reason for their visit. The mother had divorced Jace's father a few years back and remarried. Cool Jace had to spend time with both parents, which created much confusion for him. The mother and her new husband wanted to uphold Christian values in their home while Jace's father had abandoned himself to a permissive life of drunkenness, worldliness, and crudeness. Poor Jace was caught in the tug-of-war between the two lifestyles, and his father seemed to be winning. Jace had begun wondering if he even wanted to be a Christian. The parents were concerned that all their efforts to draw in Jace seemed to be pushing him away instead. They admitted that when they finally reached the point of delivering consequences, they were usually angry and frustrated. Cool Jace had taken on an air that he was tough and that nothing could touch him. Could we help?

We all gathered at the river and began playfully throwing stones into the swiftly flowing North Fork River. My family made friendly conversation specifically with Jace and his brother. After our walk we played freeze tag at our home. I made it a point to chase Jace, to reach out to him in fun and play. We incorporated Cool Jace and his brother into our home training program of preparing meals, washing dishes, and doing chores with my sons. Jace fit in nicely, and trust was being established.

Groping for his heart

But the next evening, during a walk to the river, Cool Jace began throwing stones at my sons. Jace's brother, Matthew, and Andrew tried mildly reasoning with him, but he spitefully continued hurling rocks at them. Finally Andrew came and told us what was happening.

"Lord, what would Thou have us to do?"* I cried out in prayer. Jim and I discussed ideas with Jace's parents. They gave us full freedom to work with their son and to take whatever steps we felt God was asking us to take to try to gain his heart. The mother then shared with us, "Jace has had problems like this at the Christian school he attends—especially with girls. He has pulled their hair, pushed them around, hit them, and said very unkind—even cruel—things. We've talked to him repeatedly. The principal and the teacher have tried to reason with him about this, but to no avail. His behavior has been steadily declining over the last few years, and nothing seems to get through to him.

"At home Jace used to be helpful with the household chores, carrying his own responsibilities and even cooking when I needed his help—but not anymore. He has become evasive and undependable. He slips out of the house to be with rough neighborhood youth and refuses to tell us what he is doing. And our punishments only seem to intensify this rebellion. Jace is getting increasingly hard, malicious, and cruel. He has lots of free time but refuses to have his personal worship anymore. We're worried about him. Can you help?"

We decided to hold a family council right in the living room with all present.

Jim opened the discussion by explaining the purpose of a family council. "We have family council whenever there is a problem that needs to be settled. Everyone will be given a chance to speak uninterrupted. We want this to be fair for everyone. Jace, even though these are my boys, I will judge you fairly. I will not be biased against you. Andrew, you may go first."

"Well, while we were walking to the river, Jace threw stones at me. I asked him to stop. He didn't. So I talked with Matthew, and we explained he could throw stones at the trees—that would be better. So we all began throwing stones at selected trees, and we tried to make a fun game of it. It worked for a little bit, but soon Jace was throwing stones at both his brother and me."

"Could it have been an accident, Andrew?" Jim asked.

"It wasn't an accident; it was intentional." And Andrew looked tenderly at Jace. "Look at the marks on my arm where the rocks hit."

We examined Andrew's arm, and it agreed with his story.

Jace's brother spoke next, and then Matthew, each affirming all that Andrew had said.

I was praying for the Holy Spirit to come into this meeting, especially into Cool Jace's heart to redeem him from this hurtful behavior. "Lord, let us get to the root of this issue so that Jace and his family can find the freedom that is in You! What unmet need is driving this behavior? Give us wisdom from above."†

"Well, Jace, what do you have to say?"

Jace sat in the glider rocker, rocking softly with his head down—appearing cool and untouched by the testimony against him. "Well, maybe it was an accident," he muttered softly.

---

*Acts 9:6.
†James 1:5.

"Listen, Jace, we can't resolve this issue unless you are honest. You will be dealt with fairly. We are here to help you. Now if you don't choose to do right, there will be consequences in my home. You are under my authority here—not your parents',￼" Jim explained firmly, but lovingly.

"Jace, we love and care for you," I added. "I think you have evidence of that already with how we all have treated you. We are praying that you want help so you can be helped. We are not your enemies, but your friends. The truth is always the best way to work through a difficulty. Just tell us the truth."

He was still in the same stance as before with his head down, not looking at any one of us. Then he said so softly it was hardly audible, "Yes, I did that."

Twice, we called for his heart to say it loud enough for us to hear, and he did.

"Why would you intentionally throw stones to hurt like that, Jace?"

"I don't know," was his flat response.

"Well, Jace, I think you need to do something nice to make up for your unkind treatment of Andrew and your brother. I want you to write a love letter of appreciation to both your brother and our Andrew. Will you do that?" Jim asked.

He hesitated, but with some coaxing said, "Yes."

Everyone left, but I was impressed to talk with Cool Jace about lying thoughts. In my youth I had been vulnerable to lying thoughts that led me into destructive thinking about myself. As a result God seemed so far away, and I felt like such a failure. I wanted to make him aware that Jesus could teach him the difference between true thoughts and false thoughts, and that he didn't have to believe the lies Satan poses to our minds. I shared a few experiences from my youth to help him understand how to filter these thoughts through God to know the difference. He listened, but had little to say.

The next morning, we had family worship, and Jace delivered his apology in a very nice letter. He even expressed appreciation to Andrew. It was truly lovely and appeared to be honest. His mother shared how diligent Cool Jace had been that morning, rising early on his own to compose these letters. This thrilled her soul. His letter to his brother was most touching, and with Cool Jace's approval they shared it with us. Yet there was still a heavy cloud pervading his presence, and his head remained downcast. He seemed untouchable emotionally. Even our compliments and gratitude seemed to fall on deaf ears.

We continued to pray for Cool Jace and gave him many opportunities to consciously say and do nice things. In his work, his play, and conversation we nurtured these expressions in order to exercise and strengthen the opposite trait in his character.* To his mother's surprise and joy, he worked well with my boys. We had several encounters that day, but explanations and entreaties were met with compliant obedience. He prayed when asked and changed his approaches when instructed why and how. My boys initiated good conversation with him, and he entered into it. "This touchy stallion is beginning to be comfortable in the training pen and to follow the Trainer," I said to myself. I thought we were gaining ground as Christ's power worked with all of us and enabled him to choose right over wrong. The new way seemed to be gaining momentum . . . *until* evening worship.

---

*Romans 12:21.

Challenge

"Let's sing hymn number three hundred and forty-three," Jim led out.

I was seated next to Cool Jace. Everyone began singing heartily except him. I nudged him, then whispered twice in his ear, "Jace, you can sing, too." He sat staunchly with his lips sealed tight. I caught Jim's eye, and then he, too, noticed Jace's stubborn lack of participation.

"Jace," he interjected between verses, "you need to sing. This is good for you. At my house, I'm the authority, and you need to submit to godly expectations cheerfully, not begrudgingly. Let's begin again to give you another chance to choose to do what's right."

Jace didn't even try to sing. He was entreated again. This time he mouthed the words. I couldn't hear anything so I put my ear right next to his mouth. "There is no audible singing," I reported. One more chance was given to Jace, but he was stubborn, cool, and noncompliant. He was definitely trying to be the one in charge.

"Lord," I cried out in my heart, "give Jim wisdom from above. Call for Cool Jace's heart, let him know clearly what he needs to do and empower his choices. Come near to Cool Jace and draw him unto You. Let him see the love in our expecting him to obey."

You could sense that Jim was crying out to God in a similar way. After a few moments, Jim rose from the table and said firmly, "Jace, come with me. You come, too," he turned to Jace's stepfather.

Jace didn't move.

"Jace, I said, 'come'!" Jim spoke with greater authority, and Jace arose to follow. As Jim passed the cook stove, he picked up a piece of wood and thumped it decisively on the stonework for effect. He wasn't angry, but he was very firm.

Out the back door they went—stepfather, stepson, and Jim. Those of us remaining in the house prayed for Jace. We saw that milder measures were not getting to the heart of the issue and that firmer measures were necessary for Jace's sake. We wanted him to perceive the love that motivated both the soft and the firm approach. If only we could get Cool Jace connected to Jesus, then and only then, could he find freedom from whatever it was that held him aloof, and so negative about everyone.

Jim prayed again for God to attend his words and actions. Jim didn't want to use this stick, but the time seemed right for a visual motivation. Jace had to know that remaining defiant and independent was not an option. Jim wanted him to be convinced there was no other way than to yield his ugly spirit to God and find grace in Jesus to do right.

"Now Jace, you have two choices," Jim instructed. "You can choose to submit now, kneel down, and pray to Jesus with me to help you change this nasty spirit. Or you will have to face consequences for your ungodly actions. There must be consequences for things like this or you will continue in this wrong way. I won't discipline you because I hate you, but because I love you. You are too valuable to allow you to continue in this evil way. Jesus loves you, as do I, and we want to help you to be freed from this evil spirit you carry. You don't have to obey this spirit—Jesus will help you."

Jace's eyes were beginning to soften just slightly within that stoic countenance. Jim saw that little flicker of hope and acted on it.

He knelt down and, wonder of wonders, Jace did too. "I'm going to pray to Jesus, and I'm sure you don't know what to pray so I want you to pray after me a surrender prayer. Dear Jesus, forgive me for my rebellious spirit right now." And Cool Jace repeated this.

"I want to change." And Cool Jace repeated the words timidly, but without hesitating.

"Jesus, come into my heart, my mind, my life, and change me inside.

"I want to be different today.

"I want to be the man You intend me to be.

"I can't do this without Your power and strength.

"But I can commit to submit my will to do Your will and follow whatever You ask me to do in Your strength."

Cool Jace then began to weep, his hard protective shell finally broken.

After a pause, he said from his own heart, "Lord, I'm sorry for being such a mean fellow. I do want to follow You."

All the men embraced each other, and tears of rejoicing sweetened the moment. The three men returned to the worship table, and we commenced to sing our hymn. Cool Jace sang timidly and yet with gusto. Worship was sweet. At the close of worship, we commended Cool Jace for his choices.

Jace apologized, "I'm sorry for being so stubborn and not singing. I was wrong."

God is able to reach and change the hearts of those who feel their need and respond to Him. Jace's disposition changed. His heart was made soft and tender. Now, he had a degree of hope that was new. Cool Jace was still a bundle of unmet needs, and we hoped to help him meet more of those needs by teaching him how to make Jesus his closest Friend and Savior. God knows his struggles and can provide just the needed escape from wrong thoughts and feelings.

Christlike?

Truly, love is displayed in firmness—not in the harsh inflexibility commonly seen today, but rather in the unyielding purpose to redeem the erring from the pit of sin. Christ exhibited this firmness when He overturned the tables in the temple and drove out the moneychangers. Jesus loved the erring and wanted to help them, but He needed their attention, consent, and cooperation.

The sin-loving bystanders called Christ's rebuke unfair—much like the erring child protests spankings. The real issue, however, was not Christ's method, but the fact that the sinful heart does not want to be corrected.* Sin wants to be left alone to grow. Satan wants to keep your youth under his control, so he doesn't want you to give proper consequences to motivate the child to come to know Jesus personally so that his thoughts, feelings, and habits can be changed.

We need to be strong under Jesus to wrestle them out of Satan's control. Have you ever considered that we need *Christlike* courage and force? We have often equated Christlikeness with only the softer virtues: gentleness, patience, meekness, and kind-

---

*Ecclesiastes 8:11.

liness. Christ did possess these essential graces. But His character was also balanced with courage, force, energy, and perseverance.

Jesus exemplified these firmer virtues when He cleansed the temple. Some today would call this abusive behavior. The truth is, it is abusive to allow Satan to have full reign over my youth. That's criminal neglect in God's eyes. We cripple our children when we do not instruct them in right ways and fail to bring them to Christ for power to overcome wrong habits. Spankings or correction, given in love under God, is good for them; it is the true love that is rarely seen today. We need to inspire our youth to come up higher in Jesus, to find the upright life and the strength to live it. We don't love our children when we cripple them with unbalanced parenting.

After He cleansed the temple, the truehearted people there flocked around Jesus. They were not repelled by His demonstration of firmness and authority. They saw it as just, fair, and right. They were drawn to Jesus in gratitude. They opened up their hearts and minds individually to be cleansed more deeply by Him. They wanted their thoughts, their emotions, their habits, and their concepts to be redeemed from the defilement of sin as well as to have their physical maladies healed. Jesus came into their lives to bring strength to heal them inside and out. They were drawn by His firmness. Have you discovered this proper firmness under God?

Many argue over this issue of firmer consequences. My experience with many people has taught me that most recoil from firmness because they have seen it demonstrated only in an abusive manner that communicates hatred. So they swing the pendulum in the opposite extreme of indulgence, which is just as destructive as abusive firmness. Heaven-born firmness is love. We must discover this difference with God.

Jace wasn't growing under the too soft, inconsistent program in his home. Nor did he grow when the program swung to harshness and anger. Both approaches clearly conveyed rejection and abandonment. They told him that he was no good! To protect himself, he resorted to the cold, insensitive behavior he had seen his father exemplify. His immature thinking, together with an insufficient experience with a personal God, provided him no solid foundation for emotional, spiritual, or relational health. His spiritual house was destined to fall, and he knew no other option.

Without more extreme measures to correct the present approaches, Cool Jace would remain in bondage to evil thoughts, words, and deeds. He would fall to his own destruction on the rocks below without a parent eagle to teach him how to fly in Jesus' power.

God was leading my Jim to use firmer measures. Seeing firmness demonstrated, balanced with love and caring, was something Jace had not experienced sufficiently. Jim took him to Christ where the real solution was found. Giving our youth an experience with Christ, to taste and see His power to change them, is meeting the real needs of our youth. This is the ultimate goal of our training. It allows Christ to free the tortured, troubled soul from the galling yoke of sin and kindles hope and courage for the next trial or difficulty.

Cool Jace was being changed into Kind Jace. Jesus was coming into his heart and mind and giving him a newfound freedom. That tough, "can't touch me" exterior was melting away. It seemed altogether too easy. Many others encounter a much stronger resistance before gaining these kinds of results. Apparently, these circumstances had revealed that "burr under the saddle"—the core issue—and I wanted to find out what that burr was. I asked God to lead me.

What's going on?

The next day or so, I inquired, "So, Jace, you have been a different person since your prayer with Jim on the back porch. What made the difference?"

"Jim had said that I must yield up my ugly spirit to God, for Him to take it away. I never heard it said that way before. I understood. I always fought against that spirit, but rarely ever won. Maybe I was doing it wrong. I could try yielding it up for God to take—and I did. Amazingly, as I prayed, a sweet, tender Spirit surrounded me, and I felt . . . well . . . loved, accepted—and now I belong to Jesus. Now I have Jesus' power to say no to the old ways. What Jim said worked! The thought that God wasn't there for me is a lie I had believed for most of my life. Now I am convinced He is there for me!"

"Why would you think God wasn't there for you?" I asked.

"Well, I had tried to be a Christian and be kind and good, help with the house chores, and such. But I always felt it wasn't me. I felt like I was a phony. Mother was happy, but I wasn't happy inside. When I'd pray to God, I'd think how far, far away He was and that He wouldn't care about me. I didn't belong in this home and became very unhappy, lonely, restless, and discontented, so I'd go out to find something to do with my friends that would help me forget my hopeless feelings."

"Where did you feel you belonged?"

He hesitated for some time then responded, "I see a lot of myself in my father. He is a drunkard, irresponsible, gets into trouble with the law. He is a rough and tough kind of guy. I saw myself as just like him with no hope of change!

"I'm always getting into trouble with someone for something. So I felt I belonged with him. Over the last few years I came to the conclusion that this is who I am and I should just get used to it. I can't change it. I'm just like my dad—incorrigible and destined for jail one day. God isn't there for me because I am too bad. He couldn't possibly help me."

"Did you really believe God wasn't there for you?" I asked.

"Yes. Because I'd try and try to be good and it didn't stick; it didn't work, I thought He wasn't there for me. I had thought these might be those lying thoughts you told me about. But when I prayed on the back porch, I felt God wanted me to come to Him and that I was important to Him. I sensed God telling me these were lies and that I should cast them away. He would help me like your husband was trying to help me. Somehow it all seemed different," he said.

"You have chosen to connect with God in a new and different way, then?"

"I guess so. When you asked me to write those letters, I thought at first that I couldn't write them. I can only say rough and nasty things. That's why I'd treat the girls so bad at school. The bad ways were easy to do, while the kind ways were hard. Since I was going to be just like my dad, I might as well act the way that seemed most natural. And so I decided to be bad."

He continued, "Your boys shared with me how they had overcome wrong thoughts and feelings, but I shrugged it off as nonsense. But God brought those thoughts to my mind when I was sitting to write those letters. In prayer I asked God to help me write the letters, to take the rough, ugly thoughts, and give me His good, loving thoughts instead. I needed Him to put His heart in me—like we talked about in worship. I was kind of surprised at what I wrote. It wasn't me. It must have been God doing this through me.

"Then doing chores with your boys here was really fun. I never thought doing work could be fun. Everyone treated me so nice. I began to wonder if God could change me too. I decided I wanted to be good again. It was fine until I was asked to sing."

"Why didn't you sing?"

"I didn't feel like it! That's all. And I felt no one could make me. This comes very naturally. So I followed my feelings for sure. My rebellion is that I feel like doing bad things, and I do them no matter what.

"Then God spoke to my heart—not in an audible voice, but through a thought in my mind—that I didn't have to continue to obey that lie. I began to believe God was there for me. You have said that we must follow the truth and not lies. And that we need God to help us change inside. So I surrendered my heart deeper and deeper as we prayed, and I thought on these things. I was sure God would help me, and He did. It's strange, but I kind of enjoyed singing, and, Mrs. Hohnberger, I don't sing well. I could tell Mr. Hohnberger loved me and wanted to help me even though he was very firm. And I wanted to do right. God came in and made it possible just like you were telling us at worship."

"So you just tried God on that back porch?"

"Yes."

"But, Jace, you have changed so quickly! You do well with whatever we give you to do. You are participating in worship. You're learning to treat everyone kindly. Do you like the new you?"

"Oh, yes, I do. I've always wanted to be like this, but when I tried by myself I couldn't be. I don't fully understand why, even now, something is different."

"Jace, you let Jesus in your heart. You're thinking His thoughts and feeling His feelings instead of your old ways. You are in Christ instead of in self. You're depending on Jesus to change you inside while you cooperate on the outside. Your old nature is like a wild stallion brought under restraint. Jesus wants to be your Trainer, leading you, but you must stay in the pen and follow Him instead of your wrong ways that come so naturally. You belong to Jesus now and no longer to Satan."

"I'm determined to follow Jesus from here on out. I've decided to start my own morning worship again. I started this morning."

"That is wonderful. You will be happier the more you come to know His voice to your heart. Your mother tells me you hang out with a pretty rough group of friends."

"Yeah, I do."

"What is God asking you to do when you go home?"

"Well, first I want to tell them what happened to me. I want to witness about the real Jesus to them—if they'll hear me. I want God to give me the right words and approach. They are hurting worse than I was, and I'd like to tell them about how kind and helpful God can be to them. They have some pretty rough homes they come from. But right now I know I'm going to have to let those friendships go somehow, because what they do is against God. I want to serve God and be happy like this for the rest of my life."

"Jace, you can be all you choose to be, as long as you keep your hand in Jesus' hand, your will on His side, and depend on Him to change all the yuck inside you as you cooperate with His leading. We are very happy for you, and we will pray for you. Thank you for sharing from your heart."

"You are welcome. Thank you for caring for me when I was not very lovable. Thank you for correcting my wrong ways and showing me the right ones. Our family is going home with a commitment to make our home as pleasant as yours—with Jesus. I'll like that."

Cool Jace's unmet needs were being met by realizing that he belonged to God and not to Satan. That brought hope to his mind, heart, and soul. All that the world has to offer can't fill that void—only God can answer this need. This relationship puts to flight all the lying thoughts that otherwise cripple the Christian walk. This primary need was met because a properly firm and loving parent was able to recommend Christ as He really is. Our youth need a parent who takes them to Christ and sees to it they connect with Him as their Trainer.

When we meet real core needs of our youth and take them to Christ, real miracles happen! God proved His presence to Jace as he reached out to God. His parents tried to come closer to God, and the family grew together. God loves to help each of us to change into His image. Won't you be next?

THE LONE EMBRACE
A SPECIAL WORD OF ENCOURAGEMENT FOR SINGLE PARENTS

Your youth are a byproduct of your parenting practices. If you want a change in your home or in your youth, you must let that change begin with you.* It is our unbalanced parenting that has produced the youth of today. Parenting without Christ will always be unbalanced—either on the soft side or the firm side—and needs will be left unmet.

We cannot teach what we do not know. So we must gain the experience—not just the understanding—that Christ is there for us! *He is your personal Trainer.* He is all you need! Jesus can change your wrong thoughts, feelings, responses, habits, inclinations, and even your history when you come to Him to be led by His Spirit.

Thankfully, Christ knows just what you and your youth need in your peculiar circumstances. He will direct your steps to meet your teen's need to know a personal God. He will walk with you and talk with you like He did Enoch. Turn to Him in your every trial and need. God wants to meet your unmet needs so that, in turn, you may meet the unmet needs of your youth in a profoundly simple and practical way and transform your Cool Jace into Kind Jace.

---

*John 17:19.

Chapter 12
Love and Limits

Love suffers long and is kind; love . . . does not rejoice in iniquity, but rejoices in the truth.
—1 Corinthians 13:4, 6, NKJV

Fourteen-year-old Despairing Danny lay face down on the hallway floor, his head buried in his arms. He was that fearful stallion cowering in the corner of his training pen. His mother came upstairs expecting to find him busy with schoolwork.

"Danny, are you OK?" she inquired with concern. "Are you sick?"

"I'm not going to do my schoolwork or my jobs today, Mother. So just leave me alone!" Despairing Danny's voice had the sound of someone in a deep, dark pit.

"Danny, that's not like you. What's wrong?"

"It's no use, Mother. I'm dumb. I'm stupid. I never do things right. Christianity doesn't work for me. It might work for you, Mother, but it doesn't work for me. I'm headed for hell, and there is nothing I or you can do about it. So just get used to it and leave me alone!"

Stunned momentarily, Mother paused to reflect. Obviously, there must be a "burr under the saddle," but what to do about it? A fourteen-year-old boy is too big to pick up and comfort on your lap. He's too big to physically coerce. Besides, Mother knew that forced compliance was worse than doing nothing. She decided to try reasoning with Danny.

"Danny," she ventured, "those are lying thoughts from Satan. You don't have to cooperate with them."

"Mother, I don't care what you say. I'm giving up on myself, and you might as well get used to it."

Now what? Should she just leave him to work it out on his own? What could she do? Old familiar feelings of helplessness threatened to take over her thoughts, but then God called to her heart.

"Remember—love and limits."

"Oh, God, You are here—my present help in trouble. I forget You so quickly in difficulty. You are not overwhelmed by Danny's despair, and You know how to rescue him from this pit. What would You have me to do?"

The thought repeated itself: *"Remember—love and limits."*

Flashback

Mother's mind quickly reviewed what she had learned in recent years.

When Danny had been about ten years old, Mother had begun to grasp, in a new and deeper way, her responsibility to train Danny for usefulness in this world and for fitness for the world to come. As she had examined his character with the aid of the

Holy Spirit, she saw that Danny had a strong tendency to slothful work habits. She labeled him Distracted Danny.

Immediately, she had begun to try to address those habits. She thought that if she just told Danny to be diligent, he would immediately become diligent. Well, he did express the desire to be diligent, but the old habits were stronger than his desire, and slow work habits continued.

Confident that God had a solution for this character defect, Mother prayed, studied, and then implemented a plan based on God's "replacement principle"— cultivate the right character trait and weed out the wrong one.*

First, she attempted to teach Danny the right way. She led him through an in-depth Bible study about diligence. They drew a picture depicting the path of the diligent worker. On one side of the path was the ditch of slothfulness. On the other side was the ditch of hastiness. Diligence goes right between both ditches.

Next, Mother sought to train Danny in the right way. She prayerfully invented programs using charts and stickers, games and rewards—all intended to make diligence as positive as possible.

She struggled with negative motivations. Giving corrections and consequences for slothful work were hard, even painful, for her. She would avoid them as long as possible—coaxing, persuading, even nagging—hoping she wouldn't have to actually "do something." It was always very stressful to her when she would finally enforce a consequence for slothfulness—extra work, grizzly runs, essays. But she would finally do it. However, there was no lasting change. Distracted Danny would make attempts to be diligent but inevitably would fall back into his distracted, dilatory ways.

"Lord," Mother moaned, "I think this is one of those incurable cases. This program is just not working. We are not getting to the bottom of the problem, and I don't know what else to do." She was hoping to be let off the hook and to find some easier work to do for God.

But into her mind came a sweet little Scripture song: *"And let us not be weary in well doing: for in due season we shall reap, if we faint not."*[†]

"I can't give up, Lord?"

"Weary not in well-doing, Mother."

And so Mother continued the program, wondering all the while what she was missing. One day, as she and Distracted Danny were discussing this problem, he turned to her with tearful intensity and said, "Mother, if you only knew how badly I *want* to be diligent."

Mother felt utterly helpless. What was missing? Hadn't she begun this program with God? Why was it not giving lasting results? In her frustration, she turned once again to God.

"Lord, Danny has the knowledge, he has been given incentives, and he has been corrected and given consequences. He has the desire and the will to be diligent. What is missing? Why aren't we seeing lasting change?"

---

*Romans 12:21.
†Galatians 6:9.

Dig deeper

In the quiet recesses of her mind, the thought came that the behavior she was seeing in her son was a fruit. And every fruit has roots.

"This habit has not developed in a vacuum. It is there for a reason, and you, as his mother, need to discover the reason and begin by dealing with that. You have labeled your son Distracted Danny, but your label might not be accurate. Put yourself in Danny's place and go back in your mind and heart to his very beginnings to see what has molded his character."

Why did God ask this mother to explore her son's beginning? He can't remember what happened in those early years, so how can it affect him now?

The Scriptures teach that the earliest influences on a child, through his mother's emotions, have a powerful impact on his character formation—how he thinks, feels, and responds.* If his early learning is peaceful, its influence is for good. If unrest, violence, and disturbed emotions are present in his early learning experiences, he is influenced toward hopelessness.

Modern science confirms this principle: Astounding research has been conducted regarding the effects of intrauterine experiences on the unborn child. It has been found that the most profound effect on the physical and emotional well-being of a child for the rest of his or her life is the relationship between the birth mother and the birth father during the months of pregnancy. What the mother feels is transferred directly to the child. Cortisol and adrenaline (stress hormones) dramatically affect the heart rate and increase the emotional stress the child experiences. Just imagine what must happen to the child in the womb when parents argue or are violent with each other! The adrenaline response learned there is felt years later in an automatic response.

So Mother began to ponder Danny's early beginnings to find the key to the "burrs under the saddle."

He had been in her womb during the final months of her first marriage. He had heard his father's angry verbal tirades, demeaning and belittling his mother. He sensed Mother's anguish as Father made unreasonable demands on her and then slapped her for hesitating to comply. He shared Mother's stress when Father failed to carry his share of the load at home—financially, physically, and emotionally. He experienced all the negative emotions that Mother experienced—grief, anxiety, rejection, fear, alienation, turmoil, violence, and shame—as his own without the filter of reason. What kind of foundation was laid for his emotional security?

As an infant, he beheld the traumatic events of the disintegrating marriage of his parents over and over. His mother struggled to pick up the fragments of her life—returning to work and leaving him with Grandma, beginning a new relationship, and remarrying when he was two years old, getting very involved in church activities and theological controversy. Did he find in his mother a safe, dependable, and happy connection? Not at all! Instead, Mother was depressed, detached, and distracted.

In the following years of childhood, the turmoil quieted down, but Mother was still preoccupied with too many distractions. Danny was fed, sheltered, clothed, and

---

*Luke 1:41.

homeschooled. But Mother's mind was so filled with building a house, growing a garden, many church duties, needs of friends, and many other things that she lacked the time and understanding to teach Danny how to come to God for freedom from destructive thoughts and their automatic responses. On top of everything else, she and her second husband continued to carry baggage from the past that prevented them from making their home happy and emotionally safe.

So what effect did all these early impressions have on Danny's character? As God opened Mother's perceptions, she could see clearly that Danny had felt alienated and isolated. He had an intense sense of shame and guilt and feared abandonment and rejection. The way he coped with these feelings was to just "check out." Distracted Danny was who you saw on the outside, but Distracted Danny was there only to hide the real Danny—Despairing, Doubting Danny.

Could this history be the "burr under the saddle" causing Danny's problems? Could connection and cooperation with God erase history's pathway of responses? Yes! God is big enough to redeem us from any wrong thought, feeling, or response.

With this hope, Mother began to realize that she needed to minister to Despairing, Doubting Danny if Distracted Danny was ever to be redeemed. A longing rose up within her to do all in her power to remedy the damage inflicted unwittingly on the mind and heart of her son. And yet, she had not a clue where to begin.

Not long afterwards, as she was grieving over her neglect and acknowledging the pain she had unknowingly inflicted on her son, she picked up one of her favorite books and found herself reading a chapter titled "True Love." Two sentences struck her forcefully. First: "Love will gain the victory when argument and authority are powerless."

"Lord," she inquired, "how can this apply to me? I love my son. That's why I am making him a priority. I've put away many of those distractions, and he has my time and interest before anyone or anything outside of my home. That is why I am trying to help him overcome slothfulness."

Second she read, "Wherever the power of intellect, of authority, or of force is employed, and love is not manifestly present, the affections and will of those whom we seek to reach assume a defensive, repelling position, and their strength of resistance is increased."

Again, she asked, "Lord, how does this apply to me? I love my son."

The question came back to her mind, *"Yes, you love your son. But is your love 'manifestly present'? In other words, does your son see your love and feel your love when he is being slothful and distracted?"*

"Well, I'm not sure, Lord, since You put it that way."

"What kind of thoughts are you thinking when Danny is not being diligent?"

"Well . . . thoughts such as, What is wrong with this boy? Why can't he get his act together?"

"And what do you feel like on the inside?"

"Oh, Lord, I feel frustrated, tense, helpless—and a failure as a mother."

"And what does your countenance and your tone of voice reflect to your son?"

"All that I am thinking and feeling," she admitted.

"What does your son feel from you?"

The picture was becoming all too clear now. This honest mother had to admit that her son felt coldness, disapproval, nonacceptance, and a withdrawal of affection.

"Lord," she confessed with remorse, "I censure him, bear down on him, and wish I could get inside of his head to make him think right. That's not Your Spirit, is it?"

"No it's not. Your love, Mother, is conditional, and your son feels the pain of his early childhood every time you respond to him this way. The only way he knows how to deal with this pain is to 'check out.' You are strengthening Despairing, Doubting Danny by all your good intentions to root out Distracted Danny because your love is not 'manifestly present'!"

"But, Lord, this is the only way I know to be firm with my son. If I am all sweet and happy, he won't be motivated at all to do what he should."

"Mother, your difficulty is that you are putting limits where love should be—and love where limits should be."

"What do you mean by that?"

"Picture a lovely house with a large, beautiful yard. It is all enclosed by a neat white picket fence. The fence defines the property lines and makes very clear where home is and where it is not. The fence doesn't move. It stays in one place.

"The fence of a Christian home defines what is acceptable and what is not. It should be very easy to know when you are within the fence and when you are outside of it.

"Within the fence are freedom, encouragement, room for their personality, spiritual development, responsibility, individuality, safety, love, and joy. It is a happy place to be. Outside the fence are danger, death, and bondage. It is a dangerous place to be."

"Well, Lord, what establishes that fence? I'm not very good at having consistent expectations."

"The boundaries of a true Christian home are not established by the whims, moods, or inclinations of the parent. Rather, they should be established by the principles of God's law. Parents learn what God expects and then educate their children to know where the 'fence' is. Principle is exacting and unchanging. How it is applied will vary from family to family and from individual to individual. For example, having a well-ordered schedule is a principle of My government. But how that is expressed will appear differently in your family than in your friend's family. You need Me to teach you how best to apply My principles in your home.

"You have been educating Danny about diligence—a godly principle that makes up part of that fence. And that is right. And he has a right to know when he is inside the fence and when he is outside of it.

"On the other hand, redeeming love is like the sunshine. It has no limits. You can be in or out of My will, but you can never be out of My love. Remember those Scriptures that have assured you of my love.

" 'Whither shall I go from thy spirit? or whither shall I flee from thy presence? If I ascend up into heaven, thou art there: if I make my bed in hell, behold, thou art there. If

---

*Psalm 139:7–10.

I take the wings of the morning, and dwell in the uttermost parts of the sea; Even there shall thy hand lead me, and thy right hand shall hold me.' *

" 'Who shall separate us from the love of Christ? . . . For I am persuaded, that neither death, nor life, nor angels, nor principalities, nor powers, nor things present, nor things to come, Nor height, nor depth, nor any other creature, shall be able to separate us from the love of God, which is in Christ Jesus our Lord.'* *

" 'The LORD hath appeared of old unto me, saying, Yea, I have loved thee with an everlasting love: therefore with lovingkindness have I drawn thee.'* † *Notice the verse says 'drawn thee'—not 'driven thee'!*

"Mother, this is redeeming love. This is the kind of love and acceptance that provides fuel for real change. It is the love that embraces the sinner and then draws him back into the safety and security of the fence by connection with Me.

"Your human love has limits, and when you emotionally withdraw from your son, you make it virtually impossible for him to do what you are asking him to do. He resorts to the only survival mechanism he knows—'checking out.' You two are locked in a vicious cycle of frustration and failure. I can help you to set things straight. Will you let Me? The change must begin with you."

"Yes, Lord," Mother responded seriously. "Whatever it takes, I want to redeem my errors of the past."

"Then you must do three things: First you must place limits where limits should be. They should be simple and based upon the principles of My Word. Make the location of that fence very clear to your son. He must know without any question just where that fence is and how nice it is to be on the inside and that there is no peace on the outside.

"Second, you must begin to cultivate redeeming love for your son. Put your effort toward making the atmosphere about you one of sunshine and pleasantness. And third, you must agree with Me that whenever these negative thoughts and feelings arise in you and you are tempted to be cold, to censure, or bear down on your son that you will not deal with him at that time—even when he is in the wrong. You need to come apart with Me and let Me deal with you until that disposition is subdued."

Mother began by apologizing to Despairing Danny for her wrong attitudes and approach. She told him of the new approach into which God was leading her. She gave Danny permission to respectfully let her know when he felt she was treating him coldly or withdrawing from him.

Mother faced fierce battles against self. When God alerted her that wrong thoughts and feelings were beginning to rise, she would cry out to Him. Sometimes her wrong disposition could be subdued very quickly—in a matter of moments. Other times she had to go for long walks before all the negative thoughts and feelings were effectively replaced with unconditional love.

She discovered, however, that once self was subdued in her own heart, she could work with her son in cooperation with God. She could hold to the requirement—the expectation—with firmness, saying, "You must do this. There is no other way." At the

---

*Romans 8:35, 38, 39.
†Jeremiah 31:3.

same time, through her countenance, tone of voice, and encouraging words she could express love, warmth, and a confidence that he would gain the victory in Christ Jesus.

Instead of waiting for her son to "get his act together" so that they could have a happy time together, she began to create happy times together so that her son would be secure enough to make the changes he needed to make. As Danny sensed her emotional presence and her commitment to see him through his trials, he began to find the freedom and safety to let go of his old habits.

How does it apply now?

But now, as Danny lay in abject despair on the floor, all that God had been teaching her flashed through Mother's mind in just a few seconds. Understanding the principles but not knowing how to apply them in this situation, she sent up a silent cry for help to her trusty Trainer. She yielded her feelings of helplessness to Him and asked, "Lord, which comes first—love or limits?"

She sensed God whispering to her heart. *"Love comes first."*

"Danny," she said gently, "you are my precious son, and I love you with all my heart. Nothing you can do or say will ever change that. I am here for you now, and as long as I live, I will never give up on you. God is here, too. He will never stop loving you and never stop being there for you either."

"Mother, will you please just leave me alone. I don't want to hear what you have to say." Danny spoke with bitterness.

"Lord, that didn't get the result I was hoping for. What now?"

"You have started applying the first part of the equation. Now you need to apply some limits to motivate him."

Mother pondered a moment, and only one thing came to her mind. She decided to test it. The results would let her know if it was of God. In the horse pen, the trainer uses not only words but hand signals and different leg nudges to direct the horse in the way to go. By going round and round the horse learns his master's will and follows, trusting him.

"Danny," she began, "I love you far too deeply to stand by idly while you wallow in this pit of despair. I want you to know that I am going to do all that I can in co-operation with God to help you get out. Just because you are in the pit of despair doesn't mean you don't have to fulfill your responsibilities in this home. I am going to go downstairs and start a list for you. I will write down the tasks you already know about, and then I will start adding to the list. The longer you stay here without getting started on your list, the longer it will become."

Getting no response from Despairing Danny, Mother went downstairs to carry out her plan.

Within just a few minutes, Danny came downstairs. "It's not fair, Mother," he fumed angrily. "I'm not up to doing my regular jobs, and now you're making me do more."

Mother didn't respond to his accusation. She just smiled and told him that the first thing he needed to do was to go on a nice brisk run to the mailbox—about a half mile away. And while he was running there he could plan the menu for lunch as that would put him ahead on one of his other duties.

Danny was silent for a moment, and Mother could see the struggle in his eyes. She prayed silently for him. He chose to surrender and went out the door.

In a few minutes he was back, but his disposition was still angry and argumentative like a wild horse defying his trainer. Mother sent him out to the mailbox again with the assignment of thinking of three things about himself that showed that God sees value in him.

This time, when he returned, his disposition had softened somewhat, but he said, "I can't think of even one thing that's good about me."

Mother replied encouragingly, "Danny, what has God given you that shows you He wants you on this planet?"

Danny murmured after a moment, "Life."

Then he continued earnestly. "But Mother, how can God love me? I'm just bad. I'm a hypocrite. No matter how hard I try to be good, I just end up being bad. I'm just worthless."

"Danny, you are in Satan's pit of worthlessness because you have been cooperating with his lying thoughts. He has you in this pit, and he's put an umbrella over the top to shut out any light. But Jesus is reaching His hand down to you. Won't you take it? You take it by cooperating with the thoughts that are from Him."

"How can I know which thoughts are from Him?" Danny asked honestly.

Mother paused a moment to ask God for wisdom and to direct her words. "Danny, remember the story we just read about Saul visiting the witch of Endor? One way to distinguish the voice of God from the voice of Satan is that God offers hope and a way out. Satan just condemns you and leaves you in despair. That's what he's doing to you now, isn't it?"

Danny nodded silently, gazing down, but his countenance softening.

Mother cried out to God, "What next, Lord?"

"Ask him to tell you what I am saying to him."

"Lord, isn't that kind of bold? What if he isn't hearing You?"

"Just trust Me. Try it."

"Danny, what thought is God putting in your mind right now?"

Mother could see the struggle on her son's face; she knew then that she had hit the mark. She persisted.

Danny answered in a subdued voice, "He's saying, 'Don't stay away from Jesus too long.' "

"Oh Danny, wouldn't you like to respond to Him now?"

They got down on their knees, and Danny prayed a heart-felt prayer of surrender. "Jesus, by faith I choose to trust You love me as Your Word says. I choose this against my emotions and history saying otherwise. Make this real inside me by Your power!" The last vestiges of resistance melted away, and God pulled Danny right out of that pit.

Mother and Danny snuggled on the couch while Danny opened up his heart about his innermost struggles with his thoughts, feelings, and emotions. Mother could see clearly the burr under his saddle that had pressed into a painful, festering wound. You see, there had been a sensitive issue that came up at the breakfast table that was not resolved before Father went to work. Danny's history told him that he was the one at fault and that there was nothing he could do about it. His history also made him believe Satan's lies when the devil took the opportunity to pour in his lying thoughts about Danny's worth. Danny truly believed that he belonged in that pit of despair and found himself incapable of service. Mother was able to help Danny by debriding the lying thoughts and replacing them with the salve of true thoughts.

Danny was truly free, and he very diligently took up his duties for the day and performed them as to the Lord. True freedom is found within the fence under God.

What is the "burr" under your teen's saddle? What open wound is causing him to resist training and service? God has the solution. It is found in putting limits where limits should be and love where love should be. Won't you follow Him?

THE LONE EMBRACE
A SPECIAL WORD OF ENCOURAGEMENT FOR SINGLE PARENTS

In your quiet alone time with God evaluate where you put your love and limits. Are they in the right proportions, and are they used at the right times to promote healthy growth for your family? Time is a limited commodity in a single parent's life. Don't let life or busyness crowd out your time with your God. God invites, "Come ye yourselves apart . . . and rest a while."* That quiet, restful time with Him is your fueling time. You need time to fill your emotional tank with heavenly wisdom, love, discretion, and power to live. That time with God can produce a plan of action to help your youth in their biggest struggle. When you allow Satan to crowd out that refueling time with God, you begin your day with the cheaper gas of sin, self, and Satan. You will find yourself using Satan's tactics and will confuse love and limits. It need not be thus.

Christ is calling to you, "Come, come, come unto Me."

Andrew, age 13, and Matthew, age 15, practice parking the car.

*Mark 6:31.

Chapter 13

Discipline Is . . .

He [God] openeth also their ear to discipline, and commandeth that they return from iniquity.
—Job 36:10

Discipline is training

Discipline is training that develops self-control, instills a proper submission to authority, and inspires orderly conduct. And while discipline lays down a system of rules, it also formulates a treatment plan to remedy wrong conduct. Even though the word *discipline* may carry a negative connotation to some people, it is an essential element of love, and our youth will not be happy without it. Let's redefine *true* discipline.

It was early summer—the time of year our deer friends bring their fawns to meet us. We had just arrived home from a speaking tour and were eager to see them. Sure enough, there was Friendly with another set of twins. Dainty Toes and Princess each had a single fawn, and Loco had twins, too. What a thrill it was to see them!

After admiring them, we all went about the task of unpacking. Suddenly, Matthew yelled, "Oh no! A wolf is chasing Dainty Toes' fawn!" And out the front door he darted.

Jim was downstairs in a flash and looked out the window in time to see the black wolf disappearing into the woods with Matthew in hot pursuit. Throwing open the window, he yelled, "No, Matthew, no!" Matthew didn't hear him, so Jim tore out the back door, grabbed an axe from the garage, and chased Matthew who was still chasing the wolf who was still chasing the fawn. Dainty Toes nervously ran around the yard snorting and calling to her fawn.

The men returned with a success story. After the excitement settled down, Matthew told us what had happened. He had managed to cut off the wolf's pursuit of the fawn, and Jim diverted it even further. Much to everyone's delight, the fawn escaped death! Matthew decided to name the fawn Baby Saved after the day's event.

Dainty Toes was too timid to eat corn directly from the bowl the boys held, but she brought Baby Saved to the feeder, and he learned early to trust the boys and come close. By early fall, he ate right out of the bowl. In fact, Baby Saved became so comfortable with the boys' routine that he began waiting for them at the bottom of the stairs every morning at 7:30 AM—or a little before!

Then Baby Saved, anxious to get the corn, started climbing the stairs of the porch and waited for the boys right in front of the door. They had to be very careful when pushing open the door because the fawn's tiny hooves could easily get caught in the spaces between the boards on the porch, and they didn't want him to twist or break a leg.

"Mother, I'm worried that Baby Saved will hurt himself on the front porch," Matthew confided.

"I am too, son. I think it is time for you to discipline Baby Saved. We shouldn't allow this habit to continue."

"How do we discipline a deer, Mother? We can't spank it."

"Discipline is far more than spanking. It's training. Like a parent, you need to ask God to give you a plan and to help the fawn understand your instruction. Establish a training program that restrains the wrong and cultivates the right. Then repetition will build the new habit."

The boys prayed, and then discussed and decided on a plan. Consistent discipline brings the fastest success, so they would both train Baby Saved the same way. They would say, "Stay there" when he was at the bottom of the stairs and "No, you may not come up" when he started up. If he was already on the deck, they would shoo him off saying, "Naughty boy! Get down." This is instructing and restraining. Then, to encourage the right response, they would carry the bowl of corn to the yard and call, "Come, Baby Saved. Eat from the bowl." Within a week, the old habit was broken, and the new habit established. Never again did Baby Saved climb onto the porch. The boys made the wrong undesirable and the right pleasant.

Baby Saved learned he was loved tenderly—even when reproved. That winter, the bond between boys and fawn deepened. They would comb the deer with a hairbrush, and Baby Saved just loved it! Discipline had been administered in a way that built trust. As he grew, the boys could pet and rub his antlers because of the trust they had earned.

What gems there are for us in this little story, parents! When our youth are forming a habit that is dangerous to them and others, fathers and mothers should both pray, then discuss and agree on a consistent course to restrain the wrong and cultivate the right. True discipline is training them practically how to trust, surrender, and cooperate with Christ. As the underteacher, we take our youth to Christ to accept Him as their Master and look to Him to empower their choices.

Discipline is disciple(ing) my child to Christ

Negative Nedley, age fourteen, was discouraged. He was sure he was worthless and stupid. Satan had successfully led him to think he was incapable of doing his schoolwork, and now he was so full of these thoughts he refused to believe anything else.

Mother tried to encourage him. "That's not true, Nedley. You are very sharp!"

"Mother, you expect too much of me! I can't do it!" he fretted.

"Here we go again," thought Mother. "This is the way it has been ever since first grade. We've gone round and round to learn, pulling out Bible texts and reciting them to replace the old thoughts with new, but the old ones always win anyway. The bridle I'm using to try to turn him to a different course isn't working. How do I motivate him to follow God's attitudes instead of following his inclination to be negative?"

Yet without consulting God, Mother required Negative Nedley to repeat "I can do all things through Christ who strengthens me."* And Nedley, in robot fashion, repeated it, although he didn't believe it in his heart. And he concluded by saying, "It will never happen, though. It can't work with me. I'm the exception." And his eyes shot daggers at his mother.

"For as he thinketh in his heart, so is he."† What a person believes deep down inside is what drives his behavior—not merely what he speaks with his mouth at his mother's insistence. How do you get the truth deep down inside so that *it* drives the right thoughts, feelings, and actions?

Mother, frustrated and confused, finally turned to God for help. "Lord, I've tried to instill Your principles and Your thoughts into Nedley. Why isn't it working? I don't know what else to do. Help me! Help him!"

" *'Without me ye can do nothing.'‡ Asking Nedley to do right in the power of self isn't My way. It's your way! I await you to come to Me that I may help you. I will not force Myself on you, although I'm here for you! You need My presence, wisdom, and power to reach Nedley's heart. Unless you allow Me to direct the battle, the best you can hope for from him is outward compliance—not a change in the current of his thoughts. Do you recall your previous talk with him? What were you going to do to help train him in a right way if he could not talk kindly to you while doing his lessons?"*

She thought a while, "Hmm, oh, yes. He would have to do his lessons without my assistance. Oh Lord, that is so hard for me; that is probably why I forgot about it. I'm too soft to motivate him to change when he asserts himself so strongly. I tend to leave his selfish ways unchallenged—only to face worse later. I'm determined to train him in the basics of hearing Your voice to his soul. He needs to come to You, make a decision, and do the right." And so she quietly left the room praying.

During break time, Mother returned to see how Nedley was doing. Negative Nedley spewed forth rude and unkind words to Mother.

"Lord, should I send him on a grizzly run?" Mother asked.

"No."

"What then?" She sensed God reasoning with her to use stronger measures to motivate Nedley to exchange his old ways of responding for better ones.

"Nedley, I'm sorry you've chosen to speak this way. I can see you are not happy. God wants to lead you in a way that will make you happy, but you must cooperate with Him. To help you learn to do that, I'm requiring you to write a page in your journal about how a young man should speak to his mother. I encourage you to do it with God—it will be much easier that way—and you must do it after your schoolwork is done and before you eat lunch."

Nedley exploded with anger.

"Lord, what now?"

"Zacharias . . ." the Holy Spirit led.

---

*Philippians 4:13, NKJV.
†Proverbs 23:7.
‡John 15:5.

She understood. "Son, because of your response, you may not speak for one hour. Remember Zacharias? He lost the privilege of speaking for more than nine months because He didn't trust God. God is here with you, and He can change your ugly disposition if you give Him your ugliness. Call out to God, take His hand, co-operate with courage, and trust Jesus. He is there for you, and you must choose to believe the truth instead of the lies of Satan. It's the only way!"

"Nedley, I am here for you," God whispered to Nedley's heart. *"I've always been here. Take My hand, and I'll lead you to walk in new pathways, happier lanes, and get you over the obstacles in the way."*

Nedley was almost persuaded, but wouldn't yield. The old, familiar path seemed easier. The loud, compelling voice of his flesh was stronger and seemed more believable.

Thirty minutes later, Nedley and his mother went out for their walk. It was springtime with blossoms all around, puppies dancing at their feet, and sunshine on their backs, yet Negative Nedley could see nothing good. He was silent, and his countenance revealed plainly that he still cherished negative thoughts while pushing away the positive ones.

Mother stopped and prayed out loud, "Lord, please bring peace to Nedley's heart as You calmed the stormy sea so long ago."

Nedley was unmoved. Twice, negative words slipped out of his mouth. Mother filtered her response through God this time and then said kindly but firmly, "Instead of one hour of silence, your unbelief and lack of self-control has earned you two and a half hours of silence."

Mother was beginning to waver inside. It was hard to be this firm when she couldn't see a positive response. God whispered to her mind, *"When mild measures do not work you must go to firmer measures in a heavenly spirit, not a fleshly spirit."*

Mother settled more confidently into the fact that this was not too strong.

Back at home, Nedley went upstairs to tackle his schoolwork again while Mother went to work in the kitchen crying out to God to intervene for her son. After a time, she checked on him. His countenance had softened; he looked very sad. He handed her a note expressing how discouraged he felt. It seemed like God was piling upon him all the wrongs he had done and there was no way to overcome them.

"Son," she said with deep love, "this is the devil discouraging you, not God. These thoughts and feelings are not God's character. God would stand before you with His hands outstretched to help you. The devil will whip you with negative thoughts and paint your hopelessness before you on a big screen in living color. Discouragement comes from the devil. Jesus is waiting to give you peace, rest, and freedom from this bondage. But you must choose Jesus' ways instead of your negative thoughts and emotions. Your emotions need not rule you; they are not to be trusted. If you put yourself in Jesus' hands, He will subdue those wrong emotions *inside*. You must trust God's words and act upon them in spite of your feelings. God can be trusted—not your present feelings."

He made no response.

Mother returned to the kitchen trusting in Jesus although there was no evidence of change. God was teaching her through this experience that part of discipline is correcting misconceptions without demeaning her youth. She was discipling her son to Christ so that Christ could come in and empower him to respond in a new way.

Meanwhile, Negative Nedley was beginning to see a different picture. Instead of seeing God as stern, unjust, and exacting, He saw Jesus with His arms outstretched, tender eyes beckoning, *"Come, come, come unto Me."*

Nedley responded, "I do want to follow You! But I'm afraid."

"Take My hand and we can walk together. If you choose to follow Me, I'll take away that fear and make you into Positive Nedley. Would you like that?"

Nedley was beginning to feel accepted for who he was. This growing trust nurtured faith that Jesus could change him, if he took His hand, and followed His lead. "I *can't* talk with Mother right now but I *can* talk to You." So they chatted.

Mother was still praying as she worked in the kitchen. She heard a footstep behind her and turned to see Nedley approaching her with a sweet smile on his face. He still was not allowed to talk, but he put his arms tenderly around his mother as he handed her a note asking if he could write a poem in his composition book for his consequence.

"Lord, is that all right?" Mother inquired, and she felt affirmed.

"Yes, that's fine," she said. Here is what Nedley wrote:

What words should we speak to our mothers?
Fretful, arguing, hateful, unkind, unloving words?
Maybe selfish, mean, unthankful, insulting words?
No, we should speak instead, kind, thoughtful words,
For after all, our mothers love us.

What words should we speak to our mothers?
Wretched, whining, sinful, unbelieving, un-heavenly words?
No, we should speak uplifting, encouraging, heavenly words.
Comforting, godly words—"pointing to Jesus" words.
For after all, our mothers love us.

Tears came to Mother's eyes as she read his poem. She saw Nedley's sincere repentance and sweet spirit. Negative Nedley had let Jesus come inside, and He had worked a genuine change—not the usual outward compliance thinly veiling a stubborn heart. Nedley's heart was completely softened and subdued. In Christ he found strength to face and deny the old way and courage to embrace God's new way and walk in it!

Mother also saw that her love expressed both in tenderness and in firmness had motivated him to risk taking Jesus' hand. Yet, the redemption was neither in what Mother *did*, nor in what Nedley *performed*. It was in knowing the voice of a personal Savior and cooperating to take His hand and follow God's way instead of the old familiar way. When Christ is enthroned, Satan must obey Christ and leave. Thus he loses his captive!

In this way, by repetition over time, Negative Nedley was transformed into Positive Nedley in an ever-increasing freedom from negativity. Nedley yielded to go round and round in the circular pen following Jesus as his Trainer.

Don't you want to help your youth know this kind of mother, this kind of God, and this kind of freedom? With God your Sassy Susie can become Sweet Susie, and Lazy Lucy becomes Helpful Lucy. A vital connection with Christ makes the liar, honest; the disobedient, obedient; the fearful, calm; the scarred, healed; the disorderly, orderly; and the unworthy, valuable. From what does your teen need cleansing? Or deliverance? Or in what does he or she need transformation? God is there to re-create all who come to Him. True discipline is disciple(ing) your child to Christ. Under Christ's discipleship, changes occur—beginning from the heart and flowing into a new life.

Discipline is a replacement principle

Interruptive Ivy interrupted Mother while she was on the phone with a friend. She did it without a second thought because she had always been allowed to interrupt and she knew no other way.

Mother prayed to the all-knowing God for direction to turn the habits of her daughter to God that He might change this wrong way.

"What would you have her to do instead of interrupting?" God asked.

Mother began to reason. Then, by faith, she cooperated to do what she felt God was leading her to do—apply the replacement principle of replacing the wrong with the right.

"Ivy, you may not interrupt me that way," admonished Mother kindly. "You need to go into the other room and pray to Jesus for strength to change. Then come here again and tap me on the shoulder and wait quietly for my response. You can do this with your hand in Jesus' hand."

Mother resumed the phone conversation with her friend, but prayerfully watched as her daughter bowed her head. Ivy was familiar with this process of a surrender prayer. In a few moments Ivy was back, gently tapping her mother's shoulder.

Mother waited for God's direction before responding to her former Interruptive Ivy. In God's time she answered her daughter's question quietly, and Ivy went happily on her way. This was the beginning of replacing a bad habit with a good one as God worked inside Ivy to give her His heart and attitude.

How much better it is to show our children what is right and see that they do it than it is to rail on them for what they should not be doing. "Be not overcome of evil, but overcome evil with good."*

Fifteen-year-old Disrespectful Darlene stomped into the kitchen complaining that she couldn't find the clothes she needed. "You didn't wash my clothes like you should have!" she accused her mother impatiently.

---

*Romans 12:21.

This disrespect was a growing problem, and Mother's first thought was to lash out in the flesh as she had done so many times before. "Am I your slave? You never help with the housework. When will you learn to be grateful or at least respectful?" But God's still, small voice interrupted her thoughts before she spoke them.

"Mother, this approach won't work! You need to come to Me for a better way. Wasn't that your prayer this morning?" God's voice was a thought in her mind, not an audible voice.

"Oh yes, Lord, I do need help. What would You have me to do with this issue?"

"Entreat her kindly. See her pent-up disgust? What's driving her?"

Mother looked into Darlene's eyes and determined that ingratitude was driving her disrespect. She reasoned, "If Darlene is ungrateful, then I need to cultivate the opposite trait of gratitude. I need to help her to see the value of work. She needs to keep her own room clean and make her bed. She needs to do the laundry and ironing regularly. Lord, help me to use the replacement principle under Your guidance."

"Darlene, I washed and ironed your clothes yesterday and put them on your bed. Let's go look for them."

Darlene grumblingly followed Mother to her room and they both explored the heaps of clothes scattered here and there throughout the room. Soon Mother found the clothes Darlene was looking for piled on the floor.

"How did they get here?" Mother inquired.

"Oh, I just threw them off last night to go to bed," Darlene recalled.

"Well I think we need to change—beginning today. You are becoming a young lady and need to take responsibility for your own room. I can see I've hurt you by doing it for you. Right now I'd like you to straighten up your room—put your clothes away properly and make your bed, and then I'll teach you how to do the laundry and ironing today."

Disrespectful Darlene began to respond with her usual complaining and arguing. Mother realized that she had cultivated these wrong habits of thinking and responding by allowing her to speak this way and doing all the work herself—to keep the peace. But this was no peace at all. She was now determined to do all that God wanted her to do to restrain the wrong and cultivate the right.

"What shall I do with this arguing, Lord?"

"Give her nothing for which she cries. Tell her nicely what you expect her to do, give her time with Me to change her attitude and enlist her will to do the right so she can find true happiness."

"Darlene, stop talking that way. That is not good." And Darlene stopped. Mother was different; she wasn't yelling, crying, or fretting as usual. "You can have nothing for which you cry," Mother told her. "You are acting like a little child; you don't want to do that. You are God's young lady. Take ten minutes to talk with God so He can change your attitude. Then make your room neat and orderly. Come out to do the laundry, and we can talk further then. It will take only twenty minutes here and a few minutes with the laundry. Then you can do what you planned."

Disrespectful Darlene continued to argue and fuss. God led Mother to send her on a grizzly run, but that didn't convince her to yield and be sweet. So God led

Mother to have her scrub the toilet and tub. Then Darlene began to listen. Mother repeated her former request and appealed to Darlene to follow Jesus instead of self. Darlene was finally convinced and surrendered to her mother and to God.

The disrespect in Darlene was starved of expression. Mother repeatedly took her to Christ—her Trainer—and He empowered her to yield to God's will and surrender her will. Cooperating with God, her feelings, thoughts, and attitudes changed over a reasonable amount of time. Mother was pleased to see Grateful Darlene emerge like a butterfly out of the cocoon. Happiness reigned in the home—what a blessing!

The replacement principle is telling our youth in a respectful, kind, loving, yet firm, way what to do right instead of what they are doing wrong. It is exchanging sassiness for sweetness, unwillingness for willingness, disrespect for respect, indolent habits for industry, hate for love, passion for self-control, an unforgiving spirit for a forgiving one, and disorder for neatness. It is winning the heart, giving consequences where necessary, and connecting them to God. God uses both blessings bestowed and blessings removed to motivate us to come to Him. We, too, can use this in our discipline if our motivation is Heaven-led and not driven by self. We want our youth to experience victory in Him rather than to serve passion and self.

God is there for you, parent and youth, and will be your personal Trainer to teach you these rudimentary beginnings of a life hid with Christ in God.* Discipline is replacing wrong with right by yielding to God.

Discipline is changing masters

Unkempt Ulrich sauntered to breakfast with his shirt, four sizes too big, hanging to his knees and oversized shorts that barely hung on his hips, drooping to mid-calf. His hair was spiked as if he had stuck his finger in a light socket, and his countenance wore a perpetual smirk. Mother requested, "Please finish setting the table."

He grumbled, "Why don't you do it yourself?"

Mother winced. Oh how she hated this response! She remembered how sweet and innocent Ulrich had been when he was eleven. However, when he turned twelve, something changed. He wanted to dress and act like all the other kids. At first, it was only pants one size too big. Creeping compromise took over, and the sloppiness grew—along with a careless and unhelpful attitude. Most of the time he was merely indifferent, but became downright sassy when approached to help with anything. He had no interest in spiritual things and loved only to be with his friends who were just like him, if not worse.

Unkempt Ulrich was listening to the voice of his flesh—his lower powers of impulse and inclination. The voice of God was speaking to his heart as well, appealing to his higher powers of reason, intellect, and conscience—calling him to upright living. But Ulrich turned away from these thoughts. God's way seemed to be too hard, too undesirable, and too unpopular. His experience told him that his efforts to be good always failed, and it just seemed so much more attractive to follow the path

---

*John 6:45; Jude 24; Jeremiah 32:27.

of least resistance. Hence he chose to make his flesh his master, and Mother allowed it.

Now he was seventeen, and Mother was concerned. Her church friends assured her this behavior was normal. Ulrich would sow his wild oats and come out of it in time. After all, he knew about Jesus, and the Bible says, "Train up a child in the way he should go: and when he is old, he will not depart from it."* And yet, Mother was uneasy.

"Lord, something is wrong with my concepts. Am I too strict, too straitlaced, too firm, or too soft? I'm so confused."

"Training a child in the way he should go is training him to follow Me. It's teaching him the right exercise of his will. It's leading him to experience My grace to transform his thoughts and feelings, empowering him to do right. Have you done this? To just know about Me and have intellectual knowledge isn't enough. Am I Lord of his life? Does he know My voice and follow Me? When Samuel was trained up in this way—he chose Me as his Master and followed Me instead of his flesh and Satan.

"What are the fruits of your son's character, his manners, and deportment? When you compare them with Galatians chapter five, who is his master—Satan or Me?"

Mother wasn't sure, so she began to study for herself. She found many texts in Deuteronomy about teaching children manners. Leviticus opened her understanding of the firm discipline God gave to His people in love—so that they might know Him and be set free to do right. When mild measures didn't work, He went to the firmest means necessary. She read in Galatians of the fruit of the Spirit and the lusts of the flesh. No, she concluded, she hadn't trained her son in the way to go. She could not claim the promise. She grasped that her son needed that new heart that only Jesus can give.†

More than that, Mother saw that *she* needed that new heart, too. She surrendered her stony heart to God and asked Him to replace it with His tender heart. She saw the need to change her parenting approach so that Unkempt Ulrich would know how to serve God instead of self and worldly ways. Her study showed her that God was not leading her to indulge her son's wrong desires and then lose her temper at him. *She* had to change, too!

"Lord," she prayed, "You are in charge of my life now, and I'm willing to learn to filter all I say and do through You before doing it. You have my permission to tap me on the shoulder to correct my misconceptions or interrupt my thoughts. My child is in Your hands; help me teach him how to become one of Your followers and let You be his God." Now, with her hand in God's hand, she timidly approached her son.

"Ulrich, sit down here. We need to talk about your life. First, I have been remiss in letting you dress as you do and have harmed you as a result. Second, your lack of interest in God is due to my bad representation of Him. Will you forgive me, son?"

"Hey, Mom, it's all right. I forgive you," he said flippantly.

"You are a young man now and need to learn to follow God—not me, and not your friends. Only God has your best interest at heart. His counsel can be trusted

---

*Proverbs 22:6.
†Ezekiel 36:25, 26.

where human counsel, ideas, and concepts can't be. It doesn't matter what I think or what you think but only what God thinks. I want you to study dress, deportment, and how to let God be your personal Friend, Savior, and Guide. You are presently following Satan but don't know it. I'm asking you to change masters because that is best for you. Our whole family has to change our ways and come back to God. Are you with me?"

"I've been noticing a change in you over the past several months, Mother. You have been struggling. But you have also been kinder and more serious of late. I like the change in you, but I'm not sure it's for me. I don't know where to begin or what to do to change. I know what I'm doing doesn't please God or you, but Mom, I like it."

"Lord, what do I say?" A thought entered her mind, and she followed it, trusting in Jesus for the rest.

"Ulrich, you are heading down the wide path that leads to destruction. I'm just veering off that road myself. I thought I was a Christian because I assented mentally to believing about Jesus. I'm seeing that just knowing truths about God doesn't make me His. I don't *know* Him as a Savior from self. A living Christian follows God; I follow self more. My present religion is powerless to change my habits. You and I have been following self, not God. We can change that by personally seeking God as a Friend, praying to know His voice, and giving Him time to talk to us and teach us."

That is where they began. Unkempt Ulrich submitted to spend time with God. Some days he was very cooperative; other days he was resistant. His mother continued to encourage him, and in time Ulrich began to recognize God's voice to his conscience. The Word of God began to become his standard. His thoughts were transformed one by one, and his feelings of resistance toward God faded away.

Unkempt Ulrich discovered by experimentation that saying no to self was the greatest battle ever fought. To act in opposition to established habits of thinking was like a hand-to-hand battle with Satan himself.* But putting God in charge of the battle brought victory. Saying yes to God made saying no to the flesh easier because God's grace empowered his choice to do things God's way instead of the old familiar way. In this way, he became a winner![†]

Ulrich began to recognize God speaking to him while he was with his associates. God revealed the cruelty hidden in joking about others. He chose not to participate. As time progressed, Ulrich began to find his friends' music, activities, ideas, and attitudes less and less attractive. Heavenly concepts began to look desirable, and earthly concepts were seen as inferior. Soon his associates began to call him Mr. Goody Two-Shoes. This was painful to him but also revealed to him just what kind of friends they really were.

He and his mother went round and round the training circle to master proper manners and regular personal worships. Family worships were added and used to

---

*Ephesians 6:12.
[†]James 4:7.

nurture their new experience with God and to address the issues they were currently facing.

One such issue was music. Satan uses the wrong kind of music to enchant his captives and hold them in bondage to wrong thoughts and feelings. God uses right music to encourage and inspire noble thoughts and feelings. God was agitating Mother's mind about this subject. One day she challenged Ulrich on this topic, and a fierce battle ensued.

Satan didn't want to lose a captive; he fought valiantly to keep this stronghold. But Mother and God were more valiant. Mother was learning how to remain Christlike even under provocation. Ulrich's emotions yelled, pushed, and demanded he listen to this un-Christlike music. His old habits drove him as if he had no choice in the matter. For a time, Ulrich's progress reached a plateau because *not* to decide for Christ *was* to decide for Satan to be master of this place in his heart.

When he began to see that he did not control his music—rather it controlled him—he began desiring freedom. Choice by choice, he yielded his musical tastes to God and cooperated in new thought patterns. God's standards won out. God evicted Satan and delivered Ulrich from the control of these musical tastes. Old things were passing away, and Unkempt Ulrich was fast becoming Unfettered Ulrich.

One day, Unfettered Ulrich looked in the mirror and was very displeased with his personal appearance, "How would Jesus dress were He me?" he wondered.

He started caring about representing Christ correctly in this world. Finally, he asked Mother to go with him to buy some new clothes; he told her how God was nudging him in this matter, but leaving him free to choose. He was choosing to serve God because of love to Jesus for all He had done for him. Mother joyfully bought some clothes that were neat, clean, and well fitting. No more clown outfits with their veneer of laughter and foolishness to hide an empty and broken heart!

Unfettered Ulrich was beginning to understand that God wanted him to dress in a way that reflected the changes that were being made in his heart. He realized that God wanted his outward appearance to show the neatness, order, and taste of heaven and that God wanted to build his sense of respect for himself as a beloved son of God.

When his old friends saw his new attire, they ridiculed him. However, he didn't feel hurt or even sorry for himself. Why? The empty void in his heart was filled to overflowing with Jesus. The need for association with the rebellious was no longer there. Their freedom was no real freedom at all. He had real freedom in Christ. He was free from careless attitudes, slouchy manners, bad music, and much more. Now he was gaining purpose, direction, and the power to live uprightly. God gave him a new kind of love for his friends and a desire to tell them about Jesus and how to be *truly* free in Him.

True discipline is leading our youth to change masters! It's leading them to leave the bondage of man's destroyer and enter the service of man's Restorer. It's learning to walk with God as Enoch did. It's finding the strength to live in harmony with upright convictions, and to find rest and purpose in the innermost soul. This is what I want for my children. Changing masters is a must! Won't you find Him too?

THE LONE EMBRACE
A SPECIAL WORD OF ENCOURAGEMENT FOR SINGLE PARENTS

Do you feel confused and frustrated at always being alone to manage the children, the finances, the schooling, and the discipline in character development? It's just too much! You know that you don't have the relationship with Jesus that is available to you—and you want it. But where do you get the time? Seeing your children following a similar path brings pain to your heart when you have time to think honestly.

Your overwhelmed feelings should drive you to Jesus, your Friend and Savior. Set your priorities in order. Get His wisdom at the beginning of every day. The cost doesn't matter. What is more important than your own walk with God so that you can share what you are learning with your youth before it is forever too late? Follow Jacob with his head on a stone, gaining the vision of the ladder. God has placed this ladder of communication there for you to see and talk with Him. He will fill the empty place in your heart, and you need never be alone again. God is there for you. True discipline is letting God lead you in the beginning of your day and at every moment throughout your day. What He has done for these mothers and countless others, He wants to do for you!

Andrew, age 14, feeding the pet deer, Baby Saved. God intends for us to appreciate and care for His creation.

Chapter 14

Useful Labor

*And thou shalt teach them ordinances and laws, and shalt shew them the way wherein they
must walk, and the work that they must do.*
—Exodus 18:20

Neglected

Twenty-year-old Haphazard Harry was a hit-and-miss type of guy who avoided work as much as possible. Once more he was trying—unsuccessfully—to land a job. His usual story was that someone else got preferential treatment while he was treated unfairly. Reality, however, was that he couldn't keep a job because he promised much and delivered little.

He had lost his last job as stock boy in a hardware store because of the trail of unfinished jobs he continually left behind him. He preferred to talk rather than work. He did not discipline himself to complete a task. No, he did not have attention deficit disorder. He was simply unwilling to apply himself in heart, mind, or will. He rather liked the slothful life. When called to account for his unfinished work, he fabricated excuses and expected to get away with them because he always had at home. God says, "Train up a child in the way he should go: and when he is old, he will not depart from it."* Haphazard Harry was living the way he was trained.

He also justified his situation by seeing himself as a "wise fellow" who was above menial labor. He felt destined to greatness in a managerial or self-employed position. Physical work was for peons. He deserved to be served. After eating a meal with friends, he wouldn't lift a finger to clear the table or help wash or dry dishes. He preferred to relax in a chair leisurely gazing out the window while others did the work.

Finally, through his parents' efforts, he was given an opportunity to be a real estate agent in a locale where he was little known. Moreover, a successful agent was willing to take him under his wing and train him—a great advantage. However, he would have to study and pass the real estate exams, and that required effort—something Harry was reluctant to put forth. He did make some efforts, however, and after the second try managed to just pass the test.

Accustomed as Harry was to get by with minimal effort, the beginning of his career was fraught with many trials, each revealing his character defects and lack of work skills. His benefactor gave him a lot of sound advice, and Haphazard Harry looked important with his new notebook and pen in hand, but little was recorded, and what was recorded was not referenced. Appointments were set up for him to show property, but often he would either arrive late or not show up at all. Consequently, he lost sales. Of course, he had his usual excuses. The car chose to run out

---

*Proverbs 22:6.

of gas. The alarm failed to go off in the morning. The secretary didn't get him the message. It was always someone else's fault!

His mentor recommended that he get on a schedule and go to bed and get up on time so that he could get to work on time. "Oh," he responded, "I just get involved with my computer, and the only time I have to read is in the evening, and the next thing I know it's after midnight. And I don't believe in missing my sleep, so I just let my body wake me up when it is ready. And I have to fend for myself, you know. I don't have anyone to fix my meals, or clean up, or do my laundry, or pay my bills. So I just do the best I can."

Haphazard Harry really felt sorry for himself. He often called his mother to tell her his woes and trials and ask for help. To her, he painted a picture of working very hard, when actually he was hardly working. He was extremely lazy, and God, out of love for him, was allowing all these discomforts to attempt to stimulate self-evaluation and awaken a desire to change for the better. Unfortunately, his mother interrupted God's plan by rescuing Harry from the natural consequences of his irresponsibility. She sent him food, gathered information he needed, and sent him money because "business was slow this time of year." For Harry, oddly enough, it was slow all year round. But Mother provided for his needs just as she always had.

Is God directing this young man's ideas and character? No! Harry is listening and submitting to the voice of another master. Jesus came to redeem us *from* serving sin, not to save us *in* sin. Does God want Harry to continue as he is? No! Does God want Mother to rescue him? No! Mother is enabling the very traits of character that God wants to remove from him. Satan is directing Haphazard Harry, and he is obeying. Why?

It is very simple. All his life, Harry had gotten away with avoiding real work. His parents accepted his tactics, allowed him to exercise slothfulness, and bought into his excuses. They neglected to identify the problem or go before God for direction or give consequences to motivate him away from wrong habits. Through repetition of these wrong habits, Haphazard Harry was convinced that evasion, lying, and laziness were acceptable.

Likewise, his apartment was a sad testimony to these same character flaws. Countertops stacked high with dirty dishes, laundry dumped wherever most convenient, books and papers strewn everywhere, an unmade bed, dirty bathroom—all told the story of his neglect to submit to good work habits. Of course he *claimed* he was too busy with all the real estate work to clean his apartment. In reality, the physical mismanagement of his apartment depicted the spiritual mismanagement of his mind and character—each cluttered, uncared for, irresponsible, without God, and—sadly—well satisfied with himself.

Haphazard Harry has been crippled by the lack of training in useful labor in his childhood years. He is totally unfit for real adult life. He will have difficulty in every job he obtains. He will not have the necessary skills to be a true husband or father. Unless he sees his need and takes hold of his Savior for substantial change, his chances for happiness in this life and the next are ruined.

How can we help Haphazard Harry?

Over and over again—until it becomes habit

The training pen for an "indolent stallion" must be something like a boot camp. The military enlists young recruits and forces them through a rather brutal program with the goal of overriding the learning of the past eighteen years and molding them into strong men, submissive to military authority. Now I am not recommending that we be brutal as parents, but there are some valid parallels for us to examine.

First, we must enlist the cooperation of our youth. Of course, we do not approach a twenty-year-old like we would an eight-year-old. A twenty-year-old is an adult and needs to be approached by entreaty and reason, like Jesus would—not force. We want to gain the mind, heart, and will. But to get a mule to move when it chooses not to is impossible without some external motivation—either from God, circumstances, or a loving parent. Often the best motivation is to stop enabling the bad habit, call him to account for neglected responsibilities, and allow him to experience the consequences of his bad choices. God can show you how to implement this for *your* youth. When your Haphazard Harry is motivated to make changes, the Trainer explains to him the program necessary to turn him into an Industrious Harry.

First, he must be willing to put God in charge. Haphazard Harry must learn to recognize the voice of his Trainer and trust and obey Him supremely. He must come to see God as his personal Friend, Savior, and Lord and commit himself to know and do His will. That's why personal worship needs to be put in place. For it is here he learns how to talk to God, to hear His voice, and want to change. Jesus said, "My sheep hear my voice, and I know them, and they follow me."* True worship is to talk with God and to connect to His power. It's a commitment to follow Him even when I don't want to. It's yielding to His will rather my own. And it's a step of faith!

The Trainer instructs and challenges Haphazard Harry to go to bed by 9:00 PM in order to get up at 5:00 AM to provide time with God. To live a scheduled life is a discipline. Going round and round in the pen, he cooperates to exercise these habits until they are established. New muscles strengthen. The new replaces the old until the new becomes a part of him—with or without a rein or trainer or the boundaries of the pen.

As parents, outline your youth's responsibilities and require them to do each task thoroughly, completely, and timely while promoting self-government.† This process is not easy. It requires determination and effort—as it would for a three-hundred-pound man who has decided to reach his ideal weight of one hundred and fifty pounds. It's going to take a lot more than mere desire and good intentions. It will take a lot of hard work, sweat, and perseverance. He must choose that new life. He must trust his fitness trainer more than himself in order to think and respond in God's way, not his own way.

---

*John 10:27.

†For more information on this point, please consult chapter 16 of my book *Parenting Your Child by the Spirit*.

Haphazard Harry will have to work just as hard as the three-hundred-pound man—except that his greatest battle will be in his mind. He must obey the Trainer in spite of all his habits, feelings, thoughts, and even his history calling him in the opposite direction. But resistive exercise builds good muscle—so be encouraged.

You can do it. Jesus, the General in the warfare of the Christian life, has never lost a battle. The only way to lose is by neglecting to obey the Commander. Not to decide to follow Christ is to decide to follow Satan, sin, and self.

As an infant learns by repeated attempts to turn over, to coordinate his hand with his eye, to crawl, and to walk, so Haphazard Harry learns to be Industrious Harry. He must keep putting forth effort to resist the old ways, to respond as Christ would and not follow the way he's learned in his earthly school of life. He must repeatedly cry out to God and do His will instead of his own.*

In the process of instilling these new habits, wrong ways of thinking will be challenged. These are golden opportunities to allow God to change wrong con-cepts.† If Harry continues to feel that work is beneath him or that he is special and deserves to be served, these lies will hinder change. To retain these thoughts would be like the three-hundred-pound man still retaining his eating habits and sitting around hoping to lose 150 pounds. Change takes effort! Exercising weak muscles is essential to gaining physical strength; exercising our spiritual muscles by saying yes to God and no to self is essential to changing wrong habits of thinking. God's grace needs our cooperation if He is going to be able to do the inner work in us that only He can do.

Haphazard Harry must put effort into thinking, and responding as though the following is true: "Work is fun; work is good for me; and through God I will learn to enjoy serving rather than being served. Jesus came as a servant, and so shall I be." Round and round in the pen the slothful stallion goes, trusting and obeying Jesus and finding new ways replacing the old.

When my boys were just learning to wash the dishes, clean their room, or build a birdhouse, I would tell them, "Don't worry! You will learn if you apply your will and effort. When you have done a task a hundred times you become a professional. You may start out awkward, but by repetition you will become quick and skillful at this task."

In the Bible record Samson daily yielded to habits of obeying his fleshly passion and immorality as a young adult. His choices developed his weaknesses that brought so much trouble into his life. He was physically strong, but was weak in character and unwilling to follow God when to do so opposed his inclination. Joseph, on the other hand, was strong in exercising the muscles of self-denial, self-control, morality, and integrity by submission to God. By choice and exercise Joseph became strong to do God's will—not his own. What we exercise becomes our strength. God did not force Samson to do right nor will He us. We have the free will to choose whom we will serve today, at this moment. God wants us to choose as Joseph did.

---

*Luke 22:42.
†Romans 7:23.

Haphazard Harry began by learning to wash the dishes. He engaged in a fierce inward battle of casting out wrong thoughts and listening to what God wanted him to think. As he persevered he became skilled at doing dishes, then doing the laundry, then adding general order in his little apartment, and progressed to tidiness in every drawer and cupboard. Seeking, hearing, and following the voice of God gave him the foundation for success everywhere. Thus Haphazard Harry was set free to become Industrious Harry.

Under God, Industrious Harry has the tools to be successful as a real estate agent.

Useful labor develops character

Andrew, age thirteen, was hired to mow the lawn for our neighbor. Mr. White watched Andrew as he made nice straight lines through the grass. Andrew was a good, trustworthy worker. He recalled that he had asked Andrew to keep the snow off the metal roof of his cabin this past winter while he was gone so that our heavy snows would not cave it in. Andrew had been very dependable and the cabin was well cared for. Little did Mr. White know how much fun Andrew and Matthew turned that job into! They would slide down the roof and fly off into the snow banks below. Oh what fun! Something else Mr. White didn't know was that good work habits had not come naturally to Andrew. Andrew was, by nature, a Haphazard Harry!

Somehow, Satan had convinced my Andrew at an early age that he couldn't do a good job and that he didn't like to do hard things. Consequently, he thought he didn't like to work and easily gave up on himself while avoiding things that seemed difficult or unpleasant. I discovered this character flaw when I began to require him to help with household duties. Over and over, day after day I found dishes put away with food left on them. He scrubbed the tub begrudgingly. His bed was made poorly.

God led me to deal with him at the level of his wrong thoughts, then his wrong feelings and habits. I repeatedly called him to turn to God, take His hand, and do the right in God's strength—not just on his own. Little by little he gave God chances to change his wrong thoughts until he was able to do hard things happily—like mowing the lawn, washing the dishes, or scrubbing the tub.

"Andrew you do such a good job!" Mr. White complimented him. "I'd like to say thank you in a special way. I run the motel in Kalispell. Anytime you are in town, you and your family may swim in the pool free of charge. Would you like that?"

"Oh, would I! Thank you very much!" Andrew smiled real big.

This was a double blessing. We had moved to our wilderness home when Andrew was four years old. Matthew had been old enough to learn to swim before we moved, but not Andrew. My swimming instructions had been limited because the water here is *so cold*. Ten or fifteen minutes in the lake or river was maximum water exposure. So Andrew could swim, but not well. He always felt like a fifth wheel because he couldn't swim like the rest of us and wasn't sure that he ever could. So this new opportunity challenged him to face a hard thing and change another negative stumbling block into a positive stepping-stone by surrender and cooperative effort with God.

On our next town day, we set aside two hours for swimming. I got in the pool with Andrew and gave him a swimming lesson. Then Jim and I relaxed in the sun watching Andrew swim back and forth, kicking his feet and trying to coordinate his strokes. Occasionally, we would stop him and give him pointers for improvement, and he took it well. He didn't react defensively or feel belittled as he had formerly. Jim and I would enter the pool occasionally to play tag or keep-away. Learning to swim was hard work for Andrew, but also a lot of fun. After several trips to town, he was swimming really well. He saw God's love and wisdom in giving him this opportunity to learn to swim—to work hard and in the process face lying thoughts and deny them. He began to see that daily duties of work are fun—if you let God put the right attitude inside.

Instruction, discipline, correction, and doing hard work all took on new meaning to Andrew. As these new attitudes, thoughts, and responses were repeated, they developed better habits to do God's will. Useful labor is a tool God uses to develop character after heaven's order and set Satan's captives free in mind and heart.

Useful labor develops purpose and direction for life

Matthew was twelve years old and Andrew was ten when the Benson brothers built our guest cabin. The Bensons agreed to train the boys in carpentry according to their abilities. Matthew enjoyed details and was soon given permission to cut boards with the chop saw. The brothers tested him by giving him measurements ending with five-eighths, seven-sixteenths, and six-fourths. He was challenged, but accurate, in understanding their directions, and soon became a valuable helper. Matthew loved learning precise skills and quickly gained confidence. After our guest cabin was completed, the Benson brothers went on to other work, but they appreciated both Matthew and Andrew so much that they hired them to help with construction work whenever they were in our area.

Matthew and Andrew were fifteen and thirteen respectively when they offered to build Jim a workbench in the garage. They would design it, and build it. Father would approve it and supply the materials.

Jim agreed heartily, and soon they had the plan all drawn out and accepted.

I stipulated, "This will be a wonderful project, but it is *not* to be done at the neglect of your daily chores or schoolwork. It is to be done only during your *free time*."

All agreed, and the work began. The boys had purpose and direction for their daily use of time. Personal time with God, chores, meals, schoolwork, and evening family fun were all done at the proper time in good spirit so that they would have all their free time to work on their new project.

Within a few months the first workbench was finished. It measured thirteen feet long, three and a half feet high, and three feet deep and was divided into five sections. It had double door cupboard combinations and a variety of unbelievably long drawers with smooth wood glides. It was beautiful and upon close inspection was built very solidly with attention to detail!

"This is a very functional workbench; you boys did great! Thank you so much," Jim said giving each boy a hug.

"Now which drawer or cupboard is mine, Jim? You are going to share, aren't you?" I asked.

"No, these are *all* mine. You have the house. I have the garage," he teased.

"Our home doesn't offer enough storage space. If you can't share, then maybe these great carpenters could build some cupboards right here for me," I pointed to a vacant corner of the garage and looked with a loving twinkle in my eye at Matthew and Andrew.

"Well, we could do that for you, Mother, but Father has to buy the materials," the boys responded.

"I'll buy the materials, but first you boys need to build me a workbench for our chain saws over here in this corner. You can design what will fit in this space. When you do good work like this, you are sought after!"

Both boys smiled. "Oh, Father, that would be great. We saw a workbench in the chain saw store. They mounted a cleanly peeled tree trunk between the bench and the ceiling and cut slots in it to store the chain saws. We have enough room here for our three chain saws! It'll be great!"

In time, both the chain saw bench and my cupboards were completed. The chain saw bench was like the workbench except that it was seven feet long. The cupboards were eight and one-half feet high and wide and three feet deep. The boys divided them into four large sections, skillfully crafted with shelves and double doors. I finally had my storage space!

The boys thrived, being needed and appreciated. Even Andrew learned to love work and productive occupation such as this, and each new experience taught both boys more valuable skills. Now, twelve years later, there is no carpentry job in their own homes they can't do or learn to do. More than this, their accomplishments instilled in them a sense of self-respect and value. It gave purpose and direction and formed a valuable heritage of both skill and character growth. Don't you want this for your youth as well?

Andrew surprised us by designing and building a swing that Jim and I could use during swing time. You can see it on our DVD, *Our Resting Place.*

At fourteen, Andrew participated in all phases of building a home with the Benson brothers. They gave him the assignment of building the generator shed entirely on his own. They were available to answer questions, and he did a very good job.

Andrew, still fourteen years old, was staining a large log cabin for a neighbor. He had become used to pushing himself to overcome his slow work habits. But now, Jim and I noticed the opposite imbalance coming in. Andrew was pushing himself past good work to overwork. We had a talk with him.

"Andrew, we are concerned that you are working too hard now! You need to either slow down your work habits or charge more per hour. You give too much work and push yourself at an unhealthful pace. God will show you the balance—seek Him," we counseled.

With a sheepish grin he said, "I never thought I'd see the day you'd tell me to slow down! OK, I'll take it to God. I'll likely increase my hourly rate *and* slow down a little."

Do you see that character development is all tied up with skills and how you view and value yourself? God has to bring us out of our wrong thoughts before He can effectively bring us into good habits and behaviors. Useful labor is the tool that both tests and builds our true character!

Matthew and Andrew came to us one day all excited. "Let's build a pathway down the steep hill behind us to the road. We can use it as a shortcut for walking, biking, or skiing. It would be great!"

We agreed it was a good idea and discussed the best way to do it. It was hard work digging into the steep hillside, chopping out tree roots, leveling and reinforcing the path with logs. The boys essentially did it all themselves, while we helped from time to time and offered suggestions. It was a simple way to learn the joy of productive work and this process enhanced our property at the same time. Jim and I now gratefully walk that path with many warm memories of our two boys. Great activities can last a lifetime!

We tried to have a home improvement project every year to build the boys' practical skills. Matthew and Andrew were now seventeen and fifteen years old and Jim wanted them to learn concrete work. The boys loved the idea. They dug a three-foot trench under one side of the house and poured a concrete footing—all hand mixed! Then they secured plywood backing between the house and the footing. We hand collected a nice assortment of large, flat, colorful river rock from the nearby North Fork River, and the boys used them to build a maintenance-free, mortared-rock wall from the footing to the bottom of the house. They did the first side together, and then each took one of the remaining sides and completed it.

The boy's next experience was helping a local carpenter hand mix and pour the concrete for a complete basement—walls and floor. Then they helped him build his entire home, including the root cellar, the plumbing, electrical, hydro system, and septic system. What a valuable wealth of experience!

Both do-it-yourself projects and on-the-job training by a skilled worker is good occupation and useful labor. When an opportunity doesn't present itself, make one. Andrew constructed bunk beds at home and then gained the experience of selling them.

Girls, too, need to become proficient in all domestic skills—how to cook healthfully, clean a house thoroughly, care for children wisely, sew skillfully, and garden successfully. They should also do physical labor such as collecting firewood. They can learn good organizational skills and how to use shopping lists to live within their means. They can master these jobs with efficiency, skill, dispatch, and thoroughness and should not require ten hours to do five hours of work. In the process of gaining this experience, girls will find that Jesus can become their Confidant, Guide, and best Friend.

Boys need to master the domestic skills as well as learn how to maintain the home and the car. They should learn a trade while cultivating faithfulness, industriousness, and thoroughness. They should be masters of work and not slaves to it. They should learn how to be leaders in social situations—how to teach, manage, and train others in an encouraging uplifting way. Jesus must become their Lord and Savior.

The hard work and discipline will more than repay all the effort put forth! Andrew, instead of remaining a Haphazard Harry, became Industrious Harry at age fourteen. He is now twenty-seven, happily married with two children, and has just completed building his own home—mostly by himself. What a heritage!

Useful labor tests character

When Matthew was seventeen, I asked him to do the dishes one afternoon, and immediately we had problems. He was very unpleasant in disposition, and I was ready to say something when that still, small voice of God made itself known in my thoughts, saying, *"Study his disposition, Sally. Look into his eyes and see what's going on inside."*

"He is doing the dishes. He doesn't look angry or fearful. All I can read in his expression is stubborn selfishness, and it needs correction."

"You want to enlist your son's heart—his thoughts and feelings—from the path he is in and into a new path, don't you?* Sympathize with him," God reasoned in my mind's thoughts.

I didn't like this suggestion one bit. My inclination was to stomp on this wrong behavior. Matthew knew better. I was irritated!

At last I prayed, "Lord, I must have too much corrective spirit in me right now. Make my disposition sympathetic like Jesus would be."

I didn't feel any different, but I had made my choice and trusted that God would empower me to carry it out as I cooperated. Matthew was big enough that I had to reach up to put my arm over his shoulder.

"Do you feel mistreated having to do these dishes?" I asked tenderly.

He almost jumped in surprise at my words. Then he opened up. "I feel like all I do is 'your' dishes! I not only take my turn at dishes every morning, but you ask me more often than you do Andrew to do your extra bread dishes, too. It's not fair!"

"Really? Well, let me think for a moment," I responded. But in my thoughts, I prayed, "Lord, what do I do with this? He is justifying himself. Am I wasting my time?"

"Is what he said true?"

This made me stop and really think it through, "Well yes, it is true, Lord."

"Then you are in the wrong. Make amends and pray with him."

"All right—be with Matthew and direct his thoughts. But Lord, won't admitting my wrong be detrimental to his respect for me? We shouldn't be wrong, especially with a teen—should we? He'll take advantage, won't he?"

"No, you will gain more respect by being honest and fair rather than being autocratic and above correction. Try it and see."

This takes longer to write than the fragments of time in which it took place, but I turned to Matthew and said, "Matthew . . . um, it's just that . . . Well, I see your

---

*Isaiah 30:21.

point, and you are right. You have done dishes more often than your brother. I will be more sensitive to this. I give you permission to remind me—if you do so nicely—when you see you are being treated unfairly. Thanks for telling me honestly what you think."

Cooperating with God is often like exercising a paralytic muscle that doesn't think it can work. It's awkward, almost painful. I don't know about you, but I don't like admitting I am in the wrong, and this is even harder when the other party's attitude isn't correct. I didn't feel like this situation was completely resolved yet and asked the Lord, "Can I speak to him about his term 'Mother's dishes'?"

"I'll be with you, but do it tenderly, Sally."

"Matthew, I'd like also to point out to you that these dishes are not just 'Mother's dishes,' are they? After all, I made bread four times this week to meet the appetites of some growing boys." I spoke tenderly.

Matthew hesitated, and then said, "Well, I know they are 'our dishes.' I'm sorry; you may correct me in the right spirit if I say it again. I want to change and do what's right, too."

I saw my experience mirrored in my teen through the influence of the Holy Spirit. God was speaking to him and to me, even while I was in the correcting process. We both prayed that God would keep our thoughts, mouths, and commitment to each other to change. Matthew didn't avoid the dishes and proceeded to do them cheerfully, because Christ was on the throne of his heart—and all was well between us.

Useful labor brings out the best and the worst in all members in the home. When we see good traits growing, we can rejoice and nurture them. When we see weeds, we can recognize that God is giving us an opportunity to pull them up. God uses our work to refine us like gold. He calls us to choose against self and turn to Him for direction and power to change. As we thus cooperate, God removes our dross and thus we can help our youth.

Making decisions for the right is so essential and yet so misunderstood today. In the next chapters, let's take a deeper look at how we, under God, can help motivate our youth to make right decisions to follow God and do the right.

THE LONE EMBRACE
A SPECIAL WORD OF ENCOURAGEMENT FOR SINGLE PARENTS

God told Moses to go down to the people and instruct them to wash their clothes, get their tents and belongings in order, sanctify themselves, and cleanse their hearts to be prepared to meet their God before He gave them the Ten Commandments.

God was asking Moses to use the practical duties of daily life to teach them about Him. Where else could you gain a better barometer of what's happening in their thoughts and feelings than through activities that may cross their selfish natures? How better could you know which God they were serving than by looking at their attitudes while they were performing these duties? With every task that you help your young adult to learn to do skillfully, there comes the privilege, under God's direction, to help them to learn to do it cheerfully surrendered to God. On a practical level, this is the cleansing of the heart, and it is what Moses was teaching Israel. In every task, duty, or skill they learn, your youth meet their God by choosing which master is in charge of their lives. Don't let these blessed opportunities fall by the wayside.

Useful labor can be an excellent tool to learn and teach the science of salvation. Learning how to manage keeping a kitchen in order—little attentions often, diligence, and thoroughness—teach us what it takes to keep our spiritual hearts clean and orderly.

There is no better preparation for running their own business one day than to have gone through this process of learning how to do tasks in Christ, skillfully and efficiently. God is with them to bring solutions to every problem. And they stand free in every situation *knowing how* to serve God instead of their flesh. They can stand with integrity and the ability to uphold God's ways in their business just like Joseph. God is there with you to help you in the management and training of your youth in useful labor.

Below: Matthew, age 16, and Andrew, age 14, build their first workbench, then (above), the storage shelves. Learning to build is a practical use of time.

Chapter 15

The Wings of Decision

So then every one of us shall give account of himself to God.
—Romans 14:12

Nicodemus, have you ever heard of anything like that before?" exclaimed Serious Simon. "It stirred me to the bottom of my soul! I felt so drawn to this Man, Jesus, yet He was shaking the very foundation of my view of religion. We Pharisees have always considered ourselves the chosen people, children of Abraham, but He says that we are not—*unless* we do the works of Abraham. At first, I was offended because the realities of my shortcomings so overwhelm me, but deep inside I know He is right. I don't live what I preach, and I know it. It makes sense that a mere lineal descent from Abraham, a mere connection with a church, is of no value without a viable connection with the God of heaven. Do you realize what this means? Do you see the implications if we accept it? It means radical change!"

"I know what you mean, Simon," Nicodemus replied earnestly. "I, too, was stirred! I see that my church attendance, my religious endeavors, aren't enough. Somehow, for years I thought they were, but now I see how ridiculous that is. It's abiding, it's a new birth experience. I need a new heart that only God can give me. In Him, I can live above the pull of my flesh. He said He speaks only what His Father says, so I, too, can speak God's words if I know Him and learn to recognize His voice. Simon, I'm at a crossroads. I want to let God in heaven be the Lord of my life and no longer be in charge of myself. No more doing things my own way. I will follow Him. Instead of using the Scriptures to support my views, I will allow the Holy Spirit to use the Scriptures to teach and change me.

"The idea that Satan is my lord while I'm doing all the right things and going through all the right motions is a startling one. But I see it clearly now—the motivation for my works is what makes the difference. Works are the evidence of my faith and connection with God—glorifying Him, not me."

Nicodemus and Simon seriously pondered Jesus' challenge to accept true religion of the heart. New desires and impulses were springing up within them. Would they be willing to swim upstream against the current of the majority?

Serious Simon made a decision. "Nicodemus, God is calling me to surrender my heart entirely to Him, to give Him permission to rule over me. I want to have what Jesus has—what He said we can have. Subjection to God is restoration to oneself. This divine law of oneness with God through Jesus is the law of liberty as He said so well. Will you join me in prayer right now to commit ourselves to God's keeping and to let Him cleanse us from our wrong ways? I want God to rule over me."

Nicodemus reflected, "Yes, I'm willing to change from trusting in my own good works, deeds, and my church affiliation, and from thinking we are the chosen ones while leaving God out. That's just so crazy! Let's pray."

These two men responded to conviction that the Holy Spirit was bringing to their hearts. Though they didn't understand everything clearly and they knew they would be at odds with their colleagues, they knelt on the ground and made a decision to let Jesus be Lord over all aspects of their life—every thought, word, and deed. They wanted Jesus to be the center of their life and religion. Their hearts were drawn to Him in trust.

Rising from prayer, they were abruptly interrupted by the approach of Rabbi Doubting. They glanced at each other, caution in their eyes.

"I know what you are thinking," he told them, "and you are fools. The church has been around a long time, and its leaders know better. This Jesus is creating division among us with His deceptive ideas. God doesn't want division—we need a united front! If you follow His line of thinking, you'll oppose your leaders—and that is wrong! You must submit to your leaders, gentlemen! If you disregard your church's authority, you are disregarding God Himself. The voice of the church is the voice of God! Don't follow this man Jesus who does these works of Beelzebub. You must submit to godly leaders like Rabbi Blind Judgment and Rabbi Don't Rock the Boat. They know better than you do."

Rabbi Doubting glared at them, hoping to engage them in an argument. When they remained silent, he stomped off in a huff. Simon and Nicodemus watched him go, both recalling a statement from Jesus—"I came not to bring peace but a sword."[*] There would be a cost for this choice, but they wouldn't turn back.

"Oh, I really dislike that man!" Simon burst out. "He is always dumping guilt trips on me. Absolute submission should be given only to God—not to any man. No one mind should rule over another this way. He is so pushy and compelling—it's his way or no way. I'd like to tell him to back off, yet I feel guilty for even thinking it. I've been raised to respect the leaders, but something is wrong with this picture. Should we submit to unrighteousness just because a leader endorses it? I'm confused. What do you think, Nicodemus?"

Nicodemus was thoughtful and quiet while he called out to God for wisdom. "I've been under this yoke of submission to the church my whole life, and what has it gotten me? I've performed the prescribed duties, obeyed the church's dictates, attended numerous functions, even put the church before my family, but it has not changed my heart. I'm a whited sepulcher—full of the emptiness of self.[†] I am missing the indwelling Christ. Yet, I'm one of the leaders, and I've been taught to maintain a united front before the people.

"But now I'm seeing that I ought to obey God rather than men—regardless of the consequences. How can we come out of misconceptions if we have to obey those who are still caught up in these misconceptions? If the only way to be restored to

---

*Matthew 10:34.
†Matthew 23:27.

God's image is to be in subjection to Him, and if our leaders require a conflicting submission, then we ought to obey God rather than men! If any authority does not have the earmarks of the voice and character of God—it *is not* of God no matter whether it is from the church, the world, or my own head. Does this make sense, or is it heresy?"

"Oh yes, I'm wrestling with the same thing," Serious Simon said. "As you talk I can see two contrasting spirits working here. The spirit of Satan is the spirit of compulsion and force—like the spirit of Cain. That is what Rabbi Doubting brought with him. He had no desire to listen to us or to wrestle this truth honestly. He is interested only in us blindly submitting to *him*. And he will use guilt, force, or oppression to gain his ends. Oh, and I've done this to others too! We are usurping God doing this!

"In contrast, the Spirit of God says, 'Come now, and let us *reason* together.'* He presents evidence, gives room to sort and sift, and allows us to make a choice free from compulsion or pressure. Jesus had this Spirit. I see that He is offering to save me from myself and to instruct me in righteousness, but He leaves me free to choose. That is totally different from the Rabbi.

"There are only two spirits in this world—the Spirit of God and the spirit of Satan. We can't be neutral. Either we are for God or we are against Him. If we neglect to choose to serve God, we are serving Satan by default. Many who profess to serve God are in reality serving Satan. How can we know? By testing their spirit. If they appeal to our flesh or seek to compel us or send us on guilt trips, they are not of God regardless of their profession. We must come to recognize which voice, which thought, is from which master in order to know to obey it or not! This is becoming clearer, isn't it?"

"Yes, yes." And the men proceeded down the road, talking.

Whether you are a parent or a youth, the ability to make right decisions is absolutely vital. The development of that skill is as important to successful adult life as is the proper maturing of wings to a butterfly. We must individually choose Christ to be our Lord. That is what redemption is all about. Every soul that refuses or neglects to give himself to God is under the control of another power. He is not his own. He may talk of freedom, but he is in the most abject slavery. He is not allowed to see the beauty of truth, for his mind is under the control of Satan. While he flatters himself that he is following the dictates of his own judgment, he obeys the will of the prince of darkness. Christ came to break the shackles of the slavery of sin from the soul. "For the law of the Spirit of life in Christ Jesus" sets us "free from the law of sin and death."† We can soar like an eagle above the pull of our flesh in Him.

There is no compulsion in the work of redemption—no external force. Under the influence of the Spirit of God, we are left free to choose whom we will serve. Our decision is the key that connects our soul with the divine energy of the Holy Spirit.‡

---

*Isaiah 1:18, italics added.
†Romans 8:2.
‡James 4:7.

Then our faculties—our thoughts and feelings—obey the dictates of God's will. Then all we have to do is cooperate with God in this process against outside sources discouraging us. We ought to obey God rather than man.

Let's look at our youth and see how all this works practically for us and them.

Restricted wings

Amiable Ada was a sweet, caring, seventeen-year-old who had been raised in a very conservative home. She was an obedient daughter who loved to serve and please.

"Mother, I want to be a nurse," she said one day. "I've given a lot of thought to it and prayed about it. I love helping people—old, young, and in between. I'm wondering where you think I should go to school."

"Honey, let's talk. There are lots of drawbacks to nursing."

And thus began a rather lengthy discussion that concluded with Mother saying, "I don't believe God wants you to be a nurse because of the things I have just listed. You need to seek God again for another idea. Why don't you consider being . . .?" And Mother listed her ideas.

After some consideration, Amiable Ada still honestly believed God wanted her to be a nurse. She approached her parents with an honest, pure heart, but a differing view of God's will for her life. "I've prayed about this further, and I long to please you, but still God is clearly leading me to be a nurse. Surely there is some field of caring for people that would be acceptable to you, Mother?"

Another long discussion began that concluded with, "Honey, in order for God to bless you, you must surrender to the will and understanding of your parents. We know better. You are young and can't properly discern God's voice. We can save you from wrong choices. You must honor your father and mother. If you don't, you will lose God's blessing in your life."

Heavyhearted and confused, Amiable Ada retreated to her bedroom. She must be wrong, but she wasn't sure why.

"It would be better for me just to ask my parents what to do, rather than ask God. It's so confusing to ask God. I get excited, then have to give up those ideas. It's easier to just seek my parents' counsel and avoid these emotional situations. That is what I'll do!"

All through her growing-up years, Ada had been maneuvered in this way. When she was corrected for some behavior, her mother would tell her what her motives were and demand agreement. Experience proved that no amount of discussion could convince her mother otherwise. The only way to resolve the situation was to submit to it—whether or not it was reasonable or honest. Consequently, Ada learned to doubt herself, to doubt God's willingness to relate to her as an individual, and to yield an absolute submission to her parents that should be yielded only to God.

What's the use of praying if you're only going to do what your parents tell you anyway? Ada read, "Children, obey your parents in the Lord."* "In the Lord," she mused. "What does that mean, I wonder?" To question her parents, or to obey God

---

*Ephesians 6:1.

against her parents would bring unrest. Peace in the home was achieved only when she agreed with her parents. Her own heart ached for some time, but this was the cross she must bear—or so she thought.

In her teens, Ada clearly saw differences between her understanding of God's Word and that of her parents'. She shared these thoughts openly—only to be reproved, corrected, and sent to her room to repent. There was no other way. Over and over this was enacted. She learned there was only one way to resolve differences—absolute obedience to the will of her parents—even when she honestly disagreed. Is blind submission to a human God's will?

So, instead of pursuing nursing, Ada went into a sales career and was moderately successful, but not fulfilled. Then she tried another field her parents suggested, but she was poorly paid and abandoned it. A third career proved semifulfilling. For a time, she sensed it was not God's will for her to take this course, but she couldn't stand the silent treatment she got when she questioned her parents' wishes. Consequently, she became very dependent on her parents—not God—for direction in life. Her confidence in God's voice to lead her was squelched. Although submission to her parents brought an outward peace, she felt empty. But she learned to override the emptiness with an outwardly bubbly attitude.

Now in her twenties, Amiable Ada was away from home starting yet another career that her parents thought would be good for her. When her car broke down on the highway, a man older than herself stopped to help her. He asked her name, phone number, and where she was living—and she gave the information to him. She didn't know how to say no to an adult. Later, he called her and talked for long periods of time on the phone. She learned that he was married—unhappily. She wasn't comfortable talking with him on the phone.

Since her parents weren't available at this time, she called a trusted friend and asked him to intervene.

What would you do? Would you call for her? To do so would not train her to stand on her own with God. It would increase her dependency upon others—not on God.

Her friend was willing to intervene for her, but he recognized the need to encourage Ada herself to tell this caller to leave her alone—and to say it in no uncertain terms. The struggle was severe. Three times Amiable Ada tried to resolve the situation—and couldn't do it. Her habit of wrongly submitting to the will of adults—even when they are not right—had crippled her. After much encouragement and reasoning and pointing her to God, she did manage to take care of the unwanted caller. But it was a one-time event and had little effect on her overall life.

Nothing changed when Amiable Ada wanted to get married. At first, her parents loved her suitor. Then just before the wedding date they changed their minds and counseled her to call it off. She was heartbroken and reluctant to yield. She tried to tell her parents that she believed this was God's will for her, but they refused to see her viewpoint. She loved this man and had allowed her feelings to grow, believing her parents approved. She was confused and in pain. She tried to seek God, but her parents' voice in her conscience was loud and compelling, drowning out His voice.

What was the use of seeking God anyway? Wouldn't He just tell her to obey her parents?

She called off the wedding and went into a year-long depression. Her parents changed their minds again and consented to her marriage with the same man who had waited patiently for her. Again, just before the wedding, the parents tried to call it off. This time, her fiancé talked with her; God talked with her; and for the first time, she went against her parents and married the man she loved. Her parents flogged her with Bible texts, accusing her of disobedience and telling her that she was lost.

Even after the wedding, the parents continued to interfere and plague the couple, until her husband realized the only option for preserving his wife's sanity was to move far away from her parents. How painful this was to Ada!

When the couple decided to have a baby, the parents advised them not to. Once again, Amiable Ada was caught in the turmoil of trying to please her parents and following God—even after she was married. After the child was born, the parents undermined Ada's confidence in her husband to the point that she separated from him to keep peace with them. A year of turmoil later, she realized God didn't want her to leave her husband, so she returned. Soon, a second child was born—against the counsel of her parents.

Her husband, a godly man, took his position as priest of their home. He worked with Ada to help her find freedom to follow God instead of man. No mind—not even that of a parent—is to control another. Together, Ada and her husband laid down some firm boundaries for the parents. Life improved, but Amiable Ada continues to wrestle with the old ways.

Parent dependant?

This is the topic Nicodemus and Serious Simon were discussing at the beginning of this chapter. No man, no priest, no church affiliation, not even parents have the right to come between us and God. Jesus is to be our Lord—no one else. He is the only safe pattern to follow. His life of submission to the heavenly Father, His power to live an upright life, is to be ours as we learn how to cooperate with God. We are to give total submission only to God. Our conscience is not to be a puppet to any institution or individual. It is to be free to serve God and God alone! Not even parents are to usurp the position of God in our lives.

We need to train our youth to have a real experience with God for themselves. They begin by knowing about God, then knowing God personally, then experiencing God speaking to them and directing their steps, and finally learning how to cooperate with God to find victory over the self that still rules them. We are to counsel, encourage, and give input, but young adults need to be given opportunities to learn how to fly on their own under Jesus' guidance. We must sever the umbilical cord somewhere. We were to be mind and will for them when they were very young, but at the age of accountability, we are to begin the process of disconnecting them from us and connecting them to Christ.

Won't you, with Nicodemus, pray the surrender prayer and put God in charge—both you and your youth? Won't you let Him lead you out of your wrong parenting approaches and your overly controlling nature that puts you in the place of God? Won't you let Him teach you new concepts so that you can help your youth to cross over from being parent-dependent to becoming God-dependent, to cross over from a self-directed life to a God-directed life? This is training the wings of decision. Herein is true happiness for parent and youth alike.

Handel was a youth with the strength of character to see things differently than his parents. His parents wanted him to be a doctor, but he felt a calling to be a musician. He followed God, and that's why we have *The Messiah* and other inspiring compositions today. Handel's parents did not know the will of God for their son. If he had submitted to them, we would not now have these works of art to the glory of God! Would any parent want the responsibility of taking their child out of God's hands?

Remember what Jesus said to Peter? "Follow *me.*"

Peter pointed to John and asked, "Lord, and what shall this man do?"

Jesus said, "If I will that he tarry till I come, what is that to thee? *follow thou me.*"*

Christ is calling our youth to follow Him. Do we help them to hear and answer His call, or do we usurp His position? Do we manipulate our youth, thinking we have the wisdom to choose their life work? Let's seek, instead, to give our youth the skills and opportunities to determine God's will for their life that they may compose their *Messiah* under God's direction. We give input and counsel, but we don't decide for them.

So every youth from a very young age should direct his or her own life—right? No! That is not what I am saying. Above all else, youth need to come under God's guidance with the help of their parents' nurturing and training. Parents should not usurp God's position in the lives of their children, and the children should obey their parents, *in the Lord*, and submit to proper authorities that are in Christ. The youth must be honest in following God's leading and not use it as an excuse to sin.

We should submit to the authority of an Abraham Lincoln under God. But we should not submit to a despot leader like Hitler under Satan.

Backlash

Many youth today, in the name of freedom, can't wait to get away from home when they turn eighteen. Why? They don't know the real, personal, powerful God that can change them inside or who can solve their problems. Some run away, some rebel, some marry to get away, others follow more cunning maneuvers, but the motive is the same—they want out, perhaps from a bad home environment, an unfair home, a dictatorial home, a nontraining home, a manipulative home, an abusive home, or even a sweetly overly controlling home.

They want freedom from undue restraint, restrictions, and guilt trips. If they do not know God personally, if they do not seek His will, if they are not accustomed to yielding to His will and way, if they do not know His voice from all the other voices clamoring in their ears, they will go down to bondage in Egypt.

---

*John 21:19, 21, 22, italics added.

One young man, who had been raised in a very conservative home, went away to school and on the side gained an education in pornography, martial arts, fist fights, and other vices enticing to his nature. He did not know God's voice personally nor how to make a decision under God. His outward good behavior had been a response to his parents' domination, but it was never in his heart. When that restraint was removed, he had no moral foundation of his own on which to stand under God. He calls obeying his flesh "freedom" and thinks he can turn from these vices whenever he chooses. The truth is, these vices bind him tightly, and only when he ventures to pull away will he find how tight a hold this master has on him.

A young lady friend of mine was raised in a home where the parents could not—or would not—teach her what it meant in practical terms to follow God. She tired of the protracted effort in self and gave up on *their* God—thinking that was all there was. She never knew the real God. So she turned to a frivolous life of gaiety, laughter, and her friendships with boys became her favorite pastime. A friend tried for years to help her recognize that God was there for her and that He was different than her parents had portrayed. She was encouraged to experience the real God herself. She was given ample instruction. But while this young lady understood, she was not willing to act. She trusted no one but herself; she wouldn't let God be *her* Lord. At eighteen, she left home to do her own thing. Where will she go with this lack of knowing God and how to make right decisions?

The rich young ruler desired to be good. He claimed that he had kept all the commandments from his youth. What tripped him up? Why did he turn away sorrowfully from Christ? It was because he would not have Jesus rule over him. It was a control issue. He wanted to be the one in charge. Will our youth turn sorrowfully away from Christ because we have not taught them the joys of making Christ their Lord?

Another young lady, who grew up in a miserable home, had deeply ingrained habits of demeaning herself and being slothful. God provided an opportunity for her to see the real gospel that would save her from her history. She toyed with the idea, talked about it, even tried it a little at home, but never made the decision to give herself entirely to God. Again, the biggest issue was trust. She trusted no one but herself—not even God. She had a support group of people who loved her, nurtured her, and encouraged her, but indecision reigned. Not to decide is to decide. Like the rich young ruler, this young lady chose to not let Jesus rule over her. She left home to claim her supposed "freedom." Her anger ruled her as she despairingly went from bed to bed, from friend to friend, trying to find the easy, carefree life. She doesn't realize that she will find what she's looking for only when she puts God in charge. Until her wings of decision for right are exercised, there will be no change.

Metamorphosis

Our children, as they enter their teen years, are like a caterpillar going into his cocoon. A metamorphosis is about to take place. The caterpillar is being transformed into a butterfly. The youth is being transformed into an adult.

Have you ever watched a butterfly come out of his cocoon? It is a very vulnerable time, and he needs a safe environment. It takes time and effort to crawl out, to stretch his legs, to uncurl his antennae, and to begin to straighten his wings. He doesn't fly immediately. He perches near his old cocoon and gently begins to move his wings. Back and forth, he exercises them until they are dry and his muscles have begun to strengthen. Then he takes short flights, increasing them in length until he is ready for long migrations.

Our youth need a safe home environment where their growing powers can develop—not too fast and not too slow. They need encouragement to exercise their wings—their ability to go to God for themselves and put Him in charge of their lives. As they gain experience in successful flight with little things, they can be stretched with bigger challenges.

The butterfly that is not allowed to emerge from his cocoon at the proper time either dies or is crippled. His wings don't open properly, and he is vulnerable to predators. Likewise, a youth that is not allowed freedom to exercise his decision-making ability under God is crippled. His trust in God is stifled. His confidence that God can and will direct him personally is confused. He becomes vulnerable to Satan's snares.

On the other hand, a caterpillar forced from its cocoon too early faces similar disadvantages. Any youth that is launched out into the world without the proper preparation of knowing God and how to exercise his wings to do God's will instead of the will of his flesh will fall prey to Satan. Without the wings of decision for a godly life being developed, there is no true flight.

These butterflies will be crippled for life unless they find God, trust and submit to Him being in charge of their life, and follow His lead to face the misconceptions from their childhood and replace them with right concepts. All can mature in Christ by letting Him re-parent them. These wings can be healed and developed in Him.

One young man, at age sixteen, left a very bad home environment just to survive. He viewed God like his parents—stern, vengeful, and distant. He determined that he was not going to be like his parents—no way. He managed to make a humble living but was driven by his unmet need for love. He tried to fill that void with inappropriate relationships, substance abuse, and pornography. He had a desperate need to control others and did so through manipulation. He used and abused his wife until she divorced him. His intense pain drove him to seek help, but he was still unwilling to decide to fully trust Jesus. He would not look to his past to see why he responded the way he did—he didn't go there no matter what. He would not go to God to see himself for who he truly was—that was too painful. He'd rather live in an unreal world and excuse himself and perpetuate his history. He refused to take responsibility for his wrongs or make real changes. That seemed too scary. Thus his second and third marriages ended in the same mess.

Until he lets God be in charge of His life, until he is ready to let Jesus direct his steps, until he puts forth effort to come under Christ's Generalship, he will remain in his indecision under Satan's rigorous rule—obeying his thoughts and feelings with their corresponding responses—no matter how painful it is.

Which youth are you?

Samuel, about age four, was sent to live in the indulgent home of Priest Eli. But he knew the voice of God; his wings of decision were exercised even at such a tender age to choose the way of the Lord.

Joseph was likely a youth, in his teens, when his brothers sold him into slavery. He had a decision to make as he rode that camel past his father's tents. Would he make his father's God his God? Or would he lie down in abject despair? His parents had given him freedom to experience God's voice personally. They allowed him to shoulder responsibility so that his skill, efficiency, and thoroughness grew. Would he now be angry with God and cast it all aside?

Joseph chose to be a child of God, to let Him have full rule over his life and direct it as He deemed best. Arriving at Potiphar's house, he chose to make the very best of his situation. He would be the best slave there was. He would obey God and not allow his circumstances to master him. All the training of his mother and father under God shone through. He excelled. Soon Potiphar put all his possessions under Joseph's management.

Satan did not like Joseph's choices and made life hard on him. He resists those who don't serve him. He makes sin look enticing or at least advantageous. So Satan attacked Joseph's purity and morality. What did Joseph do?

He would not sin against God. Accustomed to doing God's will, sensitive to right and wrong, Joseph chose once more to follow God. He left his coat behind to get away from the temptress. Thrown into prison for doing right, he accepted his lot. He probably asked God for freedom, but he was content when God didn't seem to answer. He knew God could free him, but trusted Him even when He did not. He accepted his lot and helped all those in jail in any way he could, trusting in God's timing. He would obey God rather than circumstances, wrong feelings, inclinations or emotions.

The unseen God became closer to him than a brother. This was God's chosen testing ground for Joseph. The wings of decision were continually tested—tested for fidelity, submission, trust, and loyalty to God in the most cruel of situations.

When Joseph was exalted to the throne of Egypt, he was also tested severely with the peculiar pitfalls of prosperity. He passed here as well because he let God be Lord of his life.

Every youth today may stand unspotted amid the evil of the world as they exercise their wings to trust God and choose Him for their Lord. Even if your parents cannot—or do not—teach you how to make decisions properly, you still can be a Joseph or a Samuel and let God teach you personally. Don't be the prodigal son who runs away and loses his inheritance! Your inheritance is Christ in you, your hope of glory!

"If the Son therefore shall make you free, ye shall be free indeed."* If the law of the Spirit of life in Christ Jesus sets us free from the law of sin and death, then we

---

*John 8:36.

can mount up on wings as eagles—flying above the pull of our natural thoughts, feelings, and responses.*

Join Joshua in the decision: "As for me and my house, we will serve the LORD."†

Now take flight with the God-given wings of decision in Christ Jesus!

In the next chapter, we will look at the exercise of the will to see the process that takes us from knowing what is right to being empowered to do it.

THE LONE EMBRACE
A SPECIAL WORD OF ENCOURAGEMENT FOR SINGLE PARENTS

"Woe, I am undone," you say. "I have done it wrong all my parenting years, not knowing, not understanding. I had no idea how important it is to train my children in the art of making decisions led of God. I thought I knew better than they. In my children's young years I was having all kinds of marriage problems and let my children come up like weeds.

"My own parents dominated and crippled me. I didn't think I was like them, but I am just a milder form of the same thing. My parents yelled, were angry and ugly, and dominated me. But I dominate my children, thumping them with the Bible. And I'm sure they see God as a stern, unjust God by my example. I can relate to the stories in this chapter of youth leaving their homes and sowing their oats in the name of freedom; it's my greatest fear for my children.

"So in their teens, I have been ruling over them more than when they were little, making decisions for them against great odds. I haven't been doing it to dominate them; I've been doing it to save them from making wrong decisions like I did. But the truth is that I'm leading them the same way my parents led me—except with quieter domination. The fruit will be the same because I'm not teaching them to make decisions under God."

You may have made many mistakes. But praise God that you see that now. God is the greatest Teacher! He will teach you and your youth how to make real decisions even now. When your teens see a change in you, fairness instead of an arbitrary spirit, a program that develops in them a proper independence from you and a proper dependence upon God, they will rebound. Every youth rebels in his heart against undue control. But every youth also has in his heart a desire to be truly loved by his parents. Our children are forgiving. They will respond to the changes you put in place in order to follow God's wisdom. God, too, is there for you. Turn to Him often, and He will teach you to find true freedom in Him.

---

*Romans 8:2; Isaiah 40:31.
†Joshua 24:15.

Chapter 16

The Youth's Will

Jesus saith unto them, My meat is to do the will of him that sent me.
—John 4:34

Raging Ramsey, age sixteen, and his mother faced each other in yet another battle of the wills. Mother, who hated to cross her son, was determined not to be intimidated. Raging Ramsey was just as determined not to submit. He stood over her, glaring and curling his fists, while pouring forth a torrent of nasty insults.

Trying to gain some control, she commanded harshly, "No more arguing, crying, or complaining! You did not do your chores this morning, so you must scrub the stovetop as a consequence. End of discussion! Hopefully, it'll teach you to be responsible!"

Raging Ramsey suddenly took a swing at his mother. She dodged just in time, and the shouting match escalated. By backing up one step at a time and working her way around, Mother was able to get Raging Ramsey out the back door. By God's grace, she was spared physical blows, but her son was in a fit of passion that took hours to resolve before he was safe to return to the house. Mother slumped exhausted into a nearby chair. This type of confrontation was becoming all too common. Why? And just as importantly, what could be done about it?

It is foolish to think that our youth will outgrow their passions—whether they are displayed through anger, promiscuity, foul language, control tactics, or wrong appetites. The longer their passions are indulged, the stronger they will become. In this case, the mother's example had contributed to this negative trait in her son. But his lack of control was mainly the result of the lack of training in the right use of the will. Giving this training later in life may be more difficult, but is not impossible. Let's look behind the scenes to understand what's happening.

Identifying the pharaoh of Egypt

The problem of sin and passion ruling our lives—and the solution—are both well illustrated in the story of the Israelites and the Pharaoh in Egypt. Pharaoh treated the Israelites like Satan treats us. He forced them into slavery and set taskmasters over them. Any attempt they made to find freedom or to lighten their bondage was met with ever increasing cruelty. In the same way, Satan enslaved Ramsey and compelled him to wholeheartedly serve the taskmasters of his wrong thinking and passionate feelings.

As Moses was God's instrument to lead Israel to freedom, so each parent is to be God's instrument to lead their youth out of the bondage of sinful passions into the freedom of Christ. Under God's direction, Moses approached Pharaoh and commanded, "Let my people go." We parents must be willing, under God's direction, to confront the taskmasters ruling our youth with the same confidence and perseverance. Moses did not accept "no" from Pharaoh, and neither should we. Our youth must learn to change masters, to exercise their will in the right way, and to walk away from their taskmasters. Realize that you are fighting, not against flesh and blood, but against powers and principalities of darkness.* You need Jesus as your General in the warfare against self, for it truly is a battle.

Satan, like Pharaoh, threatens our youth, "I will not let you go!" He does not want to lose his captives and will fight to retain them in his service. Like Paul, we must fight the good fight of faith against Satan, doing whatever God asks us to do in order to leave Satan's service.

First, we must show our youth that they can choose whom they will serve—God or Satan. Most youth don't realize that they *don't have to yield* to rage or any other passion. They think they must. They are just like the slaves stomping the straw into the mud to make bricks. Surely they must stay in the mud pit, for the taskmasters in Egypt will whip them if they don't. Our youth feel they do not have a choice. Some have obeyed their feelings for so long that they have no clue what else they can do. Others seem to enjoy serving the taskmasters of perverted appetites or temper. Still others want freedom but don't want to make the changes necessary to find it. In any case, we, their parents, must become the Moses under God's direction to teach them that *they need not continue to obey* the pharaoh of their sin. They can choose to serve God instead.

This changing of a master requires an exercise of the will. We choose which master we will serve by yielding to the suggestions of one or the other. We can serve either Satan or God; there are no other choices, no neutral ground. If we fail to actively yield to God and His ways of thinking and responding, we automatically choose Satan to rule as pharaoh on the throne of our heart.

We cannot leave the bondage of Egypt unless Christ is our Master and we are following His suggestions. "Which way do I turn, Lord?"† "What should I think, Jesus?"‡ "How do I respond against the compelling nature of my anger and rage, God?"§ As we learn the art of communicating prayer with God, we ask, and God speaks to our reason, intellect, and conscience. It's not an audible voice—more of a reasoning voice that leaves us free to accept or reject Him.**

Let's see our part and our youth's part in coming out of the Egypt of our passions to serve the living God.

Raging Ramsey rages under pharaoh

Although Raging Ramsey obeyed his fleshly passions, deep down in his heart he longed for freedom. He heard some messages that stirred his soul and caused him to

---

*Ephesians 6:12.
†Isaiah 30:21.
‡2 Corinthians 10:4.
§Jeremiah 32:27; James 1:19.
**For more detailed information about discerning the voice of God and the voice of your flesh, read chapter 4 of *Parenting by the Spirit* and *Parenting Your Child by the Spirit*.

think that maybe God could do something to help him. His mother timidly did her best but vacillated between overindulgence and harshness. Finally, she asked a dependable friend, Communing Carl, for help.

Communing Carl befriended Raging Ramsey. They chatted about mutual interests, and after some time, Raging Ramsey invited Communing Carl to join him in the backyard to practice target shooting with his bow and arrow. Secretly, Ramsey was wondering if this guy was worth respecting and decided this would be his test.

"Oh, it has been so many years since I've shot a bow. I don't know, Ramsey. But I'll try," Carl said. He breathed a short prayer, "Lord, to gain the respect of this young lad, I pray You help me do well."

His first shot hit the bull's-eye. Raging Ramsey's eyes bulged with admiration. "This guy is for real. He is my kind of guy," he thought.

As they continued shooting at targets, Communing Carl guided the conversation around to deeper matters, and Ramsey opened up. "Yes, I do have a temper that gets out of control sometimes. I'd like not to respond that way, but once Mother gets me all riled up I have no control. If only she . . ."

"Your mother is *not* the real problem," Carl countered. "You realize that don't you? It's your lack of surrender to God that is the real problem and the reason why you have little self-control."

"Well, yes," Ramsey finally admitted after some discussion. He saw the fallacy of blaming his mother for his behavior. He recognized that he didn't know God as it was his privilege. He glimpsed the glorious possibility that he could be free from his rage from the inside out. He began to wonder, "How do I put my will on God's side of the issue instead of giving way to passion?"

Carl shared, "for as ye have yielded your members servants to uncleanness and to iniquity unto iniquity; even so now yield your members servants to righteousness unto holiness."* They discussed the practical application of these words to Ramsey's anger and rage, and he began to understand.

They went for a walk and came upon two neighborhood dogs—a large pit bull and a miniature schnauzer. The pit bull was just charging into the schnauzer's yard and attacking the smaller dog when they stopped to watch. The smaller dog rolled over submissively, but the larger dog showed no mercy and continued attacking.

"So which dog are you?"

"I'm the pit bull," Raging Ramsey admitted.

Carl was quiet while the Holy Spirit took the analogy home to Ramsey's mind. Then Ramsey asked, "Carl, will you help me with my rage problem?"

"Are you saying I have your permission, if you get out of control, to deal with you? And will you cooperate when I show you how to overcome it by turning to God?"

"Yes, I will," Raging Ramsey promised.

The opportunity came the very next day. Raging Ramsey failed to do his chores, and Mother again gave the consequence of scrubbing the stovetop. Raging Ramsey

---

*Romans 6:19.

was out of control almost before he knew it—his response seemed automatic. Communing Carl, hearing the raised voices, cried out to God for His wisdom and presence and came upon the scene just as Raging Ramsey was clenching his fists.

"If you are going to hit someone, you need to hit me." Communing Carl stood between Raging Ramsey and his mother—firm, yet calm and loving, while communing in his heart with God.

"I can't hit you!" Ramsey said desperately, respect coming into his eyes. But his rage still overpowered his reason. He refused to pray when invited, and the arguing started to escalate.

"Come with me, Ramsey. We are going to run and run hard."

Raging Ramsey refused. Carl pressed, "I promised to help you out of your rage, and you promised to cooperate with me. This is the first step. Now come with me."

Out the door they went, but Raging Ramsey collapsed awkwardly on the porch grabbing his ankle and whining, "I can't run. I just broke my ankle."

Communing with God for direction, Carl sensed that Ramsey was bluffing. He examined the ankle and ordered, "You can still run. Let's go!"

They ran. Communing Carl had to hold on to Raging Ramsey's arm because he was inclined to run away. When that didn't work, he pretended to twist his ankle again. He was accustomed to evading discipline and implicitly obeyed every suggestion that Satan put in his mind. Carl knew that Ramsey needed to surrender to God in order to experience freedom from those evil emotions, desires, and habits. Then he would be more inclined to choose God in the future. He didn't allow Raging Ramsey's foul language or other tactics to sidetrack him.

After several miles of running, Ramsey was getting tired. He became quiet and no longer tried to get away. Carl glanced at his face and saw that his countenance was much subdued.

"Is this enough Lord?" he asked.

"Yes. Now draw out his heart to do what he needs to do."

"Let's head back," Carl told Ramsey.

As they started toward home, Carl encouraged Ramsey to choose to follow God instead of his flesh. This run was to get the evil spirit out so that he could think clearly. They stopped and prayed to God for strength to do the right. They ran some more, but this time Ramsey willingly ran beside Carl. He chose to cooperate with Carl and surrendered his will to do right. When they arrived home, Raging Ramsey was exhausted.

Raging Ramsey submits

Communing Carl encouraged, "Well, I don't need to tell you what you need to do now. You just need to do what God is telling you right now—don't fight God."

Ramsey at first was troubled, then confused, and then irritated at Carl. But instead of giving way to those feelings, he chose to turn to God. "Lord, what would Thou have me to do?"

His conscience nudged him to apologize. Raging Ramsey then went directly to his mother. He knelt down before her, looked into her eyes, and said, "I'm sorry, Mother.

I was very wrong. By God's grace, I shall never again raise my hand to hit you. Please forgive me. I'll do my chores right away like I should have done to begin with."

Mother was stunned. She couldn't believe the peace she saw in his eyes so soon after giving way to the raging current of passion. As tears of joy flowed down her cheeks, she sweetly reminded, "I gladly forgive you, son! But in addition to your chores you need to scour the stovetop like I said—this is fair."

To everyone's surprise, Raging Ramsey set out to do his chores cheerfully and diligently without any argument. His brother, watching from the sidelines, saw God, instead of Satan, having control over Ramsey and was astonished. When all his chores and the stovetop were done, Ramsey came to Mother, "Please check my work and see if it passes your inspection." *Reposed* Ramsey awaited Mother's reply.

He had done his work well, and Mother and son embraced in a special never-to-be-forgotten way. When God comes in, the stormy heart is subdued—just like the stormy Sea of Galilee was calmed when Jesus quietly commanded, "Peace, be still."

Raging Ramsey had always *known* what was right, but he did not know *how to do* what was right in Jesus. In self, he had consistently failed, but with this experience, he tasted grace. It was different. He experienced God transforming his character—his thoughts and feelings and thus his response—as he cooperated. He was to learn, though, that yielding once is not yielding always. He would have to face these old impulses again and choose this new way repeatedly before his character was permanently changed.

When we choose to yield and serve God, He opens to us His floodgate of power and strength to oppose our fleshly inclinations. Our cooperation permits Him to dethrone Satan and to cleanse our hearts from the filth of sin. When Christ comes in, Satan and rage must leave. When we make no effort to resist the pull of the flesh, we go under Satan's control and remain in bondage.

Does it take firmness to cooperate with God to extricate a soul from Satan's clutches? The battle against self is the greatest battle ever fought for parent and youth alike. It's a hand-to-hand battle with the devil himself. Are you willing, under God, to do whatever it takes for your youth to connect to and experience God? We need to hearken diligently to His voice guiding us. Of ourselves, we are no match for Satan. But with God as our General in this warfare, success is ours and our youth's.

God wants to deliver us from serving the pharaoh of Egypt and bring us out of the mud pits of rage to serve Him instead of our wrong thoughts, feelings, emotions, and responses. Our passions need not rule over us. When we invite God into our heart, we hear, believe, and choose to think His thoughts. The exercise of the will helps us move from *knowing* what is right to *doing* what is right. It takes a resolute decision to follow Him against the clamors of our flesh. God empowers that decision.

Let's look a little closer into this exercise of the will to discover how to choose, how to yield, and to see where the battle is and where it is not.

My will is ...

My will is simply my choice. I have a bundle of choices I make all day long. Will I serve God or self in this specific instance? Will I do God's will or mine? Do I choose to think and speak His will? God calls me to use my will to surrender all my choices to Him. Will I yield up my will to do His will? Surrendering with my will involves two parts: First, a choice to do His will, not mine. Second, an action to carry out my decision.

Jesus illustrates this for us. He said to His heavenly Father, "Not my will, but Thine, be done."* Once He determined His Father's will, He got up and went to Calvary. He showed us by example how He let God be in charge. So it must be with us. Jesus successfully kept His flesh subdued by depending upon His Father's divine power and direction and then acting upon it. He trusted in God, not in Himself.

We, too, must give God permission to work by depending upon His power to subdue the rule of sin in our lives. Our act of cooperation does it. This is our Calvary where self dies. When I step down from the ruling position and let God be my Pilot, miracles happen just like they did with Ramsey.

First, my will surrenders with my mind to the reality that God is in charge of my life. I will seek to know His will at the beginning of every day and at each step throughout the day. When it's time to worship, to do my chores, to eat, to study, or to relate to someone, self watches for every opportunity to resume the pilot's position. I need to continually reaffirm that I want God to be the One in charge by saying, "Not my will but Thine be done." By these choices, I learn to filter all I say and do through Christ before I say or do it. Indecision leaves me in the very trying valley of decision where I feel the pull of Satan and the pull of Christ to choose. The decision of the will can get me out of this tug-of-war valley. Let's decide for God.

Second, my will makes its choice an action. I intellectually decide to follow God, but unless I take tangible steps to do so, I'm still enslaved by my sinful or wrong practices. That is where Raging Ramsey's miracle of a changed disposition took place. When he cooperated *to do* the right (the exercise of the will) then God had his permission to come into his heart (emotions) to evict the pharaoh-Satan and redeem him from his slavery to rage. To be under Satan is a forced bondage. To be under Christ is freedom.

My will is not . . .

My will is *not* merely restraining the wrong by my human willpower alone. Raging Ramsey tried to control his rage through his human willpower alone but could not do it. He knew he was out of control even as he yielded to it. He gave up on himself to control it. He blamed his mother. Satan impressed on his mind these thoughts and feelings of indignation against her, and he habitually obeyed them. He believed that if only he could control his mother, he wouldn't get so angry. He didn't know how Christ could empower his human willpower. So he remained under servitude and bondage to respond in rage at her. We need not stay here when we understand the right action of our will under God.

---

*Luke 22:42.

The true surrender of my will to Jesus to be empowered, requires tuning my ear to heaven to know my Master's will. It requires choosing God as my Master, and then cooperating to do whatever God puts on my heart to do.

God wants us to yield up the old ways of following Satan and to follow His character traits instead. We do the opposite of what we are used to. For example, instead of yielding to rage, we yield to God controlling us, and we become reasonable and peaceful. We can choose to be happy when we're inclined to be sad. We can choose to be hopeful instead of despairing. A lasting transformation can be accomplished only *in Christ,* not apart from Him. In time, with repetition of this process of choosing and doing, Christ in me not only restricts but eventually evicts Satan and the despair he brings. Little by little, choice by choice, we choose to do God's will until there is no more answering chord to the old way. The expulsion of sin is the act of the soul itself. This is the right exercise of our will. God said that we should be doers of the Word and not hearers only. Keep giving the wrong to God and doing the right until the wrong is gone by divine power accompanying our human effort. In this way God re-creates His character in us.

Exercising my will is not just stuffing down despair and pretending I'm joyful while the sadness tortures me inside. This is not the exercise of the will that will bring success and a transformation of character. This is humanism—trying to do all that God says in the power of your human will alone.

Instead we need to submit the wrong thought, feeling, or passion to God for Him to subdue. My will is to be surrendered to God and let Him evict the wrong while I cooperate to do whatever He tells me to do according to His Word.* My will is not to fight the sin or wrestle with the sin itself but to submit it to God and wrestle to trust and follow Him by faith and not by sight.

In James 4:7 the picture is clear. We are to submit ourselves to God, then we are to resist the devil, then he will flee from us. Submitting my will and way to God is *first,* and resisting in His divine power which is sufficient to expel sin is my *second* step. Once I resist in Christ, then the devil must go because I have made a free-will choice to follow God, and God is stronger than Satan.

I'm enabled to obey by the indwelling Christ through choosing to let Him be Lord over my life here and now. And my cooperation proves my choice to be of my free will. It's really a simple concept, isn't it? Psalm 55:19 says, "Because they have no changes, therefore [it gives evidence] they fear [know] not God." If we rightly exercise our will, we will be changed in our mind (thoughts) and heart (emotions) and habits just like Raging Ramsey.

The pharaoh of fear vs. the God of freedom

Fearful Felix was seventeen years old and terrified of the dark. In fact, he had never ventured into the dark since childhood for fear of an unknown "something." He and his parents came for a visit, and the issue was soon evident. We talked

---

*Isaiah 8:20.

with his parents and made a plan with God how to help this fellow face his task-master—fear.

"Felix, do you want freedom from your fear of the dark?"

"Oh yes, very much. But I've never known anyone to have victory over a case as bad as mine. I must stay inside or surely my heart will stop beating or I will be eaten by some horrible wild creature. My parents seem to think you might help me?"

"Satan wants you to believe this lie in order to keep you as his servant under fear. He is a compelling, forceful pharaoh, and laughs with glee at your discomfort. He stirs up your feelings by feeding you lying thoughts, and you believe him. But God came to redeem you from having to obey this fear."

"Yes, oh yes! I've sensed that this fear is not from God. But how do I change?"

"God also speaks, but His is a still, small voice. He speaks to your conscience by impressions. He speaks through His Word to your reason, saying that you need not fear. God does not stir up your emotions like Satan does. He wants a free-will service. To free you from this bondage, He invites you to come to Him, believe His Word, and follow Him. You have nothing to fear with Him beside you. God wants you to trust Him instead of letting fear run over you."

"But I don't know when I hear God's voice." We all entered into a lively conversation about knowing God's voice.*

"Your will is the governing power in your nature. The will is not the taste or inclination, it is the deciding power that can work in you to set you free. God says you don't have to trust or obey those lying emotions any longer. It is for you to yield your will to Jesus. As you do this, God will immediately take possession of your wrong thoughts and feelings and purify them for you. Under the control of the Spirit of Christ, these lying emotions, feelings, and even your thoughts will be subject to Him. You cannot control your feelings of fear, but God can, when you yield up your will to Him."

"How does He do that?"

"Well, let's practice this to see how. I want you to go into our dark root cellar, leave the light off. I will shut the door, and we'll experiment with this."

"That's scary! Are you sure it's safe?"

We discussed how safe it was. No wild animals could possibly be in there. His parents were present. He needed to choose to give his wrong fears and emotions to God and see what He would do with them. So, taking a deep breath, Felix climbed down into the root cellar, and we closed the lid.

"I'm afraid," Fearful Felix called out as the darkness embraced him.

"Cry out to God. Ask Him what He would have you think in place of fear," I responded.

" 'Perfect love casteth out fear,' "† Felix responded out loud. "Lord, save me now.

---

*To see what we discussed, go to chapter 4 in both of my books, *Parenting by the Spirit* and *Parenting Your Child by the Spirit*.

†1 John 4:18.

I'm Yours, not Satan's. I'm not fear's possession, but Yours. Jesus is right here with me; I am not alone; I'm not afraid." Then it got silent.

We rejoiced as Felix quietly waited in the dark. Then, as he told us later, fear welled up within him again, and he again exercised his will. "Lord, I'm Yours, not Satan's. I want to come out from under the pharaoh's whip of fear to serve You, God. I'm not Satan's any longer, I'm Your child. Yes, I trust You, Lord."

"Doing God's will against the pull of your flesh to fear—this is faith. Go against the knowledge of your former failures," I encouraged him. "Go against your inclinations that feel so impossible right now. They are all lies."

"I'm doing all right," he responded. "It's not so bad anymore." A little while passed, then he said, "Here come the fears again."

"At times you'll feel like the paralytic that Jesus told to rise up and walk. Don't trust your wrong feelings and emotions. Choose to trust God and walk. Whatever He says to you, do it, Felix. We are all right here."

"When I walk with the Lord, I need not fear. I give my fears to You to take. I will to walk, like the paralytic," Fearful Felix responded, cooperating with these new thoughts.

Five minutes passed—which seemed like an eternity to him. He began to sing "Trust and Obey" and lasted another five minutes before asking to be let out. The lid was opened immediately, and he was warmly and affectionately received into the light.

"You did well. What happened?" And Fearful Felix recounted the battle in his mind and his efforts to remain on the Lord's side. "It's really working," he exclaimed. "Wow!"

"My fears escalated when it first got dark," he told us. "I chose to cooperate with God, and they subsided notably. I began to think of the fears, and then the battle worsened. I went back to listening to God again, choosing to reject those emotions. I feel I failed by giving up."

"No, not at all! You lasted ten minutes in the dark! That's good! Felix, you didn't die or get eaten by wild beasts. Doesn't that prove those thoughts are lies?"

"Well, yes, it does," he realized. "I was like the paralytic at the pool of Bethesda being told to walk. I could identify clearly with him. This was a hard thing!"

"But a good one and the first step in coming out of Egypt, facing the pharaoh that says he will not let you go. You learned about hearing and recognizing God's voice and experienced God changing you inside at the level of your thoughts and feelings."

We discussed the principles of the exercise of the will further. As our will—our choice to follow God—cooperates with God's will in action, it becomes omnipotent. Why? Because it links us with God, who is far stronger than any of Satan's fears, bad habits, or lying thoughts.

"God did help me, then!" Fearful Felix exclaimed.

That evening, God led a further assault on the pharaoh of fear to give Fearful Felix the opportunity to gain greater freedom. "Felix, I need this compost taken to the compost bin. Take Jesus with you and face your fears. We will stand on the porch and watch you all the way."

Away went Fearful Felix, running at top speed through the dark from the cabin to the greenhouse. For a moment, he was out of sight, and then he came running lickety-split back to the house. After several experiences on successive evenings, his fears subsided notably. He was learning how to cry out to God to protect him and to trust that God would protect him. "These fears are lying thoughts. I can reject them. God will take care of me," he recited to himself. He collected Bible texts to memorize that told him the truth. Greater belief brought greater freedom.*

"Felix, would you go into the garage and get me another bucket of oats? Its dark in there, so you may want to take a flashlight so you can see."

Again and again, his fear was faced in many differing ways. Did Pharaoh let Moses and the children of Israel go the first time? Will Satan let our children escape wrong ways at our first request, correction, or exercise? No! Then let us not weary in well doing. Persevere, knowing God is with you. The pharaoh of self is God's problem, not yours. Give the wrong to God until it is gone and finds no more answering chord. This is what Felix did. He went to the garage, choosing to turn off the flashlight while denying Satan's lying thoughts and crying out to God. To his joy, his fears diminished.

One day, victory became his. Fearful Felix just loved hide-and-seek. So we decided to play hide-and-seek *in the dark*. Felix was given the option of using a flashlight, but he decided of his own accord to turn off the flashlight and hide in the dark. This was becoming fun. Fear gripped him only a few times. Each time, he gave his fears to God, and they were quickly subdued. As we hid quietly, we heard a pack of coyotes howling in the distance. They seemed to be chasing something and came closer and closer to where we huddled. We all waited with joyful expectation.

"There, over there, do you see the three coyotes?" The graceful little creatures stepped out of the shadows into the spotlight of the moon. We all admired them quietly—even *Fearless* Felix. There was no answering chord of fear in his heart, for he knew he could trust God to keep him safe and that there was no beast in the woods God could not control. As it was with freed Felix, so it can be with you. "To be strengthened with might by his Spirit in the inner man."†

"For the weapons of our warfare are not carnal, but mighty through God to the pulling down of strong holds; Casting down imaginations, and every high thing that exalteth itself against the knowledge of God, and bringing into captivity every thought to the obedience of Christ."‡

---

*To read additional illustrations and explanations of the exercise of the will over lying thoughts, fear of bears, overwhelming emotions, and how the higher powers of the mind under Christ rule over the lower powers, consult chapter 7 of my book, *Parenting by the Spirit*. To read about the place the will has in changing our emotions, habits, and character traits, read chapter 14 of *Parenting Your Child by the Spirit*.

†Ephesians 3:16.

‡2 Corinthians 10:4, 5.

THE LONE EMBRACE
A SPECIAL WORD OF ENCOURAGEMENT FOR SINGLE PARENTS

Parents, whether single or married, we must fight the good fight of faith to put our youth on God's side—to do battle at the level of the thoughts and feelings, to let God be enthroned there that we might think His thoughts, feel His feelings, and do His will. It's the sure pathway that God will use to evict Satan from our heart. We have invited Jesus in and exercised our will over and over to choose for God to live in us instead of any pharaoh. Truly, perfect love does cast out all fear. God knows how, step by step, to lead us out of Egypt into the Land of Canaan.

Your hardships, unique trials, unique character defects don't daunt God, He invites you to come to Him, take His hand, and let Him lead you to this Promised Land in Him. He can successfully fight any foe you meet as you trust and follow Him. You cannot change without Him. God knows this and that is why He beckons you to come to Him to have His wisdom, His strength, and His presence to help you.

The covenant God made with the Israelites was that He would be their God and they would be His people. With God as their King there was no need to be under the rule of any pharaoh or human king. God freed them from slavery. He wants His children today to be under His special care, management, and authority. God promises that if we will obey His voice, He will bring us into the Land of Canaan. There is no habit, no cultivated or hereditary tendency, that can hold us captive if we grasp Christ's hand and follow Him out of the land of sin, self, or Satan.

Parents, we are training our youth how to face the pharaoh of fear, rage, or passion and not remain under their bondage in Egypt. Set your youth free to serve God with the right use of their will.*

The rock work foundation that Matthew, age 19, and Andrew, age 17, built.

Andrew built the swing (to the right of the cabin), and Matthew built the jungle gym.

Rockwork builds men.

*Joshua 1:5.

Chapter 17

Exercising Their Wings

I bare you on eagles' wings, and brought you unto myself.
—Exodus 19:4

Two young eagles surveyed the vast horizon from the edge of their nest built high on a rocky crag. One said to the other, "I want to fly to worlds unknown. I want freedom to do as I please, with no one to tell me what to do. I want to live life *my way.*"

His sibling replied, "I want to follow our faithful father. I've seen him soar successfully, and I want to fly *his way.* I want to be like him."

The first eaglet spread his wings and launched himself confidently off the nest. Father eagle offered help, but the youngster ignored him. He thrilled as the wind rushed over his wings and he veered right and left. He exulted, "Yes! This is what real flight feels like!" But he failed to notice the direction he was heading was down. He thought he was flying when, in reality, he was free falling. Too late, he saw the earth coming up quickly toward him, and CRASH—he landed in a crumpled heap. Sadly, this picture represents the life of many youth today—independent from their Creator God and free-falling toward eternal death.

The second eaglet trustingly waited. He listened carefully to distinguish his father's voice from the other voices around him, and when he heard his father call him to jump, he launched himself off the nest. He, too, thrilled as the wind rushed over his wings. He watched his father closely, listened carefully for instructions, and imitated his movements. Suddenly, he saw the earth coming up rapidly toward him. However, just before he crashed, his father swooped under him and carried him on his back safely to his lofty mountain nest. The eaglet repeated this experience over and over, gaining strength, until he learned to fly well. This experience represents those youth who trust and follow Jesus. True spiritual flight and the hope of eternal life are found in Christ.

Spiritual flight is offered to parents and youth alike. Are you exercising your wings under Jesus' direction?

Free-falling

Laid-Back Larry, age eighteen, shuffled slowly out to the counter to receive a payment from a customer. His hair hung in wispy curls over his eyes. He brushed it back to examine the check, only to have his hair fall forward over his eyes again. Oh well! He was used to peering through his locks.

"Does your hair bother you, son?" the elderly customer asked.

"No, I like it this way," Larry insisted, pulling on a yellow-and-green-striped stocking cap and tucking the reckless strands out of sight.

"I know a barber I could recommend," the gentleman teased.

"No, thanks."

"So you like your hair this way?" he pressed further. You see, this man had known Larry when his hairstyle and dress were clean-cut. He wanted to understand what had made the change. Why would Larry want to look so unkempt?

"Yeah, I really like it 'cause it's so easy to care for. I wash my hair, towel it dry, run my fingers through it, and that's it. I get up in the morning and don't have to do anything to my hair if I don't want to. I don't like to have to bother combing my hair."

"I sure liked your hair the way you used to wear it. Now you look so . . . so . . . untrustworthy."

"Well, my parents told me I'm of age and can decide things for myself. They fought me for years to keep my hair cut, and I begrudgingly went along. But now I'm doing it *my way*."

"So what does God think of your hair?"

"Oh, I don't know. He probably doesn't like it. But I'm of age now and get to do things *my way*. My dad wore his hair long when he was my age. I just want to sow my wild oats. I'll probably cut my hair soon anyway."

What's wrong with this picture?

Is Laid-Back Larry exercising his wings of decision? Yes, he is. Is there a problem, though? I believe there is. Laid-Back Larry's hairstyle is a symptom of a deeper problem—a problem that existed even when his hair was cut in a neat, manly style. He is like that first eaglet—intent on flying his own way with no care for the guidance of his heavenly Father. He is worshiping and bowing to *his* wants—not what *God* wants. God is not in his equation of choices at all.

To give self free reign is very dangerous. One thing leads to another: demoralizing associations; corrupting reading, music, and entertainment; ungodly dress; health-destroying vices such as alcohol, tobacco, and drugs; and immorality. Some young people may not become corrupt outwardly, but their independent flight carries them into selfish attitudes, bad relationships, following peer pressure, covetousness, or despair. They can refuse to recognize all these steps away from God by consulting only "What would I like to do?" To accustom oneself to be laid back, to be indecisive for God, and to do what comes naturally or is exciting, is disastrous. In addition, if Laid-Back Larry does decide one day to return to God's service, what scars will remain?

Do you see the harm we do to our youth by not giving them *spiritual* flight lessons so that they know the difference between true flight and free fall? Do you see the importance of training them to recognize Jesus' voice guiding them and to choose to serve God in all the little things of life—including their hairstyles? Do you recognize the need to empower their flight feathers of decision within the framework of God's integrity?

It is not safe to sow wild oats—especially in the years of youth. What did Samson gain for sowing his wild oats? What about the youth that taunted Elisha? Or think of Esau. All these young men thought they were going to gain something—at least a little fun—by sowing their wild oats and that then they could settle down and live upright lives. But their wild oats played a large part in determining the direction of their lives and ultimately their destiny.

What did Adam and Eve gain from sowing their oats of "my way" apart from God in the Garden of Eden? Did Judas benefit by sowing his oats of financial gain, selling out Jesus, and being self-directed instead of God-directed? Did King Saul gain by sowing his oats of "I'm the big shot," acting the part of a priest, and not waiting for Samuel the prophet as God directed him? These steps of independence from God—the same steps Satan took in heaven—turned Saul into an evil king. Each of us must answer the question, Who is in charge of my life? Will I let God direct my hair, my dress, my conduct?

Every youth will decide his own destiny. Every youth exercises his wings and will fly. If we don't help them learn to fly in Christ, above the power of their flesh, the gravity of self will plunge them down to disaster on the rocks below. Can we stand by complacently and watch it happen? No! No! A thousand times No!

Who has the heart?

Sad to say, Laid-Back Larry's training in good habits had been only *external*. What do I mean? Larry had complied with his parent's choice regarding his hairstyle only because they out-argued him or sent him on a guilt trip or simply forced him to follow their wishes because they were bigger than he was. His heart's desire and opinion still opposed the obedience he was forced to render! The best that physical and emotional domination can produce is *external* submission, which is of little long-lasting value.

Laid-Back Larry lacked *internal* discipline. He didn't learn to recognize God's voice to his soul and to surrender to God's will! He didn't seek to determine God's will for his hairstyle. God says, "Let all things be done decently and in or-der."* God cares about every detail of our lives. He desires clean-cut, upright, young men who represent Him in their thoughts, words, and deeds. He wants their outward appearance to reflect the inner order of their hearts. Sadly, Laid-Back Larry represents the *self-directed* rabble-rousers of rebellious youth today that leave God out of their life's decisions! They aren't seeking the Lord's will to follow Him; they seek another master—self—which is a disguise for being *Satan-directed*.

God's ways are so much better. He is the youth's flying Instructor, and as they seek, listen, and cooperate with Him, they experience how He bears them on eagles' wings and brings them to Himself for input, decision by decision. Every trial faced, every difficulty encountered, and every decision to be made is an opportunity to come to Him, to know His will, and to respond as God leads. He is there—calling our youth both to discern His will and to let Him empower them to live out His will from the heart. Gaining this experience requires repeated exercise.

---

*1 Corinthians 14:40.

Don't quit!

Physical exercise for strength, health, and fitness takes much effort! Spiritual exercise for strength of character, to be God-directed instead of self-directed, and to be morally strong under temptation takes just as must effort! Both take focus, decision, determination, and cooperation on our part.

To physically build muscles you begin with small weights and work up to larger and larger ones. As the muscles increase in strength through exercise, they are enabled to handle the stress of greater weights without fatigue or damage. So, too, in the exercise of your wings of spiritual flight. If you want to become strong to do the right instead of the wrong, to follow Christ instead of self, to seek *God's will* and not only *your will,* you can best accomplish this by beginning with small "weights"— small decisions to follow God. These give Him permission to direct your steps. You will gain experience in allowing God to lead in every detail of your life, and this will gradually become the norm instead of the exception.

A small "weight" might be, "Lord, what would You have me to do with my hair, my dress, my deportment, right now?"* "Do You want me to go to this party or stay home?" "Shall I participate in this youth activity? What is Your will for me?" "Shall I accept this gift or decline it?" "Shall I think this thought, react this way?" "Should I follow my friend's idea?" "How can I resolve this misunderstanding, this conflict?"

Heavier "weights" might be, "How do I overcome lying to protect myself?" "Why do I respond in the evil way I do?" "Show me how to enjoy being helpful around the home." "How do I put You on the throne of my heart and keep You there?" "I sense Satan putting doubtful thoughts in my mind that You aren't interested in me, that I'm too bad, that You can't help me, that I'm a hopeless case. How do I get rid of these thoughts?"

To exercise filtering our thoughts and decisions through God is an exercise of faith, of will, and of action. It requires constant repetition, just as does physical exercise. In the morning, it may be easy to commit to following God, but as the day wears on and old ways pull and push on you to obey them, you will see that it is as much an effort to stay connected with God as it is to stay on the treadmill and complete your physical workout. It takes making a decision over and over again to remain under Christ.

As our youth are exercised, nurtured, and encouraged in this process of choosing to come under God, their "moral muscles" will increase in strength and prepare them for the even greater stress and pressure of *staying* on God's side in honesty, integrity, and moral purity as did Joseph. They will face many issues as they associate in this world and try not to be of the world.

Don't be afraid to let your youth engage in some hard spiritual exercise—to make decisions about what to do, under God, regarding this or that issue. They need to flap their wings, to sort and sift, to search to know His will, to wrestle to make the right decision, and to work through the process of following Jesus their Savior. Don't

---

*Acts 9:6.

save them from this vital wrestling process. Nurture it, promote it, exercise it, pray and counsel them through it. This muscle needs exercise! These are their wings! This spiritual exercise is not a one-time thing but a way of life requiring focus to establish these habits. At times tenacious exercise of certain muscle groups is necessary to bring health and strength to them.

Challenging the wings

Matthew, age sixteen, approached his father. "I've been reading Sam Campbell's books, and I want to find that mysterious Sanctuary Lake he talks about. Let's plan a family outing to the Quetico area of the Boundary Waters to search it out."

"Matthew, we live in the most beautiful, vast wilderness area in the United States. Glacier Park offers all that Minnesota and Canada can offer without the myriad of bugs and mosquitoes. We have yet to climb all the peaks or explore all the lakes here. Let's play in our own backyard."

Jim hoped that would be the end of the matter, but it wasn't. Instead, it was the beginning of some very interesting discussions and differing opinions of what to do with our family vacation time. This was a test. What happens in families when there are differing opinions and one or more family members "exercise their wings" independently of God? It produces conflict and tension in the home, doesn't it? On the other hand, what happens if each family member "exercises his or her wings" under God? That is what we wanted to do. When Jim spent time to know God's will, he got a surprise.

"Jim, you need to get into your son's dreams. You need to go to Quetico and go on that quest for Sanctuary Lake. It will be good for everyone."

"But I don't want to, Lord. It is going to cost me time and money, and I'd rather explore something close to home . . . but I'm willing to yield to You."

"Jim, think about what this will mean to your son—not only that you are willing to get into his dreams, but also how it can motivate him to face and do hard things. It will help him in his future career."

"Matthew, let's take that trip to the Quetico!"

"Really, Father? Really?"

"Yes, really! However, to get ready for this trip you need to do some work. You need to locate some maps and try to narrow down where to look for Sanctuary Lake. You need to see if you can find anybody that personally knew Sam Campbell to help you plan our search. Then you need to find a place for us to stay when we get there and canoes to rent."

Matthew's eyes got big, and he was a little less enthusiastic.

"Oh, Father, you're asking a hard thing of me. I don't like to talk on the phone."

"Well, that will be the price for going, son. I don't have time to investigate all of this. And if you are really going to get into selling real estate someday, you may as well learn now how to make cold calls, talk with people, get information, and do research. This is good. God is by your side, and I am here to counsel and coach you as well."

Matthew consulted God and decided to accept the challenge. This was a jump out of the nest into a new, uncharted experience for Matthew. It wasn't easy; his thinking, reasoning, and planning abilities were stretched. He prayed to God for help to figure out where to start and what to do next. He talked with Jim for added direction, and our anticipated adventure became a favorite topic at mealtimes and family times. He made phone calls that led nowhere. He was inclined to give up, but Jesus would "catch" him on His eagles' wings, return him to his place of safety, and encourage him to keep trying. He chose to persevere and face his fears with God. He learned to work different options to obtain his goals. He often wrestled—and turned to God for ideas. As God gave him those ideas, his determination grew. After a couple weeks, he really got into it all. God blessed. Muscles of dependence on God, decision, and confidence grew with repeated exercise.

His tenacity eventually paid off. God's providence led him to a man named Sandy. Sandy had known Sam Campbell when he was alive, and this contact led Matthew to other key people. He gathered important information, but no one could tell him exactly where to find this special lake. He went back to the book and highlighted all the hints he could find. Along with Andrew and his father, Matthew pored over the many topographical maps of the area, guessing and reasoning where this mysterious place might be that is "somewhere east of sunset and somewhere west of dawn." He planned our itinerary, made arrangements for our stay, and reserved canoes for us to rent when we got there.

All of us faced challenges as we made the necessary preparations and were tempted to exercise our wings in self—to get frustrated or irritated and give up. I had to come up with meals that were economical, lightweight, yet very nourishing—to last two weeks in the wilderness! Jim and the boys had to figure out how we would pack in two weeks of supplies. As we sought God and surrendered fleshly attitudes to Him, He supplied the ideas we needed. I made granola, cooked and dried pinto beans and dried peaches, pears, strawberries, broccoli, red and green peppers, chives, onions, herbs, and much more. Jim and the boys found the best affordable gear possible.

Finally, our vacation time arrived. Off we went on this high adventure far away. On the way there, Jim tried once more to interest Matthew in Glacier Park, but Matthew's heart was in Quetico.

Time to dig in

Arriving at the Boy Scout camp where Matthew had arranged for us to stay the first night, we met Sandy and got into a lively, fun discussion about Sanctuary Lake and Sam Campbell. Early the next morning we put our two canoes in the water, loaded our gear, and were off. Matthew and Andrew took the lead position, full of the excitement of exploration. Jim and I followed in the second canoe. This area is dotted with a myriad of lakes—some small, others very large. There are no trails to follow or signs to point the way. The wilderness traveler journeys from lake to lake, using portages where no waterway connects the lakes. The boys had to read the topography, compare it with the maps, and try to find the route that fit the vague hints from the book—all to locate that one mysterious Sanctuary Lake, the proverbial "needle in a haystack." What a challenge to exercise and to strengthen their wings!

Jim and I quickly realized that Andrew and Matthew were stronger paddlers than we were. Jim had a solution. "Boys! Boys, wait up! Let us come alongside."

As soon as we caught up to them, we dumped two of our four packs into their canoe. Surprised, they looked like they were going to complain of unfairness. I sent up a silent prayer to their Flight Instructor. Then they both broke out laughing, and Matthew teased good naturedly, "Having a hard time keeping up? Need a little help, huh? We can handle it, can't we, Andrew?" The two of them dug in their paddles, and away they went—and Jim and I still found it to be all we could do to keep up with them!

I had no idea how deeply we would be tested in this high adventure. After the first ten miles, my arms felt like they were going to fall off, and my neck hurt excruciatingly. I didn't know how much farther I could paddle. I just wanted to stop and make camp right there. But I knew that to give up now would make it impossible for Matthew to realize his dream. I was that eaglet struggling to stay in the air, and I cried out to my Father to catch me. He gave me some ideas about how to vary the way I was paddling and provide relief to strained muscles and tendons. He assured me that His grace would enable me to survive this trip and that I would build strong muscles.

By this time, we had reached a large, long lake; from here there were several possible routes to take. The only way to find which route was the right one was to try them all and see which best fit the book's description. The first route we tried didn't match, and we had to return to our starting point and paddle farther up the lake to the second possibility. By that time, a strong wind had picked up, whipping the gentle waves into rollers so high I couldn't reach the water with my paddle when we were on top of one. The pain in my shoulders was getting worse, but I couldn't stop paddling. Were we to capsize, drowning would be a very real danger, with little hope of rescue.

"Focus on the big picture, not on the pain in your shoulders and neck," God encouraged.

I chose to cooperate, put on a smile, and paddled harder. It worked; I could do it!

All four of us were tested to the limits of our endurance, and it is always tempting at such times to exercise our wings of decision apart from God. The desire to give up or get angry was strong at times. However, as we yielded to the help of our Father, we continued to face our adversity as a united team.

By the end of that first day, we had paddled twenty miles and crossed eight portages. At each portage, we would shoulder our packs and hike half a mile and often more to the next waterway, going steeply up then steeply down. It would take each of us two trips to lug all of our gear and our canoes over the trail. What a relief to set up camp, prepare our simple meal, and rub each other's sore shoulders. Andrew and I were the lead paddlers in our respective canoes, and we discussed how God had helped us override our sore muscles and our desire to quit. God was good!

The second and third days were much like the first. We adapted double packing so we could manage portages with one trip rather than two. That meant I carried ninety pounds. Matthew and Andrew each hauled one hundred and thirty pounds, and Jim packed a hefty one hundred and fifty pounds per trip. We groaned as we loaded our burdens. Satan was at hand to suggest such peevish thoughts as, "Whose idea was this, anyway? Andrew, are you sure you're carrying your fair share? Matthew, you are in my way. Sally, can't you move any faster?"

But God was there too. *"Encourage each other,"* He whispered.

"Andrew, you're carrying that load like a real trooper!" "Matthew, this is a great adventure you planned. We'll never forget this!" "Father, you are doing a tremendous job with that heavy load!" "Mother, you can do it! I know you can!" As we cooperated with God, we began to enjoy the challenge of seeing what we actually could accomplish. By God's grace, we would not be defeated! Of course, we had to cooperate with God, adjusting our attitudes more than once, and this exercise built perseverance.

After eight days, we had traced Sam Campbell's route deep into the Quetico, traveling twenty to twenty-five miles a day by water in addition to the portages. We had arrived in the area where we knew only one final leg remained. Finding it among the many possibilities was not easy. We had searched out many potential lakes without success.

Pressing on

We spent the Sabbath camping on Burnt Bean Campsite. A day of rest was most welcome—physically and spiritually. The next day we were feeling great, and our hopes were high that Sanctuary Lake was just around the bend!

By this time, the details of what we were searching for were etched in Matthew's mind. He and Andrew led the way, asking God for direction. We ventured into a string of lakes that seemed to fit the description. The farther we went, the more excited Matthew became. "I think this one is it! The topography looks very much like the story." And he rehearsed all the details. "Oh, look ahead! I'll bet that's the River of Ten Thousand Umphs."

Looking where he was pointing, we could just barely pick out a shallow, reedy river entering the lake. It looked more like a swamp than a river—and hard going for a canoe!

"The water level is probably lower now than it was in Sam Campbell's day," Matthew commented as we neared it. "We are going to have to push our canoe through." Matthew and Andrew were so excited, they didn't mind stepping into the knee-deep muck to shove our canoe up this shallow waterway. Sweat streaming down their backs, they pushed and shoved until the reedy small stream disappeared.

Both boys began to search around until Andrew said excitedly, "Matthew, I found an animal trail just like Sam described in the book! Come and see!"

With mounting anticipation, we loaded our day packs and canoe onto our backs one more time. Following the well-worn game trail, we suddenly came upon a lovely, quiet lake—pristine and hidden. Was this Sanctuary Lake? Launching our canoe, we paddled around the lake looking for the one last clue that would clinch our find—the name "Joe" carved into the lichen on a big rock. "There it is!" shouted Matthew.

Human words are insufficient to express the joy of finding the object of our search. The hardness of the way was insignificant. The aching muscles were forgotten. The low food rations didn't matter. We had found Sanctuary Lake! Our search was successful. We were a real team! "Hip, Hip, Hurrah!" we all shouted.

We paddled around the lake again, rehearsing the stories and identifying the spots where they had occurred. We chose a special place to eat, and as we asked the blessing for our meager lunch, we thanked God for all we had endured for the delight of this reward. As we ate, we reminisced and laughed and reviewed our exploits together. We reflected how God had exercised our wings repeatedly to choose to follow Him when impulse or inclination would have caused us to "crash" in self.

Lingering as long as possible, we explored the lakeshore on foot.

"Look, look, look over there," Andrew yelled as he ran ahead. He had spotted a huge moose antler just off the side of the animal trail. "Oh what a find! Can I take it home, Father?"

"Son, it is so large, I don't think you can carry it out of here." We all admired it and imagined what a giant of a moose must have carried this set! "Maybe we should hang it up there in this tree. Then other adventurers can enjoy our find as well."

Andrew liked that suggestion—especially when he thought about what it really would be like to carry this giant treasure over the portages along with his already full load. He readily yielded to Father's idea. It took both Jim and Andrew to lift just one of those massive antlers into the tree.

We then turned back toward home. Our food rations were getting low, and our time was running out. We were so delighted that our search had paid off before we had to leave. With light hearts, we retraced our trail back to our Burnt Bean Campsite for one more night.

"We can set a reasonable pace on the way back, can't we?" I inquired hopefully.

"We have four days to get back to the Boy Scout Camp. Yes, we can, Mother," Jim responded.

The challenge deepens

We awakened the next morning to a change in weather. Strong gusts of wind sent angry, dark clouds scuttling across the sky; the air took on a new chill. Soon, rain began to fall—then to pour. We donned our rain gear, hurriedly packed up our camp, and loaded our canoes. All day, we paddled and portaged through the rain and wind. It seemed that in whatever direction we paddled, the wind blew against us, whipping the waves into white-capped rollers. The portages were equally difficult. The paths that had been merely steep, rocky, and mucky when we came in were now dreadfully slippery. We were all tested to our limit. We had looked forward to an easier time going out—but instead it was more difficult. Once again, feelings of anger and frustration begged to be expressed. You understand what I mean, don't you? When you are tired and things don't go the way you expect them to and really want them to, negative thoughts and feelings seem so believable.

Once again, our heavenly Flight Instructor was present. *"You can be cheerful. You can overcome this difficulty, too. Encourage your teammates, your family!"*

Evening was nearing, but we pressed on—hoping the rain would stop before we set up camp. Late that night we set up camp in the rain, bathed in the lake, and tried to pop popcorn on the fire. We finally ended up eating in our tents. But God surprised us with a special treat. As we peered out at the rain pelting down, two moose crashed through our campsite. What a thrill!

After thanking Him, we went to sleep in damp bags, hoping and praying that the next day would be better. It rained all night, and the next day dawned with no improvement in the weather. Our sleeping bags were soggy. Of course, our tents were soaked. Everything seemed waterlogged and made our packs especially heavy to portage. We paddled lake after lake in silence—tired, worn out, wet, and hungry. The portages were treacherous with big rocks and running water everywhere. Weary to the bone, we pressed forward. Ten . . . eleven . . . twelve lakes and portages. Oh, how we longed for a dry camp and a good hot meal! But the rain continued. We could see no hopeful break in the sky. We couldn't bear to set up our soggy camp again. The only other option was to go all the way back to the Boy Scout Camp—four days of pleasurable paddling packed into two miserable ones.

We unanimously decided to take the latter option. That meant we were going to have to paddle past the point of exhaustion. We took up the challenge with prayer to strengthen our resolve, and God empowered our exhausted muscles as we strained them against wind and wave. The rain continued to pelt us, and the distance we needed to travel seemed almost insurmountable. I'll never forget what happened next. As usual, the boys were leading the way. As I paddled, each stroke was a prayer for strength and endurance. Suddenly, a new sound caught my ear—a sound that contrasted marvelously with the howl of the wind and the splash of raindrops and paddles. It lifted my spirits at once! It was the sound of two weary pilgrims, yielded to God—and singing!

"A mighty fortress is our God, a bulwark never failing. Our Helper He amidst the floods of mortal ills prevailing." "Pass me not, O gentle Savior, hear my humble cry; while on others thou art calling, do not pass me by. Savior, Savior, hear my humble cry!" "Onward Christian soldiers marching as to war, with the cross of Jesus going on before. We have Christ's own promise, that can never fail." "Trust and obey, for there's no other way to be happy in Jesus but to trust and obey." "Showers of blessings, showers of blessings we need. Mercy drops 'round us are falling, but for the showers we plead."

We made it back to camp late that night. Gratitude arose to God in our prayers that evening for strengthening us in our time of need and for giving us such a joyful and successful adventure. We slept peacefully in that humble little bunk-bed cabin, listening to the melodious sound of the raindrops on the roof, savoring the pleasure of being dry, clean, and warm.

God wants us each, in our day-to-day lives, to find this experience of true spiritual flight. He calls us to exercise our wings of decision for Him, to flap our wings of self-control against discouraging odds—the wind, rain, and tide of evil that pours down all around us in this world. God is there with us. He is waiting and willing to help anytime we cry out to Him and exercise our muscles of surrender and cooperation to follow Him. God awaits our choice to let Him be the One in charge of our thoughts and responses. There is no storm of life that can swamp our canoe or dampen our attitude when He is the One in charge.

Won't you exercise your wings of decision under God's direction? Won't you let Him teach you to fly above the gravity of the world, the flesh, and the devil? Won't you help your youth to do the same?

THE LONE EMBRACE
A SPECIAL WORD OF ENCOURAGEMENT FOR SINGLE PARENTS

For our youth, exercising their wings is learning to let God be in charge of their lives—accepting His input on every aspect of their being, even the simplest things. Will our youth let God be Lord and direct their steps? Will they let God implant in them His firmer virtues of perseverance, courage, and decisiveness to endure those uncomfortable hardships that life doles out?

Single parents face their own set of peculiar storms and adversities. It is your privilege to exercise your wings of decision under God and not to be defeated by the tempests of life. As you do so, you will model for your youth how they can do the same. You can train them how to come under God for empowered flight and empowered choices.

If you and your youth will learn these basic lessons of life, together you can face any hardship that single parenting can dole out. Whatever winds of strife beat at you to knock you down, you can face it with a song—trusting in Jesus and choosing to follow where He leads in the impossible storm of life. Filter all through Christ, and you will find a happy home amidst your storms. You can then laugh at the discouragements Satan throws at you and remain under Christ's roof—directed, protected, and enabled from above to follow Him.

Chapter 18

Associations

I am a companion of all them that fear thee, and of them that keep thy precepts.
Psalm 119:63

ook at what is coming up the street," I remarked to Jim.

Fifteen-year-old Chains Charlie and his fourteen-year-old sidekick, Misfit Murphy, sauntered aimlessly down the sidewalk. Following them in a lively conversation was Tough Tommy, age thirteen, and Abused Abby, no older than fourteen. Lying Larry, Mad Music Mandy, and Despairing Dora tagged along, not wanting to miss a thing. What a sight!

But what caught my attention next aroused not only my sympathies but also my fears! I saw where this group was headed! Not far from where we stood was Brooding Becky, an unhappy, vulnerable thirteen-year-old, talking with Cool Jace, whom I knew was trying to be a Christian *without* success. Shy Sarah joined this twosome just as the first group arrived, and they all began talking.

I saw Abused Abby, a very outgoing, bubbly girl, reach out to Brooding Becky. I observed the exchange of sympathy, and soon Abby's arm was around Becky, drawing her in with concern. Chains Charlie, his pants cascading with chains, was the obvious leader of this strange group. He approached Cool Jace with an air of authority that made introductions awkward. However, Misfit Murphy, who seemed to know Cool Jace, intervened, and soon all three boys were engaged in lively talk. Despairing Dora was drawn to Shy Sarah, who seemed much taken aback by this motley group. But before long all of them were walking together down the street.

What is happening here? It is association's influence, fulfilling a genuine God-implanted desire for relationships. God did not create us to be self-sufficient entities. He made us with the need to give and receive sympathy, love, and companionship.

Observe the natural world. Nothing exists all by itself. Every living creature, from the tiniest bacteria to the largest whale, depends on other life forms to survive. In turn, each has something to give that sustains another life. Even plants relate. They depend on the carbon dioxide that is a waste product from the animal world. They take it in and, in the presence of sunshine, convert it to food and fresh oxygen, which they return to the animal world. Is your family doing as well as the natural world?

The Scriptures use the human body to illustrate the law of association.* Every part of the body both *depends on* and is *depended on* by every other part. You cannot find even one cell in your body that can live by itself. If it does not receive what the other parts of the body give, it will die, and if it does not give to the other cells, it

---

*1 Corinthians 12:12–27; Romans 12:4, 5; Ephesians 4:4.

languishes and eventually dies. If you sever a hand or a leg or an ear or remove an organ, it will die, and the body will suffer the loss.

Is there a reason God uses the analogy of the human body when He talks about relationships? Of course there is. He made us to need each other. He created us to love, and we cannot love in isolation. We can love only in relationships. Is your family meeting this need?

In a body, some members are more closely associated with each other, while others are more distant. For instance, the elbow is intimately associated with the bicep muscles, the triceps, the humerus, the radius, and the ulna. It has to learn to cooperate directly with all those muscles and bones in order to fill its place in the body. It is less closely linked with the big toe or the nose.

Even so, in life God places us in a very intimate association with our family members. Our relationships with them are critical, while other relationships may also be important but are less close. For many, the pull of family is so strong that they strive for approval or to maintain that relationship even when it is negative, abusive, indifferent, or unfulfilling. They crave to belong and be loved, whether that love is healthy or unhealthy.

Chains Charlie, Misfit Murphy, Abused Abby, and Despairing Dora were trying to fill the nurturing family intimacy they missed by substituting relationships with each other. Their problem-solving techniques, learned in the religion of self, will likely be passed on to vulnerable Brooding Becky, Cool Jace, and Shy Sarah due to the unmet needs that are driving their need of relationships and the circumstances bringing them close together. We hope they discover and try Jesus as their personal Savior rather than these associations that tend to replace God.

None of the different organs or structures in the body could function were it not for one essential member—the head. Without a vital connection to the head, the hand is useless. So is the heart or the lungs or any other member. The body can survive the loss of some members but not the loss of the head. The head is continually sending messages to every body part to guide, direct, protect, sustain, energize, and coordinate each individual member so that they function together as a synchronized whole. If the nerves connecting the head with a particular body part are severed, the messages don't get through. If part of the body is injured or attacked by disease, the body mobilizes healing forces to bring the entire body back to health.

Our Head is Christ.* He is ever sending messages to the members of His body. As we respond, He guides, directs, protects, sustains, energizes, and coordinates us in all our associations of life. Spiritually, the nerves connecting the head with the body are time and daily communion with God to give Him the opportunity to give life to right thoughts.

But there is another—Satan—who jockeys to replace Christ. He attempts to deceive us into making him our head, and many fall for his tricks—like the youth at the beginning of this chapter. The problem is that Satan sends out messages that are not good for the body. When he is accepted as the head, the body hears lying

---

*Ephesians 5:23.

thoughts. It believes them and responds wrongly. Spiritually, that is like getting sick physically. Some parts of the mind become paralyzed while others are overactive. The body does not function well, and many of its wholesome members simply die.

Who is the head? This is the key in all our associations—including associations for our youth. Whose messages are they listening to and obeying? Associations formed under Christ are uplifting, wholesome, harmonious, healing, and helpful. Associations formed under Christ's enemy demoralize, divide, destroy, and derail from life's real purpose.

That is what alarmed me as I watched that group of precious young people mingle together on the street that day. Who were they listening to? Who was their head? What would result from their association together? A lie often told will be finally believed.

What a difference the head makes!

Samson had a lot going for him. Although he was born during a time when Israel was not following God, he had parents who loved God and provided him with every advantage they could. An angel had appeared to Samson's mother before his birth to give special instructions for his care, and she followed them. Samson had every opportunity to develop physical strength, mental capability, and moral purity. God had a mission for him. He wanted to use Samson to deliver His people. He wanted to be Samson's Head, directing him in a way that would make his life the truest possible success.

Association with those who followed Satan was Samson's undoing. It probably began with seemingly "little compromises." Samson began to value the friendship of those who did not know or follow God. He enjoyed the excitement and arousal he could get out of these relationships more than he valued association with Christ. God got only a portion of his heart. Little by little, he let go of principle until, while physically the strongest man on earth, he was one of the weakest morally. He had strong passions, but not strong character. Don't mistake the two; they are not one and the same. The real strength of a man is measured by the power of the feelings he controls, not by those that control him!

Satan lured Samson on and on until he had him in the palm of his hand. You know the story. Delilah seduced him. Sexual passion has a bewitching power, dethroning reason and judgment. His reason perverted, Samson betrayed the secret of his strength to satisfy his strong passion. He had plenty of evidence that Delilah was untrustworthy, yet he confided in her. His passions controlled him. The glorious success God intended for Samson never came to full fruition. His life was full of shame. It need not have been thus.

Joseph faced similar temptations. He had, perhaps, even fewer advantages than Samson. Raised in a home divided by the contention of rival wives and sons, Joseph probably had few friendly associates. God had a mission for Joseph, just as He did for Samson, although Joseph understood it only vaguely in the beginning. His own brothers maliciously sold him into slavery. Finding himself suddenly thrust into the midst of pagans, Joseph felt alone. He had a choice to make: Would Christ continue to be his Head? Would he continue to seek and obey Him? Or would he follow the path of least resistance and join the idolaters?

Joseph had not chosen the company of these poor associates; Samson willingly did so. And this is one major factor in Samson's failure versus Joseph's success. When duty places us in difficult trials, we can be sure that God will preserve us. But when we step out of the path to which God has called us and willingly place ourselves in the path of temptation, we will fall sooner or later. It's just a matter of time.

When Joseph was confronted with seduction, his answer was quick and decisive. "How can I do this great wickedness and sin against God?" I will not sever my connection with my Head—even if I lose my life!

Joseph suffered greatly for a time because he chose to remain connected to Christ. But inwardly, he valued association with Christ above all else and could say with Paul, "For our light affliction, which is but for a moment, is working for us a far more exceeding and eternal weight of glory."* Because of his faithfulness, Joseph was able to fulfill God's mission for him in a glorious manner. Do you think he had any regrets?

Do you think Samson had regrets? Samson had access to the same source of strength, faithfulness, and purity that Joseph did. He could have chosen the right instead of the wrong.

The same choice comes to each youth today. Each faces challenges. Each have certain advantages—some more, some less. God has a special mission for each youth today that no one else can fill. Only as they accept Christ as their Head can they find the true success they were created for. The shield of grace can preserve them from the temptations of the enemy, though surrounded with the most corrupting influences. By firm principle and unwavering trust in God, their virtue and nobility of character can remain intact.

When we follow God and make Him our constant Companion and familiar Friend, we need not fear no matter what happens to us. Turn away from evil, corruption, and worldliness wherever you find it—in your own heart, in your family, even in church associations. Turn to God, asking, "Lord, what wilt thou have me to do?"† Seek associations that lead you to follow God in practical ways. Associate with those who have good manners, who can control self, who know God, who strive in Christ's strength to overcome wrong ways, who speak truth and do not lie, who are morally sound. God will direct your steps and give you wisdom to know the difference between those who make Him their Head and those who accept the counterfeit.‡

"Set down our names"

God wants parents to be the very best associates in the lives of their children and youth. In the analogy of the body, family members are like an arm or a leg—

---

*2 Corinthians 4:17, NKJV.
†Acts 9:6.
‡Proverbs 28:27.

composed of different parts with different jobs, but all working together like a team as they respond to the head. Sometimes, things are not what they should be at home because Mother or Father, brother or sister, has been listening to the wrong head and allowing sickness into the body. God calls them to unite in listening to Him! One family caught this vision and wrote to us:

> Our whole family is writing to tell you of a decision we have made together. We are reading *Pilgrim's Progress* for family worship. We just got through Christian's sojourn at the House of the Interpreter. One of the lessons there really excited us. We were discussing the meaning of the stately palace and the fierce giants that guarded it. We identified ourselves with those who stood outside desiring entrance. And we came to the decision as a family that we want to follow the example of the man who hacked his way through the giants that bar the way and got into the palace to be with Christ. So we have asked the "man at the table" to set down our names. We are arming ourselves in the armory, and we are proceeding to engage those giants in battle. We have determined that Giants Despair, Despondency, and Discouragement with all their vile relatives are banished from our home. They have too long held residence here and injured and bruised us with their swords and clubs. We have decided that Jesus Christ is Lord and Head of this home *in reality*, and we will, in His strength alone, vanquish the giants—casting them into the prison house and throwing the key into the moat. We want to enter into that "stately palace" of experience—the one David spoke about in Psalm 27—"One thing have I desired of the Lord, that will I seek after; that I may dwell in the house of the Lord all the days of my life, to behold the beauty of the Lord, and to inquire in his temple."
>
> In order to practically accomplish this, we *see ourselves as a team* with Jesus as our Commander. When we see one of our members locked in combat with one of the giants, the rest of us will come to his/her aid. We refuse to stand idly by while a fierce giant takes captive one of our number. Under Jesus' direction, we will pray fervently for the one under attack, we will speak words of encouragement, we will uphold his or her hands in the battle, and we will do whatever is needed in the strength of Jesus until the victory is gained. Failure is not an option!!
>
> Since we made this decision, we have each been approached by the giants, and sometimes their deadly blows have connected with us and caused us to stumble, "But we are not of them who draw back unto perdition; but of them that believe to the saving of the soul."* We have not suffered one of our number to be carried off captive. Praise God!!

That is true association! Wouldn't you like to be a part of such a family? I

---

*Hebrews 10:39.

would. This is the purpose for a family and all associations. We are to be all under God and the best associates of one another. Parents have the strongest influence in deciding which head rules their home. What a tremendous blessing if they are united under Christ! They can work together to connect their youth to Him.

When Christ is Mother's Head, she is like sunshine in the home—guiding, directing, motivating right choices, giving consequences where needed, all mingled with love, tenderness, and encouragement. She is her youth's most trusted friend and is a safe place to turn for nurture in a time of need. Caring for the hearts of each member, she teaches and trains child and youth alike to seek God to be their Head and direct their choices.

When Christ is Father's Head, he is like a "house-band"—drawing the family members together in the same way that Christ draws us to Himself. He is the priest of the home—caring for and instructing each member. As the head of the house, he represents Christ in all that is pure and upright and does not follow the promptings of his flesh. His leadership contributes to making the home happy. He provides financially, shares the burdens of the home, and is a real companion to his wife and children.

Parents, what do your youth see in you? Do they see genuine concern for them? Do they see you following principle rather than inclination when your own will is crossed? Do they see you consistently practicing what you preach? Do they find you attractive because you have Christ as your Head? You can associate with your youth in such a way that they desire to live a life above the slavery of sin. You can encourage them to find a vital connection with Christ so that when they see immodest dress, they have the power to choose to follow God instead of Satan. They can live above the pressure of peers to engage in impiety, sloppy hairstyles, slouchy attitudes, body piercing, perverted music, alcohol, tobacco, drugs, card playing, gambling, novel reading, occult reading, vice, vulgarities, pornography, appetites, passions, immorality, sexual matters, and everything else Satan throws at them through their associations. Through God's strong influence in their lives, they may be another Joseph—not a Samson.

It is a sad reality that many homes today are not united under Christ. Joseph's home wasn't either. If you are a parent whose spouse doesn't care for Christ, don't despair. You and Christ are a majority. Don't hide Him in an attempt to avoid conflict. Cling more firmly to Christ and ask Him to show you how to make true religion practical and attractive to your youth. Let your life demonstrate the advantage of following Christ—even if you have to go through a Joseph experience. If your youth has at least one parent who connects them with Christ, their true Head, they have a tremendous advantage.

Whose path are your youth following—Joseph's or Samson's? Don't allow Satan's enticements to be a daily temptation to your youth without the way of escape found in Christ. Remove them from dangerous associates until they are trained to be strong enough to stand with Jesus at their side. This is the family God wants us to be—not putting down our youth, but building them up in Christ.

Who will be the head?

Our boys were young teens—fourteen and twelve—when we noticed a problem. Jim and I were our boys' best friends. We worked together, homeschooled together, played together, and prayed together. Each of us was learning to recognize the voice of God and to follow Him to overcome wrong habits. My boys were happy and content in all practical household duties as a part of the team—except after attending church.

The older boys there seemed to have a negative influence on my boys. These boys would not carry their Bibles, didn't participate in singing, turned up their shirt collars defiantly, spoke sarcastically, freely chewed gum, ate chocolate at any time, and were openly indifferent to religion. By association, their attitudes eventually influenced my boys. At first, my boys had proudly carried their Bibles to church and sang enthusiastically—but not anymore. And one morning they came to breakfast with their collars turned up. We began addressing the issue. It would take us most of the week to correct the influence of that one day, and then we'd be going to church to do it all over again. Frustration!

"Matthew and Andrew, we can't continue going to these social youth activities and church if it makes you indifferent toward God, your personal worship, proper dress, and conduct. These older youth have a strong negative influence on you, and we need to do something to change that. Your thinking is very detrimental here, for you are not following the character of Christ, but another," I said.

"Boys," Father added, "when Jesus associated with foolish boys, He led the conversation onto higher ground. He didn't enter into low discussions, nor did His peers sway Him to their wrong ways. He consulted with His heavenly Father, listening for His direction, and did His will—which was often contrary to the youth He associated with. Instead of being foolish, defiant, or indifferent, He looked for someone to help, uplift, or encourage. If one of the youth didn't want to talk of good things, He looked for one who did. We need to learn to be more like Jesus. What do you think?"

Matthew spoke first, "Well, to be honest, I enjoy being silly, but I know God doesn't want me to be that way. How do I say No without offending or hurting the boys at church?"

"We certainly don't want to needlessly offend, but I've come to see that when I try to please my friends who are displeasing God, I offend God. If I must offend one or the other, which should I choose?" Father responded.

"I never thought of it that way. Well, I don't want to offend God. So how can I say we don't want to talk about this stuff, act this way, or do these things?"

I recognized that these honest questions deserved practical answers and cried out in my heart to a wise God for wisdom before I spoke.

"The replacement principle might work. Why don't you just change the conversation altogether rather than tell them they are doing wrong? You could seek God during the week for topics to talk about and write them down to refer to before going to church so you would have a replacement idea ready. God has a thousand ideas where we have none. When you get into one of those conversations, ask God to lead you to change its direction at the first available opportunity."

The boys did just that. Before going to church we had a family prayer committing ourselves to Jesus' keeping, asking for wisdom and the right spirit. God would be their Teacher, training them in the right way to go—if they tuned their ear to heaven. As parents, we kept an eye on our boys, prayed for them as we saw them endeavoring to apply what we talked about, and entered in if need be. On the way home, they'd tell us how it went—good and bad. We avoided criticizing what they did and discussed solutions instead. Open honesty is so important.

"Mother," Andrew confessed one morning, "it is so hard to be like Jesus. I just can't do it. I find myself resenting your rules of no gum or chocolate, and I'm beginning to resent reading my Bible. It doesn't seem pleasant like it used to be."

"Son, I thank you for your honesty. Keep seeking God in your personal worship time. He will lead us to the solution. It's Satan who insinuates such doubts as you are experiencing. We certainly don't want you to give up on God because of these boys' influences. We all need to seek what God would have us to do to resolve these things."

Later Jim and I talked. "I feel impressed that we need to withdraw from church for a time until the boys are strong enough to stand like Jesus, Joseph, and Daniel amidst the wrong influences. Surely God wants them to stand. Maybe some time apart to gain a fresh perspective will help. We want to train them to be leaders for God and not followers of His enemy. What do you think, dear?"

"I agree. I don't want to lose our boys by going to church when they are not strong enough to withstand the corrupting influences there. How sad that these things exist in the church! But it shouldn't surprise us. Satan works hardest there! I don't want to neglect proper Christian fellowship, but until we work this out, I think we need to withdraw for a time. If we seek God each week—what He would have us to do—He will keep us balanced on this issue. He will lead us."

And so the next week, we stayed home. It was a wonderful day. We started the day with a special study for the boys. Then Jim presented an interactive sermon, and we shared a delicious meal. Perhaps the highlight of the day was the outdoor nature activity. In the middle of our walk, we each went a different direction and found a quiet spot alone with God. We asked Him for one idea of how to exert a positive influence on the other youth. It was a great experience of listening for God's inaudible voice reasoning in our minds. We would test all thoughts by God's Spirit, character, His Word, and experimentation.

I said, "God gave me another idea to replace wrong activities with an appropriate activity. We can prepare a Bible game in which I say a text, and then all the youth turn to that text to see who can find it the quickest. Then we can discuss the verse."

"When I was out under the tree," Matthew told us, "God revealed to me that I get into foolishness because I want to be liked. You know, He is right. I like people to like me, and this is why foolishness is attractive to me. Understanding this, maybe I can say No easier. I decided to be like Joseph and let God be my Head."

Then Andrew said, "God reminded me of the fun Bible game our friends showed us where you put five letters—like those that make up the words SWORD or FAITH—across the top of the page. Down the side of the page, you list trees, flowers, birds, mammals, Bible men, Bible women. You are timed while you fill in the sections according to the beginning letter, then score points. These youth may turn their noses up on anything to do with their Bibles, but if we show them how much fun this is and pray to God, they might learn to like it too."

"Maybe we could befriend these youth," Father suggested, "and see if we can influence them into a real walk with God that is attractive to them. All youth have needs, and maybe we could meet some of their needs so that they could see Jesus as their Friend. We could plan to go canoeing and invite one or two friends; in this way we could have a greater influence on what is talked about and what we do during the activity."

Associating with Christ in this way brings Him practically into our lives.

The second and third week God impressed both Jim and me to stay home from church. The first week I had shed many tears; it felt so awkward not to attend church. But it soon became so rewarding that the awkwardness disappeared. God felt real as we studied, walked, talked, and did activities to keep Christ the center of our day and conversations. We exercised new thoughts, new ideas, new plans, and continued to consult with God for more ideas.

The fourth week, Jim asked me, "So what did God tell you we should do this week?"

"To be honest, I didn't ask Him. I just figured He wanted us to stay home. I like this new program. I like the boys not straying from our lifestyle and not having all those doubts instilled by their associations. Those are all the wrong reasons, aren't they? I'll go for a walk right now and let you know what God says to me."

Upon returning, I said, "Jim, the Lord told me we should go to church this week. I wasn't expecting that, and I must admit I don't like the idea of those old issues coming up again. But I asked God to change my mind and heart to do His will, and I know He will."

Jim had gotten the same surprising response from God. When we told the boys, they, too, had trepidation. They had grown to like being separated and apart. No one misses conflicts, do they? We prayed and went to church with our quiver filled with the various ideas God had revealed to us over the past few weeks.

We had successes and failures that day. It is very frustrating not to have an effective program in place yet. Andrew tried twice to put into practice some of his plans, then opted to stand beside us rather than face more fears and timidity. Matthew tried some of his new ideas and, although most failed, one worked, and he got into a good discussion with one older youth.

Growth requires evaluation and change

On the way home, I noticed something new. All four of us were critical of what others were or were not doing. I commented, "I don't like our attitudes today. Each of us has something to complain about—'If only the leader would . . .' 'If only I were in control.' We can't choose for others, but we can choose for us. Only by association and communion with Christ can we become like Him. We need attitude adjustments from God toward those at church."

We went home asking Christ to teach us how to view these leaders and erring youth with God's eyes rather than with our human eyes alone. What would Jesus do were He in our situation? We decided to practice filtering more of what we thought and said through Christ before doing or saying it. We would let Christ change our characters. We'd give Him permission to interrupt our fleshly thoughts, and we promised to exchange them for His thoughts. Our feelings of resentment to others must be exchanged for pity. Our frustration must be replaced with a willingness to help them where we can. Over the next several months, we made tremendous progress in being able to express our concepts and to know God's will for us at home and at church. We laid down the burden of blaming others and picked up the cross of letting God lead us.

In this way, over time, God put His mind and attitudes into our surrendering hearts; and our characters were being transformed. Jesus became more real personally. Our family was a team, watching out to help one another in our individual weak areas at church or any social function. We could share our successes without pride and our failures without despair. We could receive input from each other. Home was a safe place where one could be honest and seek new answers without fear of ridicule or rejection.

Continuing this program for a couple of years, the boys learned by experimentation to recognize His voice and follow Him. They became the leaders of the church functions! Their influence was stronger than even that of those older than themselves. Many would not be steered in better channels, but they no longer pulled Matthew and Andrew down. The boys helped each other remain under God, listening and following His direction the best they knew, uplifting the conversation where they could, leaving discussions they could not redirect to find others interested in the Christian walk, or to at least do something wholesome in nature rather than talk nonsense.

Building on this experience, we'd give them permission to go to special youth events where the associations were not all we'd like them to be. We didn't mind the activities, but we did mind the characters that would be there. We'd encourage the boys to take Jesus with them and to follow His leading. They would return home to give us a full report of all their activities and discussions. They'd tell us everything.

Following one of these events, Matthew was a bit disturbed at his ineffectiveness. He decided to study the lives of the Bible greats. He began with Joseph. The Holy Spirit pointed out how Joseph's brothers were poor influences—even hateful enemies—yet he treated them kindly. Joseph sought God and said what God put on his heart even when he was ridiculed for it. When he was sold into slavery, he turned to the God of his father and chose to trust Him instead of giving into despair. Joseph saw that God is closest in severe, discouraging trials. Difficulties help us to sense our need and turn to God for solutions. In time, it works out for good. Joseph's trials stimulated real character growth because he allowed Christ to rule instead of self. He stood strong for integrity. For doing right, he was cast into prison. Still he trusted God. He would not despair. Matthew determined that this is what he would do, too.

Andrew chose to study Daniel. He saw that Daniel chose companions who would stand for the right against the tide of evil that was prevalent. They chose to eat simple food rather than partake of all the dainties at the king's table. He saw that God was leading them and that this leading was the best for them. The Holy Spirit spoke to Andrew's heart that his resentment toward our diet principles was not of God. Andrew chose to yield up his wrong feelings and to go forward like Daniel. Communion and association with God resolved many potentially grievous attitudes. By beholding Christ in the lives of these great men, we can choose what they chose—to be changed into His image through cooperating with His power and grace. Good association!*

By the ages of sixteen and eighteen, Matthew and Andrew were well versed in elevating their associations, creating wholesome occupations, and leading interesting discussions. They needed very little input or supervision from us. God was their best Associate, and by beholding Him, praying, and asking for His direction, their characters were being molded to be like His. Nothing is more important than for parents to seek from God how to make Him real to their youth so that they can see that God is helping them and learn He is a trusted Friend to whom they can automatically turn in every time of need.

When they are not sure what to say while interacting with other youth at church, at work, or when shopping, they turn to God for His input and guidance on the spot. Then they follow what they sense God is asking them to do. While disputes arose and caused anguish, the trials spurred on growth. Successfully following God is becoming the norm, and they recognize the wisdom is from above not from within themselves.

While in nature, they enjoy being quiet and alone with God and turn to Him as a trusted friend to walk with them and share the beauties He has created. Begin building these relationships and experiences for your children when they are young, for it makes for a happier, fuller life early in their experience.

We separated our boys from evil company for the purpose of finding the tools we needed to make a difference. We withdrew from detrimental associations rather than succumbing to them. We developed a purpose and a plan. Jesus was a real Teacher, training us all. Our motto became, We go to church to *associate together for the purpose* of strengthening and encouraging one another to follow God, not our flesh. When we find an open heart, we speak of the love of God that is stronger than sin; we speak the practical, precious truths of redemption. It's good to share how to cross over from the self-directed life to the Spirit-directed life with those who are interested. Shouldn't we talk more of Jesus and less of self? Shouldn't we tell what Jesus has done for us? If we do this, we will have far more of Jesus' power and presence to give us wisdom in how to handle difficult situations, and we will gain experience in how God directs us in the moment. In this way we can demonstrate following Christ as it is—attractive.

Associations—a blessing or a curse? Which they will be is determined by whom your youth make their head, whom they listen to, and whom they obey. Let it be

---

*Psalm 119:63.

Christ, the true Head, the only safe Leader. He will be your youth's truest Friend and most loyal Companion. He will never leave them nor forsake them. He will guide them safely through all the perplexities that associations present. Nowhere is this more needed than in boy-girl relationships. Let's look at them a little closer in the next chapter.

THE LONE EMBRACE
A SPECIAL WORD OF ENCOURAGEMENT FOR SINGLE PARENTS

Don't be overwhelmed. Prayer is the answer to every problem in life. It puts us in tune with God's divine wisdom, which knows just how to adjust everything perfectly. So often we do not pray in a certain situation, because from our standpoint, the outlook is hopeless. But nothing is impossible with God, not even your case, not your special needs, nor your lack of training so far. Nothing is so entangled that it cannot be remedied. No habit is so deep-rooted that it cannot be overcome. No one is so weak that he or she cannot be made strong. No mind is so dull that it cannot be made brilliant. Whatever we need or desire, if we trust in God, He will supply it. If we trust and follow God, He has the power to change whatever we put in His care.

Make your home a sweet, desirable oasis, a safe place so that your youth do not have to go down the detour of following the course of Chains Charlie and Abused Abby and then have to come out of that pit to find Christ as their best Head. By example you can direct them to their only source of power for successfully fulfilling the mission God has planned for them.

Remember, if you associate with good carpenters, you will become a good carpenter, learning all the tricks of the trade for excellence. When you associate with the pure and virtuous, you desire to be pure and virtuous. If you walk with the Lord, you will become like Him, the one faultless Example. Try God!*

Andrew, Matthew, Sally, and Jim going to Quetico. The family is off on an adventure to find Sanctuary Lake.

---

*Proverbs 13:20.

Chapter 19
Boy-Girl Relationships

He shall cover thee with his feathers, and under his wings shalt thou trust:
his truth shall be thy shield and buckler.
—*Psalm 91:4*

Pure friendships

Disparaging Dora was a sweet, pretty, petite fifteen-year-old from a very protective, conservative family. She was quite timid and viewed herself negatively. She met me at a church gathering and asked to talk with me.

"Would you like to walk the path in the woods while we talk?" I asked.

"Yes, that would be nice. I'm having some real problems with boys. I'm generally a friendly person, as you know, but I get so nervous around men and boys. I feel if I talk with them I'll be doing something evil, so I pull away out of fear."

"Why would you think that? Surely something has triggered this thought."

"I don't really know. I'm not sure how I am supposed to act or what is appropriate to say. I fear I'll be flirtatious, and my tongue gets tied, and then I say nothing. My reason tells me it's all right to talk to a boy, but my fears overwhelm me. It's a terrible struggle within. Which thoughts are correct?"

"The world is not made up of just boys—or just girls. God intended boys and girls to mix and to enjoy getting to know each other in casual friendships. When you spend time with boys in a youth group, church group, or family group you will discover that they are human beings just as you are. God wants you to see and experience various traits in boys so that you can begin to evaluate which traits you would like or dislike one day in a spouse. It's good to begin evaluating while you're young; your perspective will mature as you get older. In encouraging a proper friendship like this, I'm not suggesting that you get emotionally or physically involved with a boy. You're not old enough for that. It's best at your age to be just friends. Does that sound reasonable, or are you still fearful?"

"Yes, it's reasonable," Dora said timidly. "But I'm afraid of boys. I'm afraid I'll displease God if I talk to them and that when Jesus comes I will be lost. I don't know what to do!"

"Why should you be afraid? You are a sweet, conservative, honest young lady! You are not forward. You're very reserved. Boys aren't evil, are they? Talking with boys isn't an evil thing when you are upright. What are you afraid of?"

Dora hesitated, then opened her heart and said, "Well, the truth is that a while back, my mother was trying to help me overcome my fear of talking with boys. She encouraged me to talk with a nice boy my age. While I was doing that, the boy's mother pulled me aside and strongly reproved me for being flirtatious and forward.

Since then, I can't bring myself to talk with a boy. Fear comes up in such a big way! I'm afraid God will give up on me for being so bad and talking with boys."

"We need to figure out the truth that God is telling you and the lie Satan is telling you," I replied. "Both God and Satan speak to you in your mind, your thoughts, and your conscience. Satan instills *false guilt* by suggesting doubts and lies about God. He wants you to see God as stern and unjust, waiting to strike you down if you make a mistake. Satan's loud voice stirs up your feelings and emotions and makes you feel *compelled* to fear or to doubt. He tells you that you must obey him if you want relief from those awful feelings. Galatians chapter five, verses nineteen through twenty-one, spells out more of Satan's character traits. God does not bring this hopelessness and fear to you—Satan does."

"Yes, that is the voice that comes to me with this fear I'm trying to describe."

"This is clearly Satan's voice and character. You need not obey it. You can turn away from Satan's lies and serve your tender heavenly Father's voice instead. He tells you the truth. He cannot lie to you, for what He says comes true. God's voice is a still, small voice that inspires hope. He never compels or forces. He leaves you free to accept or reject His thoughts to you. He gives you the time and space to be a 'Berean' and see if what He tells you is according to His Word and Spirit. God says, 'Fear not.' He brings *true conviction* to change and also offers His helping hand to do it. So, who do you think is speaking to your mind in these competing thoughts?"

"Well, my fears are compelling, loud, and make me want to doubt God. So they must come from Satan to knock me down. But what if that lady was right and I'm forward and flirtatious? I don't want to be forward or flirtatious! Do you think I am?"

"I don't see a flirtatious bone in your body! Girls don't come any more reserved than you do. You didn't *want* to talk with that boy. Isn't that right?"

"No, I didn't. I did it because Mother convinced me I needed to be more friendly and at least talk with a boy. We were praying my fears would go away if I faced them."

"Well, I agree with your reasoning. A timid, fearful person just talking innocently is neither forward nor flirtatious. You were a proper example of the saying, 'If you want to have friends, you must show yourself friendly.' Would Jesus be friendly both to you and to that young boy?"

"Why yes, He would, because He is properly friendly." The light came on. "Then there is nothing wrong with being properly, reservedly friendly!" Dora reasoned. "Jesus' example is safe to follow!"

"That is right! So the truth is you were just being a friend like Jesus would have you to be. God was asking you to come out of the ditch of being unfriendly and aloof, and He didn't want you to be afraid. Am I right?"

"Yes, that's right." And peace replaced the conflict in Disparaging Dora's countenance. God called her to trust Him, and she did.

"Then Satan was lying to you through that judgmental mother," I continued, "accusing you of something that was not true! And her rejection of you stirred your emotions of fear. Am I right or am I wrong?"

"Well, yes, I believe that is true. That is just like the devil to hurt and accuse honest people. It's Satan that calls us to fear!" Dora answered.

"So let me ask you one more question. Did you have any other desires—wrong ones, maybe—in talking with that boy?"

"I can't think of any." She paused a moment to reflect. "No, there were no other thoughts," she answered very honestly, sincerely, and introspectively.

"It's settled then. The truth is that you were acting uprightly in talking with that boy. Isn't that so?"

"Yes! Thank you for helping me. I feel much better knowing what the truth is. Summarize this for me again. And do you understand why I became so fearful over this?"

"A girl should be prayerful, listening for God's voice to guide her while she is both reserved and friendly. God will guide you, and you will learn His voice with time. A boy is just a person, just as a girl is a person. You can make a friend of a boy, and it can be totally proper before God. Is your motive right? If so, go forward cautiously, but don't be paranoid. I feel the reason this became needlessly confusing in your case is because of the overapplication of the words *flirtatious* and *forward*.

"You can overdo or underdo God's will. For some, anything goes. There is no restraint. They push themselves on boys. This is underdoing the will of God. But some—like the mother who reproached you—overapply His will. Obviously, she thinks just talking or looking at a boy is flirting or being forward. She entirely mislabeled as evil something that was very innocent and wholesome. Because you are sensitive and, perhaps, overly conscientious, you fear anything you might do now. You fear what others will think and say, and it ties you up in knots even when you are doing what God considers right and lawful.

"As a result, your thoughts freeze, and your tongue ties because you are trying to please someone while not knowing where the guideline is. In this way, Satan calls good evil and blackens the right. I think you overevaluate yourself in a condemning way. God will help you here. The Bible says not to call evil good, but neither should we call good evil. Be friendly and ask God to lead you as you study to sort out all these things. Believe the truth—not misinterpretations of it. Then you'll be strong like Joseph and have peace in spite of the lies that others accuse you of—knowing you're in God's will."

Disparaging Dora sought to let God have her fears and to follow Him to find that freedom. She put her feet in the pathway of appropriate friendships with boys.

Parents, we need to teach our young people what proper conduct is—and what it is not. Make it tangible. Help them to distinguish Satan's voice from God's voice, to know which voice is safe to obey and which to reject. Address their imbalances. If they are too shy, teach them how to be forthright under God. If they are too friendly, teach them to be reserved. With Christ leading and directing, they can remain upright in their associations with one another, as Joseph was. Neither boys nor girls are evil. They can have appropriate friendships if both seek God for balance and each has proper motives.

God plans a time for everything. There is a time for casual friendships between boys and girls that are safe and appropriate. They should get to know each other in group settings, rather than one on one. They need to evaluate their motives honestly with God. Friendships are good when there is nothing in it beyond the simple desire for friendship. There should be no fantasizing, no desire to push the relationship physically or emotionally. Keep it just a pure friendship with no hidden agendas, such as a desire to run from one's present home life.

There is a time to think about, "What type of person would I like to marry? What are my life's goals and desires? What is God's will? Who and what type of character would make a good lasting spouse for me?" All these are appropriate questions. The right time will come later to seek or to respond to a closer relationship with someone special. Then is the time to evaluate these issues even more closely. And, for some, there is a time to get married.

Above all else, don't skip building a simple friendship, which is the foundation to lasting companionship and marriage one day. Don't step too fast just for the new thrill of being pursued. On the other hand, don't let Satan fill you with fear of an innocent, proper friendship. There is a time for everything. Be God-directed not self-directed. Ask Him to teach you the proper balance. Evaluate your motives for being in this boy-girl relationship. Why are you doing what you do? Keep your motives pure and upright like Joseph. Let go of obvious wrongs. Let God teach you how to enter into proper relationships so that you will have no regrets when you are older.

Forward and flirtatious

Spirited Stella, age sixteen, flounced into the room. "Hi, Sally! How are you doing? Got some time to go for a walk with me? I'm really fed up with my girlfriends! I need to talk with you."

"We could do that right now."

"Great!" She took my arm, and off we went. After a short distance, we met two guys. Leaving me, she approached one of them. Grabbing his arm, she pulled him down to whisper something in his ear. They both laughed. She looked around to see if anyone was listening, and then pulled both young men near her to whisper something. They all laughed.

Returning to me, she remarked flippantly, "I just had to tell them what's happening with my friends; they know all about it. We e-mail all the time. They're great guys. I do so enjoy being with guys. They're so much more fun than girls."

"Stella," I reminded her, "what about your promise to stay away from guys? You know how vulnerable you are because you so strongly want someone to love and care for you. Don't I remember a promise you made to God after the last incident with a fellow?"

"Well, yeah, but I'd have no fun if I did that. My promise lasted about one week, if that. I just couldn't say no any longer. Girls are such duds. They don't want to do anything exciting."

"Was your excitement alone with that last fellow such good fun?"

"Oh, that creep. He came up to me at church last week and acted like everything was all right between us. I wouldn't talk to him. I just walked away and gave him a look that said, 'Leave me alone.' "

"And what did God say you should do?"

"He said I should leave all boys alone until I got close to Jesus and knew His voice over that of my flesh. That I was going to get myself into trouble one day. He may be right, but it's my life. My mother enjoyed guys at my age, and I want the same freedom."

"But your freedom is bondage, Stella. Freedom to sin is death to all good. You were baptized and gave up a bunch of things you were turning away from. Don't go back to your old ways; they're disastrous. You are too familiar with the boys. The way you dress, talk, hang all over them, and press yourself into their company puts you at high risk for big trouble. Remember our talk about all of that?"

She nodded and I continued. "You were doing so well for several months with your personal worships, studying how to behave appropriately around young men, and seeking to know God's voice so you would trust Him and make Him—instead of yourself—the Pilot of your life. Are you still seeking God?"

"Well, my friends keep me up late at night; that's when we talk on the phone together. And I'm too tired in the morning. I just don't have time," she excused herself.

"Then your friends are more your god than the God of heaven," I warned.

"Let me tell you about what these girls did to me. . . . " And she went on.

She was unmoved by straight talk. Was Spirited Stella open to God's leading? No! She didn't want to filter her thoughts to know God's will. She was recklessly determined to do things her way, which meant she was choosing Satan as her lord by default. It rests with the youth to choose to follow God. Many follow God superficially in word or form only. Few cooperate with Him at the core of their being where true freedom and happiness is found.

Often, our youth have large unmet needs. A lonely longing heart or the drive to be loved by someone motivates their poor associations. It's their attempt to try to fill that empty void that their parents have failed to recognize. Parenting under God's leadership can turn around this longing heart even at this age. Change can happen in Christ.

There are innocent ways for a mother to love a son that could guard him from prematurely desiring a relationship with a girl. There are proper ways to show love in a father-daughter relationship that will prepare her to recognize and resist the polished rascal who tries to entice her with phony attentions and empty words. A father's love can save her from a life of misery by giving her a proper love and a sense of belonging. There is also a father-son relationship and mother-daughter relationship that can safely meet those deep needs for love so that they are not motivated by the wrong reasons to look for Mr. or Miss Right prematurely. Above all, a real personal, workable relationship with God will guard all youth in these issues as it did Joseph.

If we don't lead them as God has designed us to do, they will find someone else who will. Perhaps Fun Time Frank, Mr. Pervert, or Exciting Eric will lead her. Or maybe Flouncy Florence, Seductive Serena, or Loose Lily will entice him. These kinds of "leaders" will suck our youth into Satan's kind of independence, flippant behavior, and disrespect to parents and authority.

Parents, we need to let God have access to our inner life. He can give us better ways of approaching our youth than being harsh, belittling, demanding, or indulgently indifferent. He longs to change us! If we know the way ourselves by experience, we are better qualified to help our youth change in Jesus.

What influence does a harsh, angry parent have on his or her youth? If you lack self-control, why would they want to follow your powerless God? Realize your youth are a byproduct of what you have or have not put into them. If we want to change them, we must begin by letting God first change us. Our example can save our youth a host of evil detours.

We can learn how to nurture them in God instead of knocking them down with pitiless hail. We can share what Jesus can do to bring them out of these wrong desires, inclinations, tastes, and habits. Maybe with God we can fill that void. If they choose to turn against their present course and turn to Christ, we can rejoice. If they will not turn to Christ, we can write out Spirited Stella's future, can't we?

Again and again, Stella came close to changing. But in her later teens, she chose to be footloose and fancy-free apart from Christ. She thought that being upright was boring. It is difficult to turn around poor training from the young years unless the youth themselves reach out to God. Sin is destructive. If your youth takes this course, let her know that God will take her back the moment she chooses to turn to Him.

Youth, that empty void you experience is best filled by Jesus as your Lord and Savior—not a romantic relationship. He can love you appropriately and even make up for your parents' shortcomings. Seek Him and find Him. Love and peace will flood your soul, and when you're ready God can lead you to that someone special. Don't be fooled by Satan's false love and excitement.

Fascination with the opposite sex creates havoc in all cases I have seen, and there is always some lie from Satan that drives it. The excessive interest in the opposite sex is often coupled with a pulling away from God and His constraints—in their thoughts, feelings, emotions, tastes, inclinations, appetites, or passions. Youth often think they will not be caught in this well-laid trap of improper familiarity that leads to immorality, and it becomes a vice that viciously rules them. This unnatural self-gratification becomes wrongly labeled "normal" when it isn't. They believe Satan's lies that God is restricting their freedom to enjoy life. The truth is, these improper relationships will scar them and plague them for eternity and bring countless, deep heartaches they cannot erase. They may try to drown these memories in drugs, alcohol, or an imbalanced mind, but the scars remain.

Should they turn to God one day they will see how close to the brink of destruction they came. Instead of passively allowing this to happen, take action now. Find the wrong drive in your youth, label it, and cultivate the true to replace it under God. God is still calling youth today, *"Come home, My son, My daughter. I want to save you from all of this. Take My hand and follow Me. I love you and will lead you home!"*

Character list of a life's companion

I was shopping in town and ran into sixteen-year-old Pure Priscilla. She is sweet and friendly, and she has a lovely reserve around young men that she has learned over the past two years with the help of Jesus and her parents. She overcame her fear of talking with boys by putting God in charge of her life and cooperating with Him to make real changes in her thoughts, feelings, and responses. Spending time with boys in group settings was teaching her much. She was learning to beware of Phony Phineas with his ulterior motives. She understood how to "depart from evil"* and the wisdom of the counsel, "if sinners entice thee, consent thou not."† She could say No. She learned a lot of what she liked and didn't like through these experiences of talking with boys. She had recently sent me a list of qualities she'd appreciate in a husband some day. She had compiled them prayerfully during her personal worship time with God as she read of the Bible greats like Daniel, the three worthies, Joseph, David, and Jonathan.

"Oh, Mrs. Hohnberger, I sent you my list of character qualities for Mr. Right. Did you receive them?"

"Yes I did. I think you did a great job formulating such a nice list. I liked your categories—Principles, Character Qualities, with Must Have, and Like to Have beside those lists. You had another list: Can't Live With and Weaknesses I Can Handle. You are recognizing that you will not be marrying a perfect man one day. That is good. We need to be realistic. Making this list now before you know Mr. Right is good. If you thought you had met Mr. Right and then made the list, it would describe him, wouldn't it?"

She grinned, nodding her head.

"Did you enjoy doing this?" I asked.

"Yes, I really did. Without making a list to use as a guide, I'd have no idea what was best or what God wanted me to have. I could be more vulnerable to Mr. Wrong. God encouraged me to look at myself as well. I'm presently formulating a list of qualities I want God to change in me so I can become Miss Right. I need to run the home better alone, and some character traits need replacing. So I'll work on that."

"Your young teen years are a good time to formulate general guidelines of what you think would be good to have in a spouse—what would make for a happy home, a safe home, a nurturing home, and good relationships between husband and wife, as you see it from both sides. As you get older and evaluate and refine your understanding, you will modify your list. Then when Mr. Right comes along, you will have some logical guidelines by which to judge his character and principles. You won't be judging merely from your emotions and feelings," I told her.

"It took me a couple years to begin to see what is really important," said Priscilla. "I watched my parents to see what factors were involved when things worked well— and when they didn't. It actually helped me to put communication high on my list. Without communication, you can't solve problems in the home. Time has really

---

*Job 28:28.
†Proverbs 1:10.

changed my list already. Do you see any area I need to work on specifically?"

"As a matter of fact, I do. One area is your list of character traits. You want Mr. Right to be a leader—strong, decisive for God and right—and to lead out as priest of your home. But you also want him to be soft, sweet, always gentle, and noncon-frontational with you when you are wrong. These are opposite traits of character. A man either is strongly firm or strongly soft—not both.

"A firm man will be a driver, an achiever, decisive, quick to judge, and strong to protect you. This man will also be strong to correct you and challenge your concepts when he sees you are wrong. If he is going to be the final say in your home, he will have to cross you at times, and that won't feel soft, sweet, and always gentle. With a driver, decisions will be made, and you will get somewhere. He may be intense rather than tender. So your desires are a bit unrealistic to begin with. These qualities can be blended as a man matures in Christ, but generally they are not there at the beginning. Take courage; God made a woman to soften this type of man under His guidance.

"Now if you want a soft, sweet, always-gentle man that does not confront you, you are describing a quiet or laid-back man. He doesn't confront because he doesn't care how things are done. Projects take a long time to get done because he isn't motivated unless he is in the mood. His softness can be indecisiveness. He wants his space or he's timid. If you want a man always soft, you will not get the firmer virtues you listed. Now a godly woman can help cultivate the firmer virtues, but she will succeed only as her husband comes under God and decides to actively cultivate these opposite traits. His softness will continue to be the stronger trait and generally dominate.

"Therefore, you start with a man who has either the softer virtues or the firmer virtues and work for balance from there. There are downsides to each personality, but there are upsides as well. You need to understand if you are strongly bent to one over the other. You can discover this through proper friendships with boys and men. Evaluate these traits and see what I'm saying here and what God is teaching you by it. Right now, you are unrealistic in this aspect. God made a woman to cultivate the weaker portion of his character. Isn't it good to know that you will have some input into the making of your man?"

"Oh, I'm beginning to see a lot of what you say is so true," Priscilla affirmed. "I see myself preferring the stronger man that makes decisions under God. I guess I'd prefer to have him be the leader and feel hurt sometimes that he didn't see something my way than to have someone who is indecisive and who doesn't get up and get moving. I like timeliness too, and that would likely fit with the traits of the firmer man. I'll give it some more thought.

"My friend, Tanya, couldn't handle the strong personality; she would be crushed because she is so easily daunted. So, for her, the softer man would be better. We have discussed how she doesn't like to move too fast and is not timely. Just wait till I share with her what you've said. Her list is very different from mine, and she feels there must be something wrong with her," Priscilla added.

"Priscilla, God made all different personalities, with differing likes and dislikes. Individually, under God, we need to seek to find the right person for us. When it comes time to look for Mr. Right, you will have your concepts basically well thought out. Then you'll need to evaluate, 'What does Christ want me to see in this relationship?' Look for evidence of God's hand in your friendships. Ask, 'Am I being logical and led by principle or by emotions?' A lasting friendship develops slowly and naturally without the physical pushing it."

"So what character traits are most important?" asked Pure Priscilla.

"I think traits that come from being a follower of Christ—such as honesty, integrity, purity, loyalty, the ability to provide, being decisive for right, and willing to communicate—are important in making a marriage strong and lasting. Dishonesty, impure thoughts and habits, carelessness, and having a pretentious religion are traits that undermine and destroy a marriage," I commented.

Serious relationships

"When you get serious, I encourage you to assess your *compatibility* with the man you are considering as a husband. Are you compatible in personality, in recreation, in life's goals and directions, and in religious concepts and direction? For example, if Mr. Right is an avid mountain climber, while you consider outdoor exercise torture, are you compatible? In marriage, will your different preferences separate you? Sure, they will. Do your religious views harmonize or conflict? If one strongly wants to be a missionary and the other doesn't, one will end up miserable or disappointed. Are we suitable for each other? This is evaluating compatibility.

"Consider your *principles* of life. Are the two of you on the same page with the same goals and direction of life? This is where your list is invaluable, for you have evaluated what is of uppermost importance to you. If one of you values honesty very highly and the other has no problem with white lies, you are set up to clash in day-to-day life. Then there are the matters of a genuine seeking of God, religious beliefs, diet, dress, music, financial management, how you keep the house (sloppy or neat as a pin), child discipline, education, and more.

"What about *adaptability*? When one is rigid, will the other be flexible? Or are you at odds when you disagree, and can't resolve the issue? Does someone have a listening heart to God? Are you able to see things differently without disaster? It is searching for solutions rather than giving a cold, hostile shoulder. If he isn't for you, find out before you are married," I concluded.

"Above all else, I want to meet Mr. Right one day, and after we go through this process with God, I want our marriage to last forever. I want us to enjoy each other in our youth and in our old age," Pure Priscilla confided. "I believe that is the way God meant it to be—not splitting up for any reason like so many couples do today."

"One more thing I'd like to say on this topic, Priscilla. When you get more involved and serious with one young man, don't say, 'I love you' flippantly. Save it for when you really mean it. God will direct you when it is right to say. Some can hold hands without being emotionally driven, while others can't. Know who you are. Also, consider withholding your kisses unless he's the one you will marry or you may cheapen their meaning. A simple kiss can be innocent and sweet, but long kissing pushes the physical passions, which clouds the logic and evaluation. So express yourselves wisely. I'd recommend saving kissing for after you are engaged to be married and you have both committed yourselves to each other. But I leave you free to follow God as He leads you when you get to this point. We can talk more then."

"Well, I have to go. My mother is waiting for me," Pure Priscilla replied. "I'll put some thought into what we have talked about and change my list accordingly. I'll send it to you when it is revised. I appreciate your sharing with me. Thanks so much. Bye!"

Our youth need direction, guidance, and counsel as they work through these things. If we stifle these talks, they will find another leader to guide their thinking, such as Worldly Wiseman, Polished Rascal, Impure Ira, or Flatterer. It's better to discuss principles for building relationships before our youth are physically and emotionally involved. Many, when they are physically involved, shut their eyes and ears unless you agree with them. Give these younger teens some guidelines and standards while their minds are more open. Give them God's standard in a realistic and tasteful way. Give them a foundation under God's leadership that will stand the test.

Worthless brambles grow luxuriantly without thought or care, while useful and beautiful plants require thorough culture. Thus it is with our youth and their characters. If right habits are to be formed and right principles established, there is earnest work to be done. If wrong habits are to be corrected, perseverance and diligence are required to accomplish the task in Christ. Work with your youth to instill solid principles for choosing good companions and friends who are faithful to God.

Under God's wing of guidance we can trust. If we are connected to Him, we can give our youth the best counsel to save them from harm's way in the Spirit of Christ. If we connect them to God, they will have a sure guide to make an intelligent choice of whom they should, or should not, marry.

To believe or not to believe

I'd like to introduce you to Naïve Nan. She is a sweet young thing, but very gullible. She quickly believes what people say rather than inspecting the fruit of their characters to see if what they *are* matches what they *say*. Satan had his snare set for her because of this weakness.

"Nan, there is a wolf over there in the woods. Better run into the house or he will eat you!" And into the house Nan ran. Of course, there was no wolf. After a long time she returned to play with the youth that remained outside. It was the boys' game to get her out of the picture so that they could play with Friendly Fawn, Nan's friend.

Naïve Nan was the tender age of fourteen, a gentle spirit, and often was made the fool because she believed what others said. One day, her girlfriend, Deceitful Diana, told her she needed some money for a missionary trip. Could Nan help her raise some money? Naïve Nan went to her parents, emptied her piggy bank, and even solicited her relatives and neighbors for money. Joyfully, Nan gave all she collected to Deceitful Diana only to notice Diana buying lots of nonessential personal items.

Nan wondered uneasily if Diana was spending the money she gave her and got up enough courage to ask, "When do you go on that missionary trip, Diana?"

"Nan, what are you talking about? I never intended to go on that trip. You must have misunderstood me. You are a very poor listener, you know!" Diana accused.

Nan began to explain what Diana had said, when Diana cut her off, "You're dreaming this stuff all up. I said I wanted some spending money, and you gave me a gift. Do you want to be an Indian giver now? You need to put the best construction upon me like the Bible says. You say you are a Christian . . . so what will you do?"

Befuddled, Naïve Nan retreated. She talked with her mother and God about it but did nothing more, yet she continued the friendship—only for Diana to deceive her again and again in different ways.

When Naïve Nan was seventeen years old, she met a good-looking young man named Polished Peter. He spoke at church and went on mission trips. His parents professed to be working for the Lord, and his family outwardly looked very happy.

Polished Peter's suave attention swept Naïve Nan off her feet.

"Mrs. Hohnberger, when would be a good time to talk?" Naïve Nan asked.

"Call me tonight about six o'clock, and we can talk," I said.

"Mrs. Hohnberger, you won't believe it. I met Peter at a meeting, and he showed interest in me and invited my family to his house for an evening of fun. We went, and, oh, he is such a godly young man! He is so spiritual. Years ago, I made my list of character qualities for the man I will marry, and I think Peter fits every point I have."

"How long have you known him?"

"I've known him for years from a distance. But I've spent one evening with him when our families were together. My parents think he is godly too."

"Have you ever read *Pilgrim's Progress*?"

"Yes, I have," Naïve Nan replied.

"Remember the man that lured Christian off the path to the Celestial City? He was dressed all in white and talked real good. But there was one time that Christian saw a flash of black under his white clothing. And where did this man lead Christian and his fellow traveler?"

"That was the Flatterer. He led Christian and his friend away from the path of right. He got them into a mess—a trap—then left them there to die. God sent an angel to rescue them, and they were reproved and put back on the path. Christian learned that you can't trust a person by what he professes or merely by the outward packaging. You must test his character being led of God," she answered.

"That is right. Evil people can behave right outwardly for a time, and you must let God lead you as you judge their real character, whether they are what they say or not."

"But it would be wrong to say that Peter is not what he says he is! I wouldn't be a Christian if I thought that, would I?" she honestly questioned.

"We can't tell a book by its cover. The cover can look beautiful outwardly and be full of evil inside, can't it? We can't judge a man solely by his outward profession either. Remember Talkative?"

"I do remember. He could talk like he knew the walk, but he didn't walk it at home," she replied.

"God called the Pharisees 'whited sepulchers' because they looked fine out-wardly, but inwardly they were full of dead man's bones, putrefying sores, and darkness. They were not what they said they were. The Israelites took Saul as their king because he had a commanding, royal appearance. They liked the outward package and display. But inside, Saul was strongly independent from God, and later he bore evil fruit. Who was taller in God's eyes—Saul or Zacchaeus?" I asked.

"Well, Zacchaeus was a wee little man. He was not very attractive, perhaps, but he had a heart to follow God. He stood tall in character as he followed Jesus and made wrongs right. King Saul was physically tall and attractive, but he was short when it came to character—like the barren fig tree."

"Yes, Nan, you've got my point here. We cannot judge character by looks or even how a person talks, but by what he or she does. Profession is worthless unless the actions match it. We show our faith by our works, not just by our profession. "Even a child is known by *his doings,* whether his work be pure, and whether it be right."* This is fruit *inspecting*—not judging a person's eternal salvation. Paul admonished us to imitate the Bereans' example. They didn't just believe what Paul said. They com-pared it with God's Word to see if it were so. Well, in special friendships with some-one who might someday be your spouse, you need to test and see if he is a true fol-lower or just another Talkative."

"That's uncomfortable for me. I feel like that is judging, and we are not to judge."

"In this special type of relationship you are considering, it is only fair to both of you that you evaluate honestly. Don't you want an honest man who follows God for your spouse?"

"Yes, that is at the top of my list," Naïve Nan admitted.

"Well, then, believe he is what he says unless, with time and circumstances, God reveals otherwise to you. Ask God to reveal his true character, if the way you see it now is not the genuine article. Pray, watch, evaluate his dealings with you. Be honest with what God reveals to you. Yes, put the best construction upon him, but also be willing to see his dark side if there is one. Let the truth rule—not what you want the truth to be. You are at risk because you have a history of putting too much trust in untrustworthy people."

We discussed the confusion she had experienced believing Deceitful Diana. "God doesn't want His followers to believe lies. A true Christian calls sin by its right name and, while he loves the sinner, he still hates the sin. He also responds as Christ directs him—not as his or her emotions direct. If Peter is what he looks and says he is, he will stand your testing process and time."

So away Nan went to sort out these new thoughts. After six months of seeing Peter occasionally and cultivating a friendship, Naïve Nan had seen little that was negative. But after a year and spending much more time together, she came to talk to me again.

---

*Proverbs 20:11.

"Mrs. Hohnberger, it is so sad," Naïve Nan, now age nineteen, reported. "God asked me to call off my relationship with Peter. Your concerns for me were right. God taught me a very hard lesson. You cannot judge if a person is trustworthy by what he says, but rather by what he does. God gave me glimpses that should have made me suspicious in the first six months, but I discounted them and believed what Peter told me over what I heard and saw.

"He was lying to me from the beginning, and I didn't see it. Before I met him, he had left home to go to school and was involved in drinking, fist fights, girls, and pornography in an ever increasing degree and was tempted to do drugs. He lived two lives. He liked his so-called *freedom* and got into lots of bad stuff. He knew he was going against God, but he liked the excitement of it all, and he didn't get caught. He could talk his way out of anything with his family, and his friends admired his open admission of all the evil he was involved in. Even while he indulged those sins, he spoke at church about the Christian walk. He was interviewed on how to walk with God while he was walking with the devil. He was looked up to by many, but he was not the godly young man he appeared to be. Under all his white outer robes was hidden a dark core! Time and God revealed it to me."

"How did you discover all this?" I asked.

"One day, Peter was talkative and bragged about a few of the episodes in the dark side of his life. I think he expected me to be impressed at his honesty." She sighed. "It troubled me terribly. When I sought God's Word, Galatians chapter five told me who he was really following. We talked again and again about these things, and he tried to make me feel guilty for not trusting him. But God doesn't want us to trust untrustworthy people. I've learned that hard lesson through this and other experiences.

"When I told him I had decided to call off our courtship, he cried and revealed even more about himself. I tried to help him, but he wouldn't give up the pornography or other things. Like Samson, he was controlled by his appetites and passions; he was not strong for the Lord. At times he would admit he had a problem, but he wasn't interested in solutions or change; he just wanted me to forget it all and love him. The fruits of the Spirit were not in him. He was not easily entreated, and his stories contradicted each other. I wanted it to work out, but I had to face the truth that was revealed. Honesty is the character trait I see as most essential for a lasting friendship and marriage. Peter led me to believe that he was a Daniel while, in reality, he was Phony Phineas. He was uncovered.

"Now God and I will look for another. I'm older and wiser and thankful that this was revealed before we got any closer or married. I thank the Lord for helping me see."

"I am a companion of all them that fear thee, and of them that keep thy precepts."* "Go from the presence of a foolish man [one who does not serve God], when thou perceivest not in him the lips of knowledge."†

---

*Psalm 119:63.
†Proverbs 14:7.

Listen for the voice of God to direct your steps. Determine as did Joseph, "How can I do this great wickedness and sin against God?" Choose to do God's will, knowing He knows best for you. Search the Scriptures to see what made successful homes and what made unsuccessful homes. Observe the principles of Christ's life and follow His pattern in His trials, conflicts, and successes. If you do this, He will give you the desires of your heart; He will instruct you and lead you in the way you should go. Make a list of the qualities you should have and the qualities your spouse should have. Let God have you to mold and fashion into His likeness.

Don't seek a friendship with the opposite sex for wrong or fleshly motives, but for pure, simple reasons. Take time developing friendships in order to see what the character of this person truly is. Ask God to reveal to you what you need to know. Make a pact with your special friend whom you are considering to be your lifelong companion that you will both keep pure throughout your friendship, courtship, and engagement. If the two of you agree, one can be strong when the other is weak. And you can have the joy of marrying pure, under God, with no regrets. It's worth it. It doesn't matter if supposed friends entice you to let down your guard, to enter into a physical relationship. Believe them not! They are the enemy in disguise—whoever they are. The Flatterer will tell you he loves you just to get you to satisfy his passions. Believe him not! You can say a hearty No, under God, to all the evil, passion, and promises of the world. Follow Joseph's example—even if you may be ridiculed for being pure. It's the best and happiest course to take, and God can empower you to be all He means you to be.

In our next chapter, we will examine sexual matters and how they relate to relationships with the opposite sex.

THE LONE EMBRACE
A SPECIAL WORD OF ENCOURAGEMENT FOR SINGLE PARENTS

A single father or mother can—under God—lead his or her children and youth into pure standards of boy-girl relationships although it may not have been the path the parent followed. Be honest with your youth. Be led by God yourself. Promise to help them as they go through these formative years sorting out upright and improper conduct. Study and search out with them God's principles and help them decide, under God, how they will conduct their lives. Give them opportunities to make decisions in Christ—this is true flight training. Train them to yield their lives to God's control in order to find the truly happy life with that someone special. Be the best example you can be in Christ. Pray for them—and with them—as you go together through the school of life, led by Christ, bringing out both your strong and weak traits for God to address. He is there for you!

Chapter 20
Sexual Matters

He found him in a desert land, and in the waste howling wilderness; he led him about, he
instructed him, he kept him as the apple of his eye.
—Deuteronomy 32:10

Four-year-old Inquisitive Ira paused as she dressed her dolly. "Mommy," she asked nonchalantly, "where do babies come from?"

Mother, who was pregnant, sent up a little prayer for tact. "Honey, babies come from Mommy's and Daddy's love. Jesus gives life, and Mommy carries the baby right here until he's big enough to be born," and Mother placed her hand on her swelling abdomen. "This is where you grew, and I loved and cared for you in this way, too."

"Oh, I was just wondering," Inquisitive Ira replied and continued dressing her dolly.

Fourteen-year-old Pondering Pat had come in the door as this exchange ended, and he, too, asked the question. "Mother, where *do* babies come from? I mean, how are they made?" Mother looked into his eyes and saw that he was asking an honest, sincere question. Placing her hand on his shoulder, she steered him into the next room. She breathed another prayer for wisdom and then responded. "Well, son, a baby truly is made from Mother's and Father's love. You have seen the squirrels come together, haven't you?" Pat nodded, listening carefully. Mother continued. "When your father and I decided to have a baby, we came together in an act of true love. Mother's body supplied an egg, and Father's body supplied the seed to fertilize the egg. Those two cells joined and multiplied and divided according to God's plan to grow into a baby. That is what the woman's cycle is all about. About once a month, a woman's body makes an egg, and we then have the opportunity of having a baby if we choose. Love begets it, and God's blessing grows that love into a new life—a baby. That is how babies are made." She waited to see if that answered his question.

"Where does the baby grow? In your stomach?" he asked a bit squeamishly.

"No. God designed a special place inside every woman for a baby to grow. It's called the uterus. It is separate from my stomach and all my other organs. A cord grows inside the uterus that connects the baby's blood supply with my blood supply. God uses this cord to supply the baby with food and water and to carry away the waste products from the baby's body. The baby does not breathe or go to the bathroom until it is born. What a mother eats nourishes her baby; that's why I'm extra careful to eat healthful food. What a mother thinks and feels nourishes her baby emotionally. That's why it's important for me to be cheerful, trusting, and calm. When I talk with God and He with me, the baby experiences God right along with me. This helps the baby to grow physically, mentally, and spiritually.* Does that answer your question?"

"Yes. But I'm also wondering how the baby comes out."

"God makes provision for everything. He made a special channel for the baby to come out called the birth canal. It is small right now, but when the right time comes, it can stretch enough to allow the baby to be born. Isn't God marvelous? Is there anything else on your mind?"

"I have other questions, but I think that is all I want to know just now," Pondering Pat replied.

"Son, I want you to come to your father or me any time you have questions like this, and we will answer your questions truthfully. God designed sexuality to be pure and beautiful, but Satan has worked very hard to twist it into something destructive. Even among professed Christians, you will come across worldly ideas regarding sexual matters. Satan is out to give you not only wrong ideas but also destructive concepts about women that will damage your views of life. So please feel free to ask me anything and beware of what others tell you about this special gift of creation that God gave to man."

"I will, Mother! Thank you for explaining. I understand now."

Pat's eighteen-year-old brother had been studying in the corner of the room, but this conversation had drawn his attention. He commented, "Pat, do you remember how I asked Mother and Father what certain swear words meant that I had heard at the real estate office?" Pat nodded. "They suggested it was best for me not to know what those words meant because knowing would harm me more than help me. After I talked it over with God, I agreed. Then later, when our neighbor railed on me with all those foul words, I could stand there without getting stirred up because I didn't understand what he was saying. I knew what he was saying was bad because of his demeanor, but the words meant nothing to me. So they didn't really bother me. I think some things like Mother is talking about are also better not known."

"Well," Pat agreed, "I want to know only what Jesus wants me to know. I don't want to know what swear words mean—or the wrong knowledge about sexuality either."

Our children and youth need a proper understanding of God's plan for love and sexuality. And the best place for them to learn it is from loving parents who are sensitive both to God's leading and to the readiness of their young people to handle the information they are given. We should not give them too much or too little. Start with general information and add the specifics as they are needed. Too much explicit detail may arouse curiosity or lead to exploring or experimenting before they are old enough to have a walk with God or have sufficient moral judgment to use this information wisely and purely. If they do not need the details to perform the function, why are we giving it?

On the other hand, parents shouldn't be fearful or embarrassed to approach this topic with their children. Honest questions deserve honest answers tailored to the

---

*Luke 1:41.

child's age, understanding, and maturity. Handle questions in a matter-of-fact manner, giving them godly information in its pure sweet form as God intended. Some parents give their young people a book to read, and this may have its place. But a book is rather impersonal. If you choose to share a book, be sure to open communication with your young person to add the personal touch and answer their questions. God can give you the wisdom and approach that is best for you and your youth.

True love and self love

The foundation for one's perception of sexual matters is his or her definition of love. We say, "I love my car." "I love ice cream." "I love shopping." These kinds of love are based on what *I* like, what pleases *me*, what makes *me* feel good. This kind of love may have its proper place, but it is not God's plan in family relationships.

God illustrated at Calvary the kind of love we need for one another. "God so loved the world, that he gave . . ."* Unselfish love for one another is God's true love. Our self must die, so that God can live and love others through us. We give ourselves up to God. The spouse that denies the impulse to express anger or to speak belittling words is expressing love in a very tangible "Calvary" way. The *I* in us must come out of the center focus of our life's circle, and Christ must be enthroned instead. Only on this basis can you arrive at a pure understanding of love and sexuality.

Our youth learn to define love by the way their parents conduct themselves in the home. If they see Father and Mother being vulgar or crude, indulging sensuality, being self-centered or angry, the framework is built for the youth to entertain those perverted ideas of love. But if they see parents denying themselves for the good of each other and demonstrating God's pure, caring love in tenderness, helpfulness, kindness, and purity in Christ, they will gain a much healthier definition of love and intimacy.

A wife and mother can demonstrate this love in many ways. I didn't grow up seeing real love between my father and mother, so God has had to teach me how to unselfishly love my Jim. God asks me to speak kindly through both the good times and the difficult times. When problems arise, I don't need to throw temper tantrums or withdraw into cold silence. I seek the right time to open communication, be vulnerable, and try to resolve the issue—not just to submit to wrong, but be willing to speak honestly.

I also make it a priority to serve Jim, to make him comfortable by having timely meals, to help him be successful in his work, and to assist with his endless projects around the house. "What does Jim need? How can I help him?" My cheerful efforts to keep home neat and pleasant speak loudly of true love through service. Tender touches like back rubs or foot rubs show that I care for him. I also enjoy telling Jim, "You are so strong, you can do anything." Or "That's my man!" In this way I'm telling him he is special. These honest words of affirmation warm his heart and draw us close.

I can love Jim by spending time having fun together—enjoying him. I like to tease him into chasing me around the kitchen table, or around the house outside. Jim and I laugh and giggle—as do our boys or whoever is visiting. Of course, he always catches me with a warm hug and kiss. It's just pure fun!

---

*John 3:16.

I do these things with the motive of "what's in it for him?"—not "what's in it for me?" What is your motive for what you do? Is it for you or for the other? That's what makes the difference between true love and self love. True physical intimacy is the natural byproduct of this habitual expression of love and helpfulness all day long on the part of both husband and wife.

The husband defines love by how he pursues his wife. He is to cherish her as Christ loved the church and gave Himself for her.* Christ did not exploit the church for what it could do for Him, did He? No way! When a husband is under God's direction, his love will be a sweet, pure, godly model that is worth imitating. He will enjoy his wife for who she is—her mind, her heart, her personality—not just what she can do for him. Self must die. True love will not vent anger, or use the silent treatment to manipulate her to give in to his way. Love will follow God by thinking, speaking, and acting kindly. He will care for her and play with her. He'll communicate in positive ways with her and seek solutions when difficulties arise. He will be approachable, helpful at home, and affirming. He will treat her like a princess.

My Jim likes to say he loves me by teasing me and by having "beauty attacks," and he is always finding new ways to affirm me with words like "you are the missing color in the rainbow" with nothing in it for him. When a man loves his wife like this, she will love to serve him and submit to him. She will open up like a flower to give herself to her man.

Our two boys observed this for more than twenty years, and they caught on. When Matthew was courting Angela, he took her hiking. As they climbed beside a waterfall, they came upon a field of red Indian Paintbrushes in full bloom. Matthew exclaimed, "Angela, look! You are so beautiful that even these flowers blush in your presence." Angela blushed redder than the flowers, and they bantered playfully back and forth. How did Matthew learn to love like this with pure motives? He was following his parents' example. Angela in turn showed Matthew that he was special by making his favorite dessert—carob kisses—just for him.

Andrew had his own version. "Sarah, you are so gorgeous! You are the brightest star in the heavens. Thank you for being you!" Shy Sarah's lovely face flushed red with pleasure. A day or so later, Andrew received a tin of carob treats made especially for him with a note that said, "You are the most perfect man alive!" Andrew enjoyed her response, too. We do learn by imitation!

Matthew and Angela, Andrew and Sarah—each had storybook courtships because they built their relationships on the foundation of pure friendship. I wish I had the space to tell you of the many sweet expressions of love they each made to their special someone. You would enjoy them all. Both couples now enjoy lovely affectionate marriages—each in their uniqueness—untainted by regrets or selfish passions.

With God, your home can be a demonstration of the pure love God wants a husband and wife to share. It's our strongest influence in the lives of our young people.

---

*Ephesians 5:25–28.

Many youth are exposed to concepts of love that are not true love at all. If a wife takes her husband for granted, fails to do her part in making the home happy, and expects him to provide for all her wants, she is caught up in self-love. If a husband treats his wife like a convenience, speaks harshly to her, or treats her well only when he's in the mood or wants something, he does not know true love.

Beyond the home, self-love is taught almost everywhere our youth turn. It's in the music they hear at the grocery store. It's advertised all over the magazines and billboards. It's shared with young people by their teachers or classmates at school or even by their church associates. Satan falsely equates love with sexual excitement apart from a committed relationship. Its focus has to do more with external attractions than the real qualities of the person's inward heart. It's all about "me"! How cheap!

Many young people become infatuated with the idea of physical intimacy. It may be that their home is unhappy. Perhaps there are unresolved conflicts. Often, young people carry an inner emptiness that they have difficulty recognizing and verbalizing themselves. They are driven to find love, but Satan has succeeded in deceiving them so that they can't recognize the difference between true love and self-love.

The false portrait of a man

Girls long for romance. They want to feel special to someone. They want to know that they are loved and cherished. They think that the right man will satisfy that deep inward longing. They expect a young man to be their "knight in shining armor" to rescue them from the hurts of life and to make them feel like a princess. I've seen young teen girls wanting a boyfriend so badly that it becomes their main focus in life. The problem is twofold. First, no young man can live up to that expectation. Second, the girl's motivation for the relationship is selfish—"what's in it for me?" rather than "how can I honor God and improve the life of this young man?"

One sweet, pretty, and petite seventeen-year-old girl pursued boy after boy. She told me she wanted to get married because she wanted a baby to raise for Jesus. That sounded noble, but when I probed deeper, she opened up to explain that her home life was terrible. Tears filled her eyes as she told me about the small, unfinished, dirty house that she called home. Her family continually argued, and she felt unloved and unwanted. If she could only get away and have her own home to keep tidy, to be loved by someone, and to have a baby, she was sure she would be content and fulfilled. Her longings are understandable, aren't they? But is her solution truly a solution? Is it motivated by true love or self-love? God looks upon our motives. He asks, Who is in charge?

This desperate young lady did find a young man that would marry her, and she had that first baby early on. But she didn't find the fulfillment she expected. She carried into her marriage the poor ways of relating she had learned from her parents while her husband contributed some of his own. He was not prepared to provide financially for her and their child, so they were forced to live in a tiny apartment with next to nothing. The instability of their marriage escalated with the second and third child; they grew further and further apart. She was devastated. She realized she had jumped from the frying pan into the fire. Now under very difficult odds she had to find the solution that had been there all along—letting God, not self, have that central position to guide and direct her!

Her case is all too common. Some girls want a young man to give them a free ticket to stay home and be a lady of leisure. Others fall for a romance that ends in physical or mental abuse. Evaluate your motive with God. If self-love is behind your desire, you almost certainly will have a bad marriage, and it is better not to marry at all than to have a bad marriage. God desires to save you from these traps.

The false portrait of a woman

Both boys and girls long for true love! They long to be affirmed and validated. They want to know that they matter and that they have what it takes to be a man or a woman. God has implanted in them this desire for true love. The problem is that Satan promotes self-love—lust—in the place of true love. And lust in the soul is like poison in the body—it destroys you and your most important relationships.

Lust is behind the false portrait of a woman that is portrayed almost everywhere you go. Men get the idea that a woman is a plaything whose sole purpose is to fulfill them. Girls, confusing lust with love, play into the game. They entice the boys physically by dressing immodestly and by being forward. The attention they get seems gratifying when they don't know the difference between true love and lust. The boys will play the game for the thrill and excitement without responsibility.

Instead of viewing a woman as a special treasure to cherish and care for, boys and young men see her as something to conquer and use for their own gratification. Much of society tells them it is manly to think and behave this way. But the reality is that it ruins their chance for experiencing true love and enjoying a genuinely happy marriage based on God being in charge of their life. Self-love and true love cannot exist together. They do not blend. When one rules, the other must bow. The base passions that God intended to be kept under the control of reason, principle, and God's Word run rampant. Lust becomes an idol that demands expression for "me."

Boys share with other boys exciting sexual ideas that focus around the false portrait of a woman. Their fantasies put sexual activity in a perverted light—all geared to please self. One thought, one action, leads to another, and the boys progress to discussing or sharing pornography, stories about masturbation, or their misuse of girls. They become physically aroused, and their desire to experiment is increased. However, the indulgence of lust never brings freedom and joy. Instead, it turns into an addiction bringing intense shame and guilt. The boys withdraw from God and from those who would help them—which distances them even more from the true love they really need. The emptiness drives them deeper into lust. Learning how to excite one's passions leads to a host of destructive, sinful practices that pervert God's pure love.

Sexual abuse

It is a very sad fact that many children and youth have to deal with sexual abuse or incest. Sometimes one of their parents abuse them. In other cases, a relative, friend, teacher, or clergyman is the abuser. For some children, this exploitation begins very young.

Sexual abuse is someone manipulating you sexually or forcing you to be sexual with them. They touch and handle you inappropriately and ask you to do things with them you should not be doing. Closely related to sexual abuse is incest. Incest is sexual intimacy within the family in any combination—other than husband and wife. Both abuse and incest are perversions of God's plan of love. They bring a heavy burden of guilt and shame. Through repetition, these perversions increase the desire for these and other addictive practices. True freedom is obtained only through an exercise of trust, union, and communion with Christ as your Savior, and by following Him in this warfare against Satan's passion.

God wants youth to say "No" to whoever is pushing them in this direction. Many people wrongly think that God wants children and youth to obey any adult in a position of authority. They twist God's commandment, "Honour thy father and thy mother,"* to serve their own selfish purposes. They forget that the Scriptures qualify what kind of obedience children are to render. "Children, obey your parents *in the Lord.*"† If an authority figure is demanding that the young person do something out of God's will, the child or youth is not expected to obey. They should obey God rather than man.‡ He will teach them how to come out of sensuality and how to say no to improper authorities.

Some abusers are outwardly kind and so sly that their victims don't even realize that what happened was inappropriate—even though they may have gone all the way! Some grade school or high school teachers take advantage of the students by convincing them that this activity is therapy for them. Too late, the naïve youth discovers he or she was deceived. I've known youth who were molested while giving Bible studies. Their "Bible student" forced them into homosexual activity. One such youth experienced extreme guilt and shame, and because he wasn't able to sort out the issues, and didn't know God's voice to his conscience and soul, he became a homosexual himself. Whew!

Sexual abuse messes up its victims physically, mentally, emotionally, and spiritually. God never intended anyone to experience this. Children and youth are not prepared to handle the implications of such an intrusion of their person. Often, because of intimidation or shame or the lack of a safe person to talk to, they keep the molestation a secret. But they should not keep it a secret. They should find someone they can trust who will help stop the abuse and guide them to find healing.

God is willing and able to help them work through the wrong thoughts, feelings, and responses that are instilled through the experience of being exploited. He can show them better ways than they have learned. If the young person will seek Him, He will teach them proper independence from man and a proper dependence upon God.

The parent with tendencies toward sexual exploitation must find freedom in God from this heritage. Only then can God pronounce His blessing to the third and fourth generation of those that love and follow Him. In this way the parent can change the curse into a blessing.

---

*Exodus 20:12.

†Ephesians 6:1, italics added.

‡Acts 5:29.

Pornography

Pornography is a baited hook that captures far too many unwary youth. It is easily accessed through magazines and the Internet, and its sole purpose is to arouse perverted sexual desire. You should avoid it as carefully as you would a cobra, because it is deadly and addictive. Both boys and girls can get hooked on pornography and find out too late that it controls them—not that they control it! I've known many people that have toyed with it, entered into it, and become hooked on it. It makes them a puppet in Satan's hands and leads into deeper perversions.

The degrading portrayals of a woman's body creates an expectation in the mind of the young man of how a young woman should perform, and when he does get married, he is set up for disappointment and disillusionment. It is not God's will. I've known married men who lost their marriages and families playing the pornography game and cultivating its tastes, leading to incest in the family. I've known seemingly good youth to get into it out of curiosity and find themselves perverse tools in Satan's hands to hurt, taint, and demoralize other youth.

Pornography is also a form of self-arousal. It has nothing to do with true love. It is the moral equivalent of committing adultery.* Usually, it goes hand in hand with some other form of selfish gratification—often masturbation. The habit of masturbation feeds on the fantasy life offered by pornography, and the two work together to destroy those engaged in it.

Secret sin

Many youth—both boys and girls—fall into the habit of masturbation, which is clearly self-love. Masturbation turns an act that God created to be a beautiful expression of unselfish love for the one and only spouse in your life into a way to gratify your own desire for pleasure or excitation. Many think this practice is normal because it is pleasurable. But in reality, it's against God!† Self-love is *not normal*—it is always harmful.

Secret sin is a form of self-abuse. Fondling your own private areas produces a short season of self-pleasure, but God never designed these organs to be used this way. A careful study of the Scriptures shows that there is only one appropriate sexual expression—within the context of a loving committed marriage. All other avenues of sexual expression are self-love. Self-love is a monster never satisfied. The more you feed it, the more it demands. Thus self-control becomes very weak. Animal passion rules. Through this habit, Satan nurtures a self-nature that compels you to obey it as much as alcohol drives the alcoholic to drink. If you doubt me, just try stopping. You'll discover that it controls you, and not you it.

This monster demands your service, but repays you very poorly. It drains the vital force of your body proportionate to the frequency of your indulgence. It steals the spiritual sensitivity needed for a mind responsive to the voice of the Holy Spirit. Many find that it produces a foggy or slow brain with poor recall and a short attention

---

*Matthew 5:28.
†2 Timothy 3:2–4.

span. Schoolwork seems difficult and undesirable. It leaves you tired, in need of extra sleep, indecisive, and prone to depression. It nurtures a selfish disposition, a "me" focus—"Leave me to my little pleasures and don't ask me to help in any practical household duties; I'm too tired." Some find themselves withdrawing from life and evading work, which often contributes to conflicts in the home. The indecisiveness makes your Christian walk shallow and ineffective. Instead of growing in Christ, the self-love nature grows and overshadows your better qualities. "Me and my comfort" is your standard for decisions rather than God's will.

Satan, not Christ, is your leader, and his whole object is to ruin your health, your relationships, and your prospects for this life and the next. He keeps whispering his lies to you that this practice is normal and harmless. When Christ brings conviction and the longing for freedom to your heart, Satan insinuates that God is restricting your freedom. Far too many youth and older people alike believe him and continue indulging the vice, reaping the consequences.

One reason this practice has become so commonplace is that it is an inherited trait. The Bible says that the iniquities of the fathers are passed down to the third and fourth generation of them that hate (do not obey) God.* You can inherit a bent toward alcoholism. In the same way, you can inherit a bent toward secret sin.

Another common cause for secret sin is the lack of true love from an early age. Many people have big holes in their hearts that God meant to be filled with wholesome healthy relationships with their mother, father, brothers, and sisters—and especially with Him. When those important relationships are strained, stressed, or just plain distant, a young person is driven to fill that void with something that relieves the pain of loneliness. Often, making love to one's self seems to be the best option. But the relief gained is only temporary and is usually obliterated by shame and guilt. Then the person feels he must hide what he is really like from God and from others, and the loneliness and isolation increase. The pain demands relief, so he indulges again, and the vicious cycle keeps repeating itself. Is there a better solution? Yes, yes, yes! We'll get to that shortly.

Many youth, finding themselves hooked on self-love, and not knowing how to conquer it, look to marriage to bring them relief from this practice. They think, *If I can just find the right partner and get married, I'll no longer need to have my secret life of fantasies and masturbation, because he [or she] will fulfill my sexual fantasies.* But this is just another lie of Satan. After marriage, most find themselves going even deeper into sexual immorality. Sadly, secret sin and the fantasy life that accompany it pave the way for the next step in the progression: fornication.

Sexually active

Sexual promiscuity and fornication is prevalent today—both in the world and in the church. Because it is so common, some see it as "normal." You must decide what your standard for normality will be—God's everlasting principles or the decaying patterns of society.

---

*Exodus 20:5.

Unfortunately, many choose to follow society and reap the sad results. Youth as young as twelve or thirteen are ensnared. Some simply don't have an opportunity to understand God's standards and how these standards are given to protect their happiness. They are exposed to explicit material, lack proper parental supervision, or have been sexually abused. Others are desperate for love and mistake lust for love. Still others are driven by overwhelming peer pressure because "everyone is doing it." They get caught up in the dating game where wrong concepts are embraced and the goal is to get the girl in bed—even on the first date.

At a time when young people are laying the foundation for their future and need solid pure friendships, many youth get caught up in a pattern of self-love that often sets the tone and direction for the rest of their lives. Physical intimacy outside of the God-given parameters of marriage brings a host of evils beginning with perverted thoughts, feelings, tastes, and reactions. Repetition strengthens the evil, and many accept the bondage for life. *It's truly self-worship.*

What to do . . .

Where are you in this picture? Are you a parent with a teen who has fallen for Satan's counterfeits? Don't be complacent and don't be discouraged. How you relate to it will significantly influence the outcome for your youth. There are real ways that you can help. We are often tempted to think that by the time our young people are teens, it is too late to make a change. That is one of Satan's lies. It is never too late to begin parenting by the Spirit! God has all the wisdom and direction you need to give your youth every possible opportunity to develop true love.

Are you the teen who has lost his or her purity? Don't despair. While Jesus condemns the sin that hurts you, He does not condemn you. He loves you. He wants to set you free! Every teen can be free. None need remain in the jail cell of self-love. Don't settle for imprisonment.

What to do if you are the parent . . .

1. Live out the experience you want your youth to have. "And for their sakes I sanctify myself, that they also might be sanctified through the truth" (John 17:19).

Does your life, marriage, and home influence teach true love or self-love? That's a hard question for many of us to face, but it is truly the starting point. We cannot ask our young people to be what we are unwilling to be ourselves. That's hypocrisy.

God's grace is sufficient for you! If your home is messy, He will direct you how to make it clean and pleasant. If your disposition is sour or selfish, He will teach you how to be a sweet servant. If you have a habit of speaking harshly, He will suggest kind words to your mind. If your private sexual practices are not driven by pure, self-sacrificing love, He will give you the steps to change. Nothing is too hard for Him!* Nothing can daunt Him. The only obstacle between you and freedom is your own unwillingness to engage in the battle with Him. Resolve tension and stress in the home—replace it with safe, fun, pure, family companionship.

---

*Matthew 19:26; Philippians 4:13; 1 Corinthians 10:13.

Which inheritance will we choose to pass down, parents? What legacy will we leave our young people? Will our influence help them or hinder them?

2. Be there to nurture and admonish them. "*And, ye fathers, provoke not your children to wrath: but bring them up in the nurture and admonition of the Lord*" *(Ephesians 6:4).*

All our youth—both boys and girls—need a safe parent to confide in about anything that concerns them. They need to be able to tell you what they hear or if someone is relating to them inappropriately. They need to be able to open up to you regarding their struggles and failures neither fearing condemnation nor being told it's OK—not to worry. They need to find tangible help and wholesome relationships to fill that big hole in their hearts. Protect them; introduce them to God.

For your youth's sake, find out what their concepts of intimacy are. Explore to see what practices they are indulging in. Secret sin is often secret. But God can lead you to discover what your youth are involved in—not merely for the purpose of exposing and shaming them, but for the purpose of bringing them to Christ for healing and help.

3. Replace evil with good. "*Be not overcome of evil, but overcome evil with good*" *(Romans 12:21).*

Often, if the soil of the heart is kept preoccupied with good things, evil cannot gain the advantage. This is one of the key ways for parents, under God, to help their young people. Youth whose hearts are full of true love for their families and God and whose lives are brimming with wholesome occupation will have little taste or desire for Satan's counterfeits.

This is one reason for a family to have a schedule. A time to rise, a time for prayer, and time for meals and work and family fun leaves little time to dawdle in bed. Keep your youth active and involved in interesting pursuits—useful occupations that prepare them for life. Give them skills, interests, and wholesome friendships and activities. Make sure they get plenty of physical exercise both through work and fun so that they go to bed tired and satisfied. Require them to get up in the morning and get involved with God in their quiet time and to help with the household duties. Allow no idle time in bed.

Consider the influence of their associations. God may ask you to change schools, change locations, or homeschool them instead of exposing them to the life of Sodom and Gomorrah needlessly. They would be better off not having these false ideas in their head. Protect your heritage by giving them the best possible environment while guarding them from all the temptations possible.

Most of all, cultivate the expression of true love in all interactions and confront self-love—the expression of "me" only—when it raises its ugly head.

What to do if you are the teen . . .

1. Admit that you have a problem and confess it. "*If we confess our sins, he is faithful and just to forgive us our sins, and to cleanse us from all unrighteousness*" *(1 John 1:9).*

You can never solve a problem that you deny. The first step to freedom is to admit you are in bondage. Admit your problem and your powerlessness to overcome it to yourself, to God, and to a safe adult—hopefully your parent. Jesus promises that if we confess our sins to Him that He will not cast us aside,* but that He will forgive us and cleanse us. When you choose to take this step—even though you may feel weak, ashamed, or even unrepentant—Jesus embraces you just as you are. He loves you with a deeper, purer love than any on earth. God is different. He will never ask you to give up what is in your best interest to keep. But He will fight for you to help you overcome that which would destroy you. When you open yourself to Him, you will find relief that you are no longer facing this battle alone.

However, many teens find it very difficult to open themselves up to God because they have a misperception about what God is really like. If parents—particularly fathers—have not been safe, loving, and dependable, it is very likely that their children will have difficulty relating to God as safe, loving, and dependable. You see, our parents stand in the place of God to us while we are young children. In a home with safe and loving parents, it becomes a natural transition to love and obey a safe and loving heavenly Father. But, if we have parents that don't rightly represent God, we tend to view God as unfair, hurtful, or not available—like our parents. Many have found release from this by separating the character of God and their ungodly parents.

It will also help you to feel less isolated if you share your struggle with an adult who is led of God and who will neither condemn you nor coddle you. Such a person can help connect you with God when the struggle becomes severe and hold you accountable to stick with your decision to find purity in Christ. Don't try to face this battle alone—Satan will overwhelm you.

2. Ask God for a clean heart. "Create in me a clean heart, O God; and renew a right spirit within me" (Psalm 51:10).

When King David had fallen into sexual sin, he prayed for a clean heart. Whenever we offer that prayer sincerely, God grants it. He says, "A new heart also will I give you, and a new spirit will I put within you: and I will take away the stony heart out of your flesh, and I will give you an heart of flesh. And I will put my spirit within you, and cause you to walk in my statutes, and ye shall keep my judgments, and do them."† We may not *feel* like we have a new heart, but we do because God has promised it. Trust Him! That new heart will be kept pure as long as we choose to serve God rather than our bondage. But Satan does not give us up easily. It will require determination to keep serving God when all your perverted desires demand that you give way to your flesh.

You may have inherited this weakness, but you have the same choice Adam and Eve had back in the beginning. You can choose to position yourself under God's rule rather than self's rule. You can choose to serve God. His strength can become your strength.‡ He can break the power of this habit if you come to Him, discard your toys of self-pleasure, and let Him be Lord of your thoughts, your hands, and your sexual organs.

---

*John 6:37.
†Ezekiel 36:26, 27.
‡Read Exodus 15 and Psalm 91.

3. *Replace evil with good.* "*By mercy and truth iniquity is purged: and by the fear of the* LORD *men depart from evil*" *(Proverbs 16:6).*

When God gives you a clean heart, He wants to help you form a plan for keeping it clean. That plan will involve cultivating right habits in place of wrong ones and will begin with new, right thoughts and concepts.

Love needs to be redefined. Instead of consulting what "I" want—which is loving self—you need to consult what God wants. "Lord, what would Thou have me to think, feel, or do here?" Christ needs to be your Head, your Lord, and your Savior. Love to God means doing His will, not your own—regardless of the opposition of your way and will. He's in charge—not your history, habits, or passions. In order to wrap both arms around Christ and love Him, we have to let go of our other lovers—the secret, or not-so-secret, sin. We must give up the "me" circle of reference and stop seeing others as existing to serve yourself.

As far as possible, avoid temptation. If your peers draw you into impurity and are unwilling to change, you must withdraw from close association with them. If the TV or Internet lures you into self-love, replace them with wholesome activities. If the fantasies of your imagination go wild at the swimming pool, you may need to stay away. If the magazines at the checkout line in the grocery store stir up those feelings, minimize your trips to the store and make a plan ahead of time what you will do with your eyes to avoid taking in those wrong images.

If you have a habit of fondling yourself at bedtime, go to bed so tired from active work that you can fall right to sleep. Pray to God for strength. He promises, "For I the LORD thy God, will hold thy right hand, saying unto thee, Fear not; I will help thee."* Covenant with God to put your hands outside your covers and keep them there, whatever that takes, until there is evidence of God's internal cleansing of your mind (thoughts) and heart (feelings). If you find yourself amidst the automatic act, yield your hands to God's control immediately and follow what He directs you to do instead.

If your weak time is in the early morning, be prepared with a well-thought-out plan of what you will do instead. God may ask you to go for a long run outside. He may ask you to occupy your mind in heartfelt prayer for His guidance, wisdom, and strength that He may teach you His thoughts, feelings, and responses. Perhaps He'll ask you to study how to connect vitally and practically to Him in order to have the power you need to change. Perhaps He'll direct you to study passages of Scripture, identifying His part in your salvation and the part you must act. Perhaps He'll direct you to learn the keys of surrender and cooperation that unlock heaven's storehouse. Under God's tutoring you can find intensely interesting studies that fill your soul to overflowing with the living water of heaven-born love.† When you experience God's true love, you will see the cheap self-love Satan has sold you as just that—cheap and unsatisfying.

Be a Joseph. When tempted, cry out, "How can I do this great wickedness and sin against God?" Flee the scene of temptation—even if you have to leave your coat

---

*Isaiah 41:13.
†John 4:10.

behind. Flee to God. He is able to save all who come to Him—regardless of their weakness or their past. Your victory or failure is not determined by the strength of your temptation, but by your willingness—or lack thereof—to trust and obey God. Take His hand freely. He knows you can't overcome without His guidance, grace, and strength. He has the keys of freedom from this or any other vice through the right exercise of your will. Don't delay and don't believe Satan's voice that you have gone too far or that you are too awful. Jesus died to save *just you* from this world of sin. You have fallen into the quicksand of vice, but God can pull you out. Follow Him. Taste and see God's love as freedom from its power. As you experience victory over and over again, the day will come when this temptation will no longer find an answering chord within you. You will truly be free!

Then, one day, you will sing with the saved of all ages, "Redeemed how I love to proclaim it, redeemed by the blood of the Lamb. Redeemed through His infinite mercy, His child and forever I am. . . ."

THE LONE EMBRACE
A SPECIAL WORD OF ENCOURAGEMENT FOR SINGLE PARENTS

God is calling every single parent to believe in Him, to follow Him, to seek His face and find that He is bigger than any mountain of difficulty you find yourself up against—be that an oppositional spouse, unfair court systems, mental confusion, rebellious youth, financial difficulties, your youth's sin, or your own sins. God can direct you what to do in your extremity. These trials are God's opportunity to show Himself as your Father, Lord, and Savior—if you follow Him and come out of your spiritual bondages and sinful practices. He is there for you always!

Andrew, age 17, building the rock puzzle to protect the cabin foundation. Working with rock taught him diligence and joy.

Chapter 21

The Touch of the Master's Hand

So Jesus had compassion on them, and touched their eyes:
and immediately their eyes received sight, and they followed him.
—Matthew 20:34

It was Sunday morning—the last day of Family Camp Meeting. Over the previous four days we had witnessed the power of the Holy Spirit upon the hearts of those who attended. Now at the closing meeting my husband, Jim, gave a stirring appeal to the congregation to respond to the Holy Spirit and to work *out* in their lives what He was working *in* their conscience. Before he ended the meeting, Jim asked if there were any who would share their testimony. My heart beat faster as I saw Procrastinating Pete, a distinguished-looking, middle-aged gentleman, rise to his feet and stride to the platform.

Grasping the podium with both hands, he gazed at the audience, his face filled with emotion. He began, "Folks, I stand before you amazed at what God has done both for me and for my family. I have been to more camp meetings than I can remember and listened to the messages on CD between camp meetings. The Holy Spirit has called to my heart again and again to let Christ redeem me. I have desired to be changed. I even prayed for years that I could change. But I never did. I want to tell you that desire isn't enough to change us! A calamity happened to our family. My younger brother was killed in a car accident. It was so sudden and unexpected that it really shook me up. For the first time in my life, I began to think seriously about my life and the direction I was headed. It was like my eyes were opened, and I began to view my character and my home life the way God must see it.

"I began to catch a picture of just how self-centered I was. Everything I did was for my own benefit. I was nice to my wife when I felt like it and thought I would get something out of it. But if she irritated me or didn't meet my expectations, I would either fly off the handle or give her a cold shoulder. I did the same thing to my children. I would enjoy them as long as they fit into my program. But if they wanted to do something that I didn't really feel like doing, or if they were noisy or uncooperative, I had no tolerance for them.

"God revealed to me that even my church work was done to please myself. I liked being considered a spiritual giant by the church members. I would very patiently and tenderly help them with their spiritual problems—even helping some of the new members to overcome addictions. It made me feel good inside, and then it was easier to ignore the gnawing conviction that things weren't quite right in my life.

"God said to me, 'You may have the knowledge of truth, but the Person of this truth (Christ) doesn't have you. You don't know Me, and I don't know you.'

"Somehow this caught me off guard. It caused me to think of the many times God had tried to prod me to find more time to spend with Him. My wife often expressed that she wanted more time for us and the children. It just seemed impossible with my job and all my other responsibilities. Too many years went by waiting for God to perform this miracle in spite of me.

"But my brother's death made me realize that I had to make a decision. So, I finally decided. No matter what it cost me, God—rather than me—would be the center of my life. The first thing He asked me to do was to simplify my life and prioritize my time by cutting out everything that was not essential for life. It seemed a hard step to take at the time, but looking back now, it was the best thing I ever did. Why did I wait so long? I cut out my TV programs, my movies, my Internet surfing, my newspapers, and my overtime at work. I replaced these activities with time to seek God—not just the formal reading and prayers I used to have—but real time to seek Him and understand what He was saying to me personally.

"He began to show me that 'my way' was a miserable way to live and began to teach me the joy of living for others. I began to see my wife with new eyes, and God taught me better ways to relate to her when she crossed me. We began to spend time talking and seeking to understand one another. She is now my partner, my best friend, not my slave. . . ." and he broke down in tears. His wife joined him on the platform and put her arm around him encouragingly.

"My children—I discovered I didn't know my children. Brooding Becky was thirteen, and we began to take time to walk and talk together. She'd play 'fashion show' because she wanted to know what I liked and didn't like of her clothes. She wanted me to be part of her life.

"Friends, I had no idea we had this much influence with our young people. She wanted to know what *I* liked! She wanted to please *me*! If I had remained out of her life as I had been, would she still have been interested in my opinion when she turned sixteen?" Tears again stopped him from speaking for a moment.

"My boys, Tough Tommy and Lying Larry, were older, and they were harder to win back than my daughter. My precious wife stood by my side praying faithfully for me to find God and stop belittling them. For years I didn't listen and spurned her gentle suggestions. I had rejected the boys by having no time for them, having no interest in their school or life, no time to play with them, and worse yet—no time to consult with God how to direct them. God let their transformation begin with me.

"He helped me see that my short-fused temper needed to be replaced with a listening heart. My own interests and conveniences weren't as important as I had formerly thought. As I learned to deny my old way by communing with God, He taught me what to say instead. My boys' skepticism melted away with time. We drew closer until I could embrace them in a true, heartfelt father's love from above. In time they believed it to be true. Oh, I wasn't perfect. But they gave me space to make mistakes and go the old way, to forgive me, and to call me back to God.

"I remember the day I went to them to apologize again for losing it. Tommy said, 'Oh Dad, I make mistakes too. You have changed so much! I never thought I'd ever have a real dad, but you are real to me now. Since you started being nice to Mom and made time for us, it's never been the same. We are the family I was sure I'd never have. Many bad things have passed away. . . . Dad you are a miracle from God just for me! Thank you for being you. I like being *your* son!' "

Through still more tears, with his wife clinging to him, he shared how much of his time had been spent with pornography. "It's an evil, wasteful substitute for true love. It never satisfies the true inward heart of a man. Why did I do it?

"Although this vice had the hardest hold upon me, God was stronger. Dear friends, God is able to save us from ourselves, from vice, from wrong habits, from whatever has us all tied up in knots. But first you need to simplify your life so you have time with God. The time you redeem from the nonessentials, the excess, the sports, and the self-gratifying things, needs to be put into God, your spouse, and your family. There is no greater work than this. Redeem your time, find God, and He will take you from that point, one step at a time, to unravel the mess you are in. The redeeming of our marriages and our children begins with us, men."

By this time, there were few dry eyes in the audience. I had to reach for a tissue more than once. Tears of joy streamed down the cheeks of his wife, and as the man ended his testimony, she timidly moved toward the microphone.

"Friends, everything Pete has shared is true. After hoping and wishing and praying for all these years, our family is really changing. I always used to blame Pete for the tension and unhappiness in our home, but God began to put on my heart the fact that my resentment of him was wrong and kept me locked in a prison cell. I excused my own failure and chose not to move forward in what God was asking me to do as a wife and mother because Pete wasn't doing his part.

"God asked me to surrender my resentment and leave my husband in His hands while taking the steps He was asking me to take—with or without my husband. It felt like I was cutting off my right hand to do it, but I gave God my resentment and asked Him to replace it with pure love.

"It was harder at first than I can describe to you, but I found such freedom and delight as God changed my disposition. I began to actually enjoy my children rather than just tolerate them. I began to look forward to my tasks in the home and to look for ways to make it pleasant and happy. God began to give me ideas of how to love my husband—even when he didn't love me back. And God also asked me to confront my husband at times—not in a fleshly way—but in a Spirit-directed way. He helped me face my fear of Pete's temper, and He made me strong.

"When Pete's brother died and Pete started making these changes, I'll admit I was skeptical to start with, but now I see the change is real and lasting. I can't believe how God is granting the deepest desires of my heart—to have a genuinely Christ-centered husband." Turning to the new *Prioritizing* Pete, she threw her arms around him and they lovingly embraced—tears flowing freely down their cheeks.

I turned to look at their three children. I had watched these children through the years and had seen that all-too-common look of longing turning to hopelessness turning to callousness—especially with the boys. Now I saw softness in their eyes—and hope, sweet hope!

What made the difference?

There is a familiar poem that explains this transformation quite well:

The Touch of the Master's Hand
    'Twas battered and scarred, and the auctioneer
Thought it scarcely worth his while
    To waste much time on the old violin,
But he held it up with a smile.
    "What am I bidden, good folks?" he cried.
"Who'll start the bidding for me?"
    "A dollar, a dollar. Then two! Only two?
Two dollars, and who'll make it three?
    Three dollars once; three dollars twice;
Going for three. . . "

But no!
From the room far back, a grey-haired man
    Came forward and picked up the bow.
Then, wiping the dust from the old violin
    And tightening the loosened strings,
He played a melody pure and sweet,
    As a caroling angel sings.

The music ceased, and the auctioneer,
    With a voice that was quiet and low,
Said, "What am I bid for the old violin?"
    And he held it up with the bow.
"A thousand dollars, and who'll make it two?
    Two thousand! And who'll make it three?
Three thousand once, three thousand twice,
    And going and gone," said he.

The people cheered, but some of them cried,
    "We do not quite understand.
What changed its worth?" Swift came the reply:
    "The touch of the master's hand."

And many a man with life out of tune,
    And battered and scarred with sin,
Is auctioned cheap to the thoughtless crowd,
    Much like the old violin.
A mess of a life, a mess of a home,
    And he travels on with no change.
He is "going" once, and "going" twice;

He's "going" and almost "gone."

> But the Master comes, and the foolish crowd
> 　　Never can quite understand
> The worth of a soul and the change that's wrought
> 　　By the touch of the Master's hand.
> 　　　　　　—Myra Brooks Welch [Lines 37 and 38 adapted.]

Each of us is like that old violin. None have escaped being battered and worn by sin. We all have an enemy who tries to sell us cheap. But the Master comes for each of us. He comes for moms, dads, grandmas, grandpas, aunts, uncles, teens, and children of all ages. He comes for you. All He asks is that you place yourself unreservedly in His hands and let Him be your Master. Abused Abby did that, and she became Happy Abby. Silly Sal from Siam learned that she was truly loved and loveable. Selfish Sophie became Selfless Sophie. Opportunistic Ona grasped opportunities to follow God rather than to evade duty. Valueless Vicki was transformed to Valuable Vicki. Cool Jace became Kind Jace. Despairing Danny turned into Diligent Danny. All these were transformed because they submitted to the touch of the Master's hand.

He is waiting to do the same for you! Won't you let the Master pick up the bow of your emotions, desires, tastes, appetites, and passions to adjust and cleanse them? Won't you let Him dust off your ideas and concepts and bring out the beauty He originally intended? Won't you let Him tune the strings of your responses to others? Won't you let Him conduct your life to orchestrate what's needed in your marriage and family?

If you do, He will play a melody on your heartstrings that will soar like the eagles above the disharmony and confusion of self. He will bring beauty out of your life you never dreamed possible because they that wait on the Master shall renew their strength. They shall mount up with wings as eagles and fly above the pull of sin.*

The motley crew revisited

Remember the motley crew from chapter 1? Chains Charlie, Misfit Murphy, Shy Sarah, and all the rest are instruments awaiting the touch of the Master's hand. They are battered, worn, and driven by unmet needs into unwise associations, vice, and immorality. The enemy tells them that there is no better way, that they are hopeless, that they are OK the way they are. They drift on with hearts out of tune—the victims of unmet needs—unmet needs that will be satisfied only when they place themselves in the Master's hand. He has promised to supply all their needs according to His infinite riches.†

The sum of our entire duty as parents—the burden of this book and the three books that precede it in this series—is just this: to lead our young people to place

---

*Isaiah 40:31.
†Philippians 4:19.

themselves in the Master's hands. We must show them the way. We must let them hear the melody the Master brings forth from our heartstrings. Sure, it will be uncomfortable to move off the shelf we're used to sitting on. It might not feel good when our loose thoughts and emotions have to be tightened and tuned to His ear—not ours. His hand guiding the bow and fingering the strings of our hearts feels close and strange. But then, He calls forth beauty and strength we never knew while we sat on the shelf. His melody warms within us. The old dusty ways are no longer inviting. We like being tuned by Him. Yielding to His playing becomes our greatest joy!

Parenting by the Spirit—it's not a method. It's a way of life! It's placing ourselves in the Master's hand and then leading our young ones to do the same. We introduce them to the Master. We teach them how to place themselves in His hands. We train them to cooperate with His tuning process. And then we step back. The Master—with His infinite skill and understanding—brings forth the music He has composed for their lives.

What is the Master saying to you? Don't be a Procrastinating Pete. Decide today to accept the touch of the Master's hand.

The Hohnberger family backpacking in the Rocky Mountains. Parents and teens need to do things together. Be there for your teen!

Parenting Your Teen by the Spirit is book 4 in Sally Hohnberger's series of four books on parenting. You won't want to miss the other three!

Parenting by the Spirit (Book 1 of 4)
with Tim and Julie Canuteson
 This book lays the foundation for winning the hearts of our children—our own vital connection with Jesus.
Paperback, 160 pages. 0-8163-2031-4 US$13.99

Coming Soon!
Parenting Your Infant by the Spirit (Book 2 of 4)
 The last book of the four to be written, but certainly not the least in importance, Sally addresses the vital needs of our precious infants to four year olds.

Parenting Your Child by the Spirit (Book 3 of 4)
 Drawing on numerous real-life examples, Sally offers helpful advice for parenting children ages five to twelve.
Paperback, 204 pages. 0-8163-2070-5 US$19.99

Order from your ABC by calling **1-800-765-6955,** or go online and shop our virtual store at **http://www.AdventistBookCenter.com.**

Prices subject to change without notice.

Empowered Living Ministries is the outgrowth of Jim and Sally's experience with God. Located near Glacier National Park, the ministry office is here to serve your needs, whether it is to book a speaking engagement, request a media appearance, or order any of a large variety of resource material, including books, booklets, seminars on CD, or a special DVD series. For more information, contact us:

http://www.EmpoweredLivingMinistries.org
Phone 406-387-4333
Orders 877-755-8300
Fax 406-387-4336